Footsteps of the Flock

365 Daily Meditations from Joshua to Malachi

Jon Courson

Footsteps of the Flock
365 Daily Meditations from Joshua to Malachi

Copyright © 2007 by Jon Courson

Published by Calvary Chapel Publishing (CCP),
a resource ministry of Calvary Chapel Costa Mesa
3800 South Fairview
Santa Ana, California 92704

First printing, 2007

All Scripture quotations in this book are taken from the King James Version of the Bible.

ISBN 10: 1-59751-030-0
ISBN 13: 978-1-59751-030-1

Printed in the United States of America.

INTRODUCTION

. . . go thy way forth by the footsteps of the flock, and feed thy kids beside the shepherds' tents.

Song of Solomon 1:8

With shepherds as founders of their very nation (Genesis 46:32), the bond between sheep and shepherd is one that God's people would readily understand. Therefore, it is little wonder that, throughout Scripture, He uses it to describe His relationship to His people . . .

The Lord is my shepherd; I shall not want.

Psalm 23:1

He shall feed his flock like a shepherd: he shall gather the lambs with his arm and carry them in his bosom, and shall gently lead those that are with young.

Isaiah 40:11

Hear the word of the LORD, O ye nations, and declare it in the isles afar off, and say, He that scattered Israel will gather him, and keep him as a shepherd doth his flock.

Jeremiah 31:10

And there were in the same country shepherds abiding in the field, keeping watch over their flock by night.

Luke 2:8

And Jesus, when he came out, saw much people, and was moved with compassion toward them, because they were as sheep not having a shepherd . . .

Mark 6:34

I am the good shepherd: the good shepherd giveth his life for the sheep.

John 10:11

In fact, the only picture God paints of Himself more often than that of Shepherd is that of Father. Therefore, it is my prayer that He will use the following portions of His Word to keep you walking day by day in the footsteps of His flock, and as His "kids," constantly feeding close beside your Shepherd.

JANUARY 1

Now after the death of Moses the servant of the LORD it came to pass, that the LORD spake unto Joshua the son of Nun, Moses' minister, saying . . .

Joshua 1:1

"I have come that you might have life and that you might have it more abundantly," Jesus declared (John 10:10). We who have been born again have life. We have eternal life - but do we have abundant life? It's wonderful and important to be saved. But there's more to the life of faith than simply being saved, for as He did His people, God not only takes us out of Egypt, which is a picture of the world, but He desires to bring us into the Land of Promise.

Perhaps you've heard sermons on, or sung hymns about the Promised Land in reference to Heaven. Yet as we make our way through the Book of Joshua, we will see that, although there is abundant fruit in the Promised Land, there are also battles to fight and wars to wage. Therefore, the Promised Land cannot speak of Heaven, for in Heaven, we will "learn war no more" (Isaiah 2:4).

> Moreover, brethren, I would not that ye should be ignorant, how that all our fathers were under the cloud, and all passed through the sea; and were all baptized unto Moses in the cloud and in the sea; and did all eat the same spiritual meat; and did all drink the same spiritual drink: for they drank of that spiritual Rock that followed them: and that Rock was Christ. Now all these things happened unto them for ensamples: and they are written for our admonition, upon whom the ends of the world are come.
>
> 1 Corinthians 10:1-4, 11

"Don't be ignorant of the fact that these Old Testament pictures were painted for our benefit," says Paul. "The Rock speaks of Christ. The manna speaks of spiritual nourishment. The parting of the Red Sea speaks of baptism." Here in the Book of Joshua, God's chosen people have been set free from the brutal bondage of Egypt just as we have been set free from the bondage of our own sin and carnality. They were "baptized" when they crossed the Red Sea just as we have been baptized in water. They have wandered for forty years in the dusty, dreary wilderness just as we wonder and wander through dry days in our own spiritual experience.

But if you're at the place where you're tired of the wilderness, the Book of Joshua is for you, for it deals with what it means to move into the Promised Land of the Spirit-filled life.

JANUARY 2

Moses my servant is dead; now therefore arise, go over this Jordan, thou, and all this people, unto the land which I do give to them, even to the children of Israel. Every place that the sole of your foot shall tread upon, that have I given unto you, as I said unto Moses.

Joshua 1:2-3

God didn't say, "I will give you the land upon which you walk." He said, "I have given it to you." The same is true today. Concerning the things of God, whenever you choose to step out and engage your "sole," that land is already yours. It's a matter of possessing your possession. It's a matter of appropriation. Where do you want to put your soul? Where do you want to plant your foot and say, "I believe You for this, Lord. I'm stepping out in this. I'm going after this"?

I read about a man who was arrested in a futile attempt to rob a convenience store. The amazing part of the story is that the gun he used was actually a Civil War-era pistol worth $23,000. He had robbed the store for $125 when all the time, right there in his hand, he held a $23,000 treasure. Isn't that like us? We strive for peanuts when the Lord has grapes for us the size of bowling balls. The Lord says, "I've already given you the land. It's already a done deal. It's just a matter of how much of it you want. I won't take you any farther than you choose. But I'll take you as far as you want to go." How far did the Israelites go? The Promised Land covers thirty thousand square miles. At the height of their power, in Solomon's reign, the Israelites claimed three thousand square miles. They took one-tenth of what God had already given them. And I can't help but wonder if we have even done that.

Concerning the Spirit-filled life and the appropriation of the power of the Holy Ghost, many people say, "If the Lord wants to empower me and baptize me, I'm open." But in Genesis 8, we see Noah on the ark, with the dove - a symbol of the Holy Spirit - circling overhead. Noah stretched out his hand and brought the dove in unto him. So too, I believe the Spirit of God is looking for a person, a people, a congregation to land upon. But this will not happen through passivity. Rather God, like Noah, responds to those who see the opportunity and extend their hand to pull Him in unto them.

Here in Joshua 1:3, the Lord says, "The land is already yours. It's up to you how far you want to go, how deep you want to be."

JANUARY 3

This book of the law shall not depart out of thy mouth; but thou shalt meditate therein day and night . . .

Joshua 1:8 (a)

Notice that God didn't tell Joshua that His Word was not to depart out of his hand or out of his back pocket, but that it was not to depart out of his mouth. The Hebrew word translated meditate simply means "to mutter." Thus, Biblical meditation consists of speaking the Scriptures over and over. It is not a matter of thinking about the Scriptures because merely thinking about them allows our minds to wander. Meditation means to speak verbally, quoting Scriptures audibly, talking to others about them constantly.

"Blessed is the man that walketh not in the counsel of the ungodly, nor standeth in the way of sinners nor sitteth in the seat of the scornful," the psalmist declared. "But his delight is in the law of the LORD; and in his law doth he meditate day and night. And he shall be like a tree planted by the rivers of water, that bringeth forth his fruit in his season; his leaf also shall not wither; and whatsoever he doeth shall prosper" (Psalm 1:1-3).

In the seasons when I have meditated on the Word, my leaf doesn't wither. Fruit inevitably abounds. I'm successful and prosper. In the seasons when I mistakenly thought I was too busy to meditate, I have found myself withering, being blown about, fruitless. In other words, I have found what David said to be absolutely true.

"Let not My Word depart from your mouth," God said to Joshua. And He says the same thing to us.

JANUARY 4

. . . that thou mayest observe to do according to all that is written therein: for then thou shalt make thy way prosperous, and then thou shalt have good success.

Joshua 1:8 (b)

Prosperity, success, and the abundant life are hallmarks of the Spirit-filled life. And the Spirit is inextricably linked to the Word . . .

> Let the word of Christ dwell in you richly in all wisdom; teaching and admonishing one another in psalms and hymns and spiritual songs, singing with grace in your hearts to the Lord. And whatsoever ye do in word or deed, do all in the name of the Lord Jesus, giving thanks to God and the Father by him. Wives, submit yourselves unto your own husbands, as it is fit in the Lord. Husbands, love your wives, and be not bitter against them. Children, obey your parents in all things: for this is well pleasing unto the Lord. Fathers, provoke not your children to anger, lest they be discouraged. Servants, obey in all things your masters according to the flesh; not with eyeservice, as menpleasers; but in singleness of heart, fearing God.

Colossians 3:16-22

According to this passage in Colossians, the result of letting the Word of Christ dwell in us will be that we'll speak to ourselves and to each other with psalms and hymns. We'll be submitted to each other. We'll be the kind of husband, wife, or child we ought to be and the kind of worker that honors God.

> And be not drunk with wine, wherein is excess; but be filled with the Spirit; speaking to yourselves in psalms and hymns and spiritual songs, singing and making melody in your heart to the Lord; giving thanks always for all things unto God and the Father in the name of our Lord Jesus Christ; submitting yourselves one to another in the fear of God. Wives, submit yourselves unto your own husbands, as unto the Lord . . . Husbands, love your wives, even as Christ also loved the church, and gave himself for it . . . Children, obey your parents in the Lord: for this is right . . . And, ye fathers, provoke not your children to wrath: but bring them up in the nurture and admonition of the Lord. Servants, be obedient to them that are your masters according to the flesh, with fear and trembling, in singleness of your heart, as unto Christ; not with eyeservice, as menpleasers; but as the servants of Christ, doing the will of God from the heart.
>
> Ephesians 5:18-22, 25, 6:1, 4-6

According to these passages in Ephesians, the result of being filled with the Spirit is that we'll speak to ourselves with psalms and hymns. We'll be submitted to each other. We'll be the kind of husband, wife, or child we ought to be and the kind of worker that honors God. In other words, being filled with the Spirit and being filled with the Word are undeniably linked together.

Spirit-filled people or congregations are those who meditate in the Word, devote themselves to the study of the Word, and gain more understanding about the Word. And as that happens, they are continually filled with the Spirit in fresh ways. I used to think a believer was either a Spirit-filled person or a student of the Word. Not so. Jesus said the Father seeks those who will worship Him in Spirit and in truth (John 4:23-24).

At the very beginning of his ministry, Joshua is told to meditate in the Word day and night because that is the key to appropriating the power of the Spirit he would need to accomplish that which God had called him to do. And the same is no less true for you.

JANUARY 5

And Joshua the son of Nun sent out of Shittim two men to spy secretly, saying, Go view the land, even Jericho.

Joshua 2:1 (a)

Joshua, a picture of Jesus, is about to take the Israelites across the Jordan River into the Land of Promise. But before he does, he does something that reminds me of what Jesus did. That is, he sends two men to go before him into the Land. In Luke 10, we read that Jesus sent seventy men out in groups of two to go before Him, to be His witnesses. The two men Joshua sends think they're going to spy. But in reality, they'll be witnesses.

The same is true of you and me. We think we're school teachers, insurance salesmen, or stockbrokers. But we're not. We're undercover agents for the Kingdom. God has planted us in those positions to be His witnesses. The two men Joshua sent out were the first of the Israelites to experience the Promised Land. So too, it is as we let the Lord shine through us in His supernaturally natural way in our work places, schools, and neighborhoods that we will experience the abundance of the Spirit-filled life as well.

JANUARY 6

And they went, and came into a harlot's house, named Rahab, and lodged there.

Joshua 2:1 (b)

Although the Hebrew word translated "harlot" can also refer to a female innkeeper, each time Rahab's name appears in the New Testament, it is in conjunction with a word in Greek that can only be translated "harlot." Why did these men go into a harlot's house? Most likely it was because, as enemies in the gated city of Jericho, Rahab's house was the only place they could hide in anonymity.

In Hebrews 11, a small number of people are singled out as heroes in God's "hall of faith." Isaiah didn't make it. Jeremiah didn't make it. Daniel didn't make it. Elisha didn't make it. But one who did make it into the hall of faith was Rahab the prostitute. Rahab's name appears again in James 2 as an example of what it means to have faith that is real. But the most important place Rahab's name appears is in Matthew 1, as she takes her place with only three other women in the genealogy of Jesus Christ. How could it be that Rahab would be exalted to this position?

In 2 Corinthians 5, we read that every believer will stand before the judgment seat of Christ - not to be judged for our sin because our sin was washed away by the blood Jesus shed on the Cross of Calvary - but to be rewarded for what we've done. In 1 Corinthians 3, we read that all of our works will be tried by fire wherein the wood, hay, and stubble - that which was done with mixed motives and carnality - will burn away, leaving only gold, silver, and precious stones. Revelation 1 describes Jesus as One whose eyes are like a burning fire. Therefore, I believe it is as He looks on us that all the stuff that's polluted and defiled by mixed motives and carnality will evaporate and disappear.

What will be left? Based on the story of Rahab, I suggest what's left will be a lot more than you think. You see, in Jeremiah 15, the Lord said, "Jeremiah, you will be My spokesman if you can extract the valuable from the vile." We tend to notice only the vile. Not so the Lord. He does the opposite. He pokes around in the pile of our rubble and stubble and finds the jewels. We would call Rahab a harlot and a liar. Not God. Simply because she believed in Him, He calls her a hero.

We have a tendency to listen to Satan who perches on our shoulder, saying, "You're not going to be rewarded for that. Your motive wasn't pure. Your thoughts weren't right. Your attitude was amiss."

But God would say, "I specialize in extracting the precious from the vile. Oh, I know there's all kinds of weakness even in your best deeds and ministry. But I will find the gold, silver, and precious stones others don't see - even in your simply giving a cup of cold water in My name" (see Matthew 10:42).

January 7

And they went, and came unto the mountain, and abode there three days, until the pursuers were returned: and the pursuers sought them throughout all the way, but found them not. So the two men returned, and descended from the mountain, and passed over, and came to Joshua the son of Nun, and told him all things that befell them: and they said unto Joshua, Truly the LORD hath delivered into our hands all the land; for even all the inhabitants of the country do faint because of us.

Joshua 2:22-24

Even as the seventy apostles returned to Jesus amazed, saying, "Lord, even the demons are subject to us in Your name" (see Luke 10:17), so Joshua's witnessing spies returned amazed by what they had seen. That's always the way it is. Whenever we set out to witness to someone else, we are witnessed to by God's power and provision. Conversely, in failing to witness, we miss out on so much.

There are people on my street I have never talked to directly about Jesus Christ because I've listened to Satan's lie that says they don't want to hear, that they're not ready, or that they're too busy. The story of Rahab says just the opposite. "Where have you been?" she asked the spies. "We've heard about what your God has done."

Isaiah 14:16 says that when we see Satan, we're going to look at him narrowly - or squint at him - saying, "Is this the one who terrorized the world?

This is the one who intimidated us? This is the one we believed when he told us our friends, family, and neighbors didn't want to hear about Jesus?"

The power of the Holy Spirit is like electricity. It won't enter something from which it can't exit. We want the power of the Holy Spirit. The question is, will there be a place for it to go? When we say, "I want to share the plan of salvation with my secretary, empower me," or, "I want to talk to my buddy about You, Lord. Make me bold," we'll be empowered in ways we never could have imagined. How long has it been since you've shared the Gospel, the plan of salvation, the scarlet cord with someone who's not a believer? By faith, receive the power to be a witness. Awaiting you is a Land of milk and honey, fruit and abundance. And you get there by going in as a witness. It's time to cross over the Jordan into the Promised Land of the Spirit-filled life.

JANUARY 8

And Joshua rose early in the morning; and they removed from Shittim, and came to Jordan, he and all the children of Israel, and lodged there before they passed over. And it came to pass after three days, that the officers went through the host . . .

Joshua 3:1-2

Here, Joshua arises early in the day just as our Greater-than-Joshua did (Mark 1:35). Isaiah prophesied that Messiah would rise morning by morning that He might hear from the Father concerning what He was to do, what He was to say, where He was to go (Isaiah 50:4).

Following three days of preparation, it was time for the people of Israel to move off the banks of the Jordan and into the Land of Promise. So too, time spent in preparation for the baptism of the Holy Spirit - of which the crossing of the Jordan speaks - is time well spent.

Of the believers worshipping the Lord and speaking in tongues, some said, "Those guys must be drunk."

"They're not drunk," Peter answered. "This is that which was spoken by the prophet Joel." Peter then quoted Joel who said, "In the last days, I will pour out My spirit upon all flesh. And your sons and daughters shall prophesy. Your young men shall see visions, your old men shall dream dreams" (Acts 2:15-17 and Joel 2:28).

It's not a waste of time to wait for three days, three months, or even three years on the bank of the Jordan if, like Peter, you can say, "I'm not simply caught up in an emotion or seeking an experience, but I understand the Biblical foundation and base for the direction into which I'm moving."

JANUARY 9

And they commanded the people, saying, When ye see the ark of the covenant of the LORD your God, and the priests the Levites bearing it, then ye shall remove from your place, and go after it. Yet there shall be a space between you and it, about two thousand cubits by measure: come not near unto it, that ye may know the way by which ye must go: for ye have not passed this way heretofore.

Joshua 3:3-4

"When you see the presence of God move, go after it," the officers of the congregation said. I like that! Our God is on the move. And we must be those who go after Him.

When they saw the Ark of the Covenant move, the Israelites were to follow it. Yet they were to follow at a distance of approximately half a mile. In this, it's as if God was saying, "Follow Me, but don't push Me."

People say, "I'm going to have the same experience that he or she or they had." God, however, wants to take us where we've never been before. Therefore, it's the wise man or woman who says, "Lord, I want Your anointing. And I'm going to give You space to work it out any way You choose."

JANUARY 10

Behold, the ark of the covenant, even the Lord of all the earth passeth over before you into Jordan. Now therefore take ye twelve men out of the tribes of Israel, out of every tribe a man. And it shall come to pass, as soon as the soles of the feet of the priests that bear the ark of the LORD, the Lord of all the earth, shall rest in the waters of Jordan, that the waters of Jordan shall be cut off from the waters that come down from above; and they shall stand upon a heap.

Joshua 3:11-13

When the priests and representatives from each tribe put their feet into the river, the water would divide. Forty years previously, when the children of Israel crossed the Red Sea, the water parted before they stepped in (Exodus 14). But not this time. When it comes to the issues of the Spirit, we're to step in by faith.

"But what if hands are laid upon me and I seek the Lord's power aggressively, yet nothing happens? I'll feel like a big drip," we say. So we stay on the bank where it's safe and dry - real dry, dusty dry, wilderness dry.

Why doesn't God part the water first? I'm convinced it's because the language of eternity is faith. This life is only eighty years long at best. So God uses every opportunity to teach us to see and hear with the eyes and ears of faith. "Step out. Step in. Step up in faith," He says. "And watch and see what I'll do."

JANUARY 11

And it came to pass, when the people removed from their tents, to pass over Jordan, and the priests bearing the ark of the covenant before the people; and as they that bare the ark were come unto Jordan, and the feet of the priests that bare the ark were dipped in the brim of the water, (for Jordan overfloweth all his banks all the time of harvest,) that the waters which came down from above stood and rose up upon a heap very far from the city Adam, that is beside Zaretan: and those that came down toward the sea of the plain, even the salt sea, failed, and were cut off: and the people passed over right against Jericho.

Joshua 3:14-16

The Israelites weren't commanded to step into a trickling stream but into a raging river. But how could it have been otherwise? In reference to the Holy Ghost, Jesus said, "If any man thirst, let him come unto Me, and drink. And out of his innermost being shall gush forth torrents of living water" (see John 7:37-38). Thus, it's appropriate that, as a symbol of the power and presence of the Holy Spirit, the Jordan would have been a roaring river.

For the Jordan to part at the point the priests stepped in, God had to have built a supernatural dam nineteen miles upriver. Because Joshua and the people of Israel couldn't see that far, this means that God was working out of sight. And He still works that way today. That's why He says, "Trust Me. Don't walk by sight. Walk by faith. I'm doing things nineteen miles upriver that you can't see now - but that you will understand in the right place, at the right time."

JANUARY 12

And the priests that bare the ark of the covenant of the LORD stood firm on dry ground in the midst of Jordan, and all the Israelites passed over on dry ground, until all the people were passed clean over Jordan.

Joshua 3:17

The priests stepped in and said, "We're not leaving until all have passed over." And they stood firm while three million people passed through the Jordan. They stood until the work was done.

> Evangelist D. L. Moody locked himself in a hotel room in New York City for three and a half days, saying, "I'm not coming out of this room until I know the power of the Spirit has come upon me." On the fourth day, God overwhelmed and overpowered him to such a degree that he knew without a doubt that he was empowered to do the work God had called him to do.

So too, as I read the Book of Joshua, I say, "Lord, I don't want to miss out on anything You have ordained for me."

JANUARY 13

And the children of Israel did so as Joshua commanded, and took up twelve stones out of the midst of Jordan, as the LORD spake unto Joshua, according to the number of the tribes of the children of Israel, and carried them over with them unto the place where they lodged, and laid them down there. And Joshua set up twelve stones in the midst of Jordan, in the place where the feet of the priests which bare the ark of the covenant stood: and they are there unto this day.

Joshua 4:8-9

Twelve men were to place twelve stones from the bed of the Jordan River on the west bank of the Jordan. Of them, they were to make a monument, a memorial. In our country, sites like the Vietnam Memorial and Lincoln Memorial help us to remember and to reflect. So too, the twelve stones would enable the Israelite fathers to tell their children how God miraculously stopped the Jordan for His people.

In addition to the twelve stones placed on the side of the Jordan, Joshua was instructed to place twelve stones in the midst of the Jordan itself. This means that when the water came rushing in after everyone had passed over, Joshua's monument would not be seen by any man - only by God. There were two monuments. One was visible. One was out of sight. And that's the way it is with any work of the Spirit. The outward manifestations are only as valid as the inward, hidden work in one's heart.

JANUARY 14

And the people came up out of Jordan on the tenth day of the first month, and encamped in Gilgal, in the east border of Jericho. And those twelve stones, which they took out of Jordan, did Joshua pitch in Gilgal. And he spake unto the children of Israel, saying, When your children shall ask their fathers in time to come, saying, What mean these stones? Then ye shall let your children know, saying, Israel came over this Jordan on dry land. For the LORD your God dried up the waters of Jordan from before you, until ye were passed over, as the LORD your God did to the Red sea, which he dried up from before us, until we were gone over: that all the people of the earth might know the hand of the LORD, that it is mighty: that ye might fear the LORD your God for ever.

Joshua 4:19-24

Paul proclaimed that the three greatest and most important components of life are faith, hope, and love. In the Book of Joshua, we see the people had hearts of hope in chapter 2 when the spies came back and said, "Truly the Lord has delivered the Land into our hands." In chapter 3, they took steps of faith as they put the soles of their feet into the Jordan River, believing God would meet them in the process. And here we see the third component - a picture of love. Twelve stones stacked together in one monument - twelve stones representing twelve tribes, fit together in unity - would be the sign that the Israelites had crossed over the Jordan, that they had been "baptized" a second time.

Peter says that, as believers, we are living stones that are fit together in unity (1 Peter 2:5). When you come to church, not out of obligation but because you want to be linked together with fellow blockheads and stones, your love for them is a sure sign of your being touched deeply by the Spirit. "All men shall know you are My disciples," said Jesus. By your speaking in tongues? No. By your gift of healing? No. "They'll know you are My disciples by your love" (see John 13:35).

In 1 Corinthians 12 and 14, Paul discusses spiritual gifts and their manifestations. But packed between them is chapter 13, a chapter that deals exclusively with love because love is the defining characteristic of one who has had an encounter with the Spirit.

"Father, let them be one," Jesus prayed in John 17, "that the world might know that I am in You and that You are in Me." In other words, love within the Body of Christ is proof positive to a world that is skeptical that Jesus is risen and real, alive and well.

JANUARY 15

And the manna ceased on the morrow after they had eaten of the old corn of the land; neither had the children of Israel manna any more; but they did eat of the fruit of the land of Canaan that year.

Joshua 5:12

It is interesting to me that it was in the Promised Land, a picture of the Spirit-filled life, that the miracle of manna ceased. If there was ever going to be manna from Heaven, I would think it would be when we're Spirit-filled, when we're moving in the arena of the miraculous, when we have the anointing of the Holy Ghost. But this passage tells me differently, for when the Israelites were in the wilderness - which speaks of carnality and dryness - miracles abounded. But now that they're in the Promised Land, the manna stops.

In the Azusa Street Revival of the early 1900s, during which there was a fresh outpouring of the Holy Spirit, the leader of the movement prophesied that three things would cause the movement of the Spirit to be quenched: more attention given to the Holy Spirit than to Jesus Christ, more attention given to praise than to prayer, and more attention given to the gifts of the Spirit than to the fruit of the Spirit.

When they were released from Egypt and as they wandered in the wilderness, the children of Israel saw more signs and wonders than any other group of people in history. Yet it was unbelief that kept them from entering the Promised Land (Hebrews 3:19) because faith doesn't come through seeing miracles. It comes from hearing the Word. Therefore, the new generation would eat the formidable fruit found produced in the Land of God's promise rather than the manna of the miraculous.

Cling to the Word. Cling to the promises of God. Not only will this please God as you walk by faith, but you will find them to nourish and sustain you more deeply than even a miracle would.

JANUARY 16

And it came to pass, when Joshua was by Jericho, that he lifted up his eyes and looked, and behold, there stood a man over against him with his sword drawn in his hand . . .

Joshua 5:13 (a)

Throughout the Word, when men find themselves at a crossroads, we see them lifting up their eyes to God in Heaven (Genesis 13:10; 18:2; 24:63; Numbers 24:2; 1 Chronicles 21:16; Daniel 10:5). In this case, Jericho is looming over Joshua. It's a formidable problem, a massive walled city. Yet Joshua didn't look down, hide out, or hole up. He lifted his eyes.

As we will see, this Man is none other than a pre-incarnate appearance of Jesus Christ. Because Joshua was on the verge of battle, the Lord appeared to him as a Man of war. On the plains of Mamre, the Lord appeared to Abraham as a traveler because Abraham was a pilgrim (Genesis 18). To His disciples, He appeared as a fellow fisherman cooking fish (John 21:7-9). So too, no matter what Jericho is looming ahead of you, don't look inward; don't look down; look up and look around. Watch for the Lord appearing to you in the unexpected time and in the unexpected way through the circumstances and people around you.

JANUARY 17

. . . and Joshua went unto him, and said unto him, Art thou for us, or for our adversaries? And he said, Nay; but as captain of the host of the LORD am I now come. And Joshua fell on his face to the earth, and did worship, and said unto him, what saith my lord unto his servant?

Joshua 5:13 (b)-14

As Joshua scoped out the city of Jericho, a Man with a sword in His hand appeared to him. "Are You for us, or for our enemies?" Joshua asked. "Which side are You on?"

But as Captain of the host of the Lord, the issue wasn't whose side He was on. It was whose side Joshua was on.

If we're to see walls flattened, the first thing we have to realize is that it's not "us against them." When there are walls or barriers in a marriage, a family, or a church, the issue will inevitably become one of us against them, the good guys versus the bad guys.

"Whose side are You on, Lord?" we ask, sure that He will answer that He is on ours.

But when He simply answers, "No," wise is the man or woman who does what Joshua did, who bows the knee and changes the question to, "What saith my Lord to His servant?"

Before he understood Who he was talking to, perhaps it was rather gruffly that General Joshua asked, "Whose side are you on?" But once he realized Who it was, he no longer gave orders. He simply reported for duty. And that's the way prayer ought always to be. We're re-learning that God always gives His best to those who leave the choice to Him.

I used to think that prayer in faith meant I was to give the plan to the Lord, stand on it in faith, and expect it to come about. I've since learned, however, that because we all see through a glass only darkly at best (1 Corinthians 13:12), I would be a fool to order the Lord around. The Bible says to have faith in God. He sees things we don't see. So we ask in faith. We share our thoughts with the Lord in humility and transparency. But we leave the choice and results with the One who sees the beginning from the end, who sees all things clearly.

JANUARY 18

And seven priests shall bear before the ark seven trumpets of rams' horns: and the seventh day ye shall compass the city seven times, and the priests shall blow with the trumpets.

Joshua 6:4

The priests, the Ark, and the rams' horns that were part of the procession around the walls of Jericho all point to Jesus. Even the Sabbath, the seventh day, points to Him for He is our Sabbath rest (Hebrews 4).

Imagine that it's Valentine's Day and you walk into your house and see your wife hugging and kissing your picture. "Surprise!" you say as you hold out candy and roses, expecting her to run toward you. But if she remains more infatuated with your picture than with you, you would say, "Why are you so wrapped up with the picture, when the one it portrays is right here?"

So too, were Jesus on the scene in Joshua's day, He would say, "I am the fulfillment of the Sabbath and of the silver trumpets. I am the fulfillment of the priesthood and of the Ark of the Covenant. They're just pictures. Focus on Me." Yet I wonder how many of us are focused on rules, regulations, and religion even in the Promised Land of the Spirit-filled life. I wonder how many of us subconsciously say, "It's Sunday. That's a holy day. I'm off to church," or "It's morning. I'm disciplined. It's time for devotions."

To us, Jesus would say, "Rules, regulations, and rituals are only necessary if I'm not present. But if I'm present, those things are replaced by relationship with Me." Gang, we know more than the early Church knew about typology and illustrations. The question is, Do we know Who they knew? They knew Jesus. And they responded to His leading moment by moment. We too will be free from religion and predictability, from legalism and traditions, from habits, ruts, and routines to the degree that we realize that the Captain of the host, the Captain of our salvation, Jesus Himself, is in our midst.

JANUARY 19

. . . and when ye hear the sound of the trumpet, all the people shall shout with a great shout; and the wall of the city shall fall down flat . . .

Joshua 6:5 (b)

For six days, the congregation of Israel marched around the walls of the city of Jericho. So too, God has you and me go round and round in circles until finally we get dizzy and realize the wall is too high, the breach is too great, the estrangement is too severe. Although we do everything we know how to do, the wall only gets higher. Before there can be a moment of the miraculous, sometimes there must be a lengthy season of helplessness.

When their circling was complete, the Israelites were not to point, not to doubt, but to shout. So too, while I'm waiting for God to flatten the walls in my life, I'm not to wring my hands in anxiety. I'm to clap them in expectancy (Psalm 47:1).

Notice that the Israelites were commanded to shout before the walls fell - not when they fell, not after they fell; the children of Israel shouted before they fell. Thus, theirs was an expression of anticipation, a proclamation of faith.

Let's join their ranks. Let's be those who have free access to the heart of all that God has for us as we believe in Him, wait for Him, and submit to Him - for that's where the walls begin to fall.

JANUARY 20

And the second day they compassed the city once, and returned into the camp: so they did six days.

Joshua 6:14

As His people marched around the walls of Jericho, God prepared them in several ways. First, He gave them a realization of the impossibility of their situation. The first time the Israelites circled the city, the walls must have looked huge. And they must have looked bigger and more foreboding with each successive trip. Thus, in their repeated journeys around Jericho, the Lord was showing His people that victory would not come through their might nor through their power, but only by His Spirit (Zechariah 4:6).

So too, there might be a huge wall between you and a family member, neighbor, or fellow believer. God will have you go around it again and again until you finally say, "I can't manipulate the situation. I can't solve the problem. I can't do a thing about this, Lord. Only You can solve this." And when at last you come to this realization, I promise you that in due season, He will do something earth-shattering. Oh, it might take six months or even six years - but there will come a time when you'll say, "It was the Lord Who brought that wall down. It wasn't my cleverness or my ingenuity because as I went in circles day after week after month, it just got thicker and higher."

Second, as His people circled the walls of Jericho, God taught them the importance of patience. Hebrews 6:12 says that it is through faith and patience that His promises are obtained. Do you have faith? Great. God wants you to have patience too. You see, His agenda is bigger than just knocking down walls. His purpose is to develop patience in us in order that we might be perfect, lacking nothing (James 1:4).

Third, as His people circled the walls of Jericho, God taught them discipline. His job was to work, theirs to be absolutely silent. If I can't control my tongue, I won't conquer the enemy. My tongue will get me in big trouble. So will yours (James 3:5-6). Therefore, it is the wise man or woman who silently - without complaint or opinion - gives God time and room to work.

God's strategy for conquering Jericho served not only to prepare the children of Israel but to provide a witness to the people of Jericho. I believe that the people walking in quietness and tranquility, the Ark of the Covenant, the trumpets playing were all to be a witness to the inhabitants of Jericho. According to Rahab, their hearts were already melted. Thus, I believe God was giving them one last opportunity to come to Him. While His people were in Egypt, God gave the inhabitants of Canaan four hundred years to repent. Then He gave them forty more years while His people wandered in the wilderness. Here, He gives them six more days as they watched His children walk in devotion and order.

What will impress people around you? Seeing you walk patiently and quietly, neither panicking nor complaining, but simply walking under the authority of your Captain. Seeing the way your homes, marriages, and lives are ordered in this march toward Heaven is a witness to the people of our own Jerichos.

JANUARY 21

And Joshua adjured them at that time, saying, Cursed be the man before the LORD, that riseth up and buildeth this city Jericho: he shall lay the foundation thereof in his firstborn, and in his youngest son shall he set up the gates of it. So the LORD was with Joshua; and his fame was noised throughout all the country.

Joshua 6:26-27

He who tried to rebuild the walls of Jericho would pay a steep price. His oldest and youngest son would die. In 1 Kings 16, we read of a man named Hiel who did this. He rebuilt Jericho - but his oldest and youngest son died in the process.

Maybe you can relate to Joshua and the people of Israel. You've been set free from Egypt and baptized in the Spirit. But before you is a wall, a fortress, a barrier between you and someone else that is keeping you from going all the way into the heart of the Land of Promise. As a father, it might be between you and your junior high son. As a mother, it might be between you and your teenage daughter. As a husband or wife, it might be between you and your spouse. As a believer, it might be between you and a brother or sister in the Lord.

If God knocks down a wall between you and another and you say, "Maybe I shouldn't be so forgiving. Maybe I'm being taken advantage of," there will be no shortage of people to hand you all the bricks and mortar you need to rebuild the wall. But you'll pay a terrible price. Don't undo what God has done. Don't harden your heart. Don't let your soul become like concrete. Instead, with the wall flat on the ground, enter into fresh fellowship with the one from whom, by God's grace and mercy, you are no longer estranged.

JANUARY 22

And Joshua sent men from Jericho to Ai, which is beside Beth-aven, on the east side of Beth-el, and spake unto them, saying, Go up and view the country. And the men went up and viewed Ai. And they returned to Joshua, and said unto him, Let not all the people go up; but let about two or three thousand men go up and smite Ai; and make not all the people to labour thither; for they are but few. So there went up thither of the people about three thousand men: and they fled before the men of Ai.

Joshua 7:2-4

Instruction for crossing the Jordan had been given to Joshua by Divine revelation (Joshua 3). Instruction for dealing with the flesh once they were in the Promised Land had been given to Joshua by Divine revelation (Joshua 5). Instruction for taking Jericho had been given to Joshua by Divine revelation (Joshua 6). In other words, all along the way, Joshua had been seeking the Lord. But when he thought he could handle Ai by himself, the Spirit was quenched.

Paul put it this way when he asked the Galatians, "Are you so foolish? Having begun in the Spirit, are you now made perfect by the flesh?" (Galatians 3:3). And the same can be true of us.

Although we were once open to the mystery and intimacy of God's Word specifically and personally given to us, a "Joshua chapter 7" mentality can creep in which causes us to say, "I can handle this little problem with my own energy, insight, and ability. After all, it's just Ai." But whenever we try to do battle in our own strength, whenever we fail to wait upon the Lord and to listen for the Holy Spirit, the same thing that happened to the Israelites will happen to us. We'll flee before that which we thought we could easily conquer.

JANUARY 23

And the LORD said unto Joshua, Fear not, neither be thou dismayed: take all the people of war with thee, and arise, go up to Ai: see, I have given into thy hand the king of Ai, and his people, and his city, and his land . . .

Joshua 8:1

Once Achan's sin was exposed in chapter 7, the Lord said, "Don't be dismayed, I'm giving you the victory" in chapter 8.

The successful person in life is the one who gets up one more time than he or she is knocked down. Too many Christians, when they are dealt a blow, lay in the dust day after day and don't get up. "Forgetting the things which lie behind, I press toward the mark of the prize of the high calling of God in Christ Jesus" Paul declared (Philippians 3:13-14). How could Paul accomplish what he did? By forgetting that which was behind and looking ahead instead.

JANUARY 24

For Joshua drew not his hand back, wherewith he stretched out the spear, until he had utterly destroyed all the inhabitants of Ai.

Joshua 8:26

Where did Joshua get the idea to stretch out his spear during the battle? I suggest it was forty years earlier at Rephidim. The Amalekites were fighting the Israelites. And Moses said to Joshua, "You lead the troops in the valley. I'll go to the mountain and pray." Moses held high the rod of God. And as he held it up, Joshua and the troops were victorious. But when his hands grew weary and the rod began to fall, the Amalekites gained the upper hand. Moses lifted his hands once again, and Israel took the lead. The battle seesawed back and forth until Aaron and Hur held up Moses' hands until the victory was completely secure for the Israelites.

"Write this scene in a book," God said to Moses. "And rehearse it in the ears of Joshua so that he will know that the reason for his victory in the valley was not due to his strategy or ability but rather because there was intercession and prayer on the mountain" (Exodus 17:8-14).

A lot of us have lost our passion for God. Devotions have become drowsy. Prayer, if we bother, is routine and repetitious chatter. But here's the good news: God cares so passionately about you and me that He will not allow us to remain in a state of passionless religiosity.

C. S. Lewis nailed it when he said that God whispers to us in our pleasure, but shouts to us in our pain. Pain and passion walk hand in hand. If you're married, you understand this. Things get routine, mundane, boring. But when she says something she ought not to, or when he does something he ought not to, there's pain. Feelings are released. Frustrations are vented. Tears flow. But it all leads to passion as the couple is engaged once again.

"I want you either hot or cold," says the Lord (see Revelation 3:16). Yes, you have morning devotions and evening prayer. But there's no smiting of the arrow, no holding up of the spear throughout the whole day, no putting your head between your knees until there's death, drought, or the specter of a Syrian attack. God will not let you reside in a passionless state with Him indefinitely. He will send you pain.

The reason Joshua held up his spear is because he was tired of seeing his friends dead and defeated. I can't afford this any more, he must have thought. The stakes are high, so I will stand here. I will prevail. And he did.

G. Campbell Morgan said that faith answers questions and is, therefore, out of business when no question is asked. If there are no questions, there is no need for faith. And when do questions arise? When I'm going through difficulty and pain. Therefore, as believers, we can have a unique outlook on pain and setbacks if we see them as the fuel of passion. We can, in fact, count them all joy (James 1:2).

JANUARY 25

There was not a word of all that Moses commanded, which Joshua read not before all the congregation of Israel, with the women, and the little ones, and the strangers that were conversant among them.

Joshua 8:35

At the beginning of their conquest of the Promised Land, all of Israel and those in their company stopped to hear the Word. Have your kids heard the Word? The tremendous task before us is to read and discuss the Word of God with our kids over and over, day after day. "We don't have time," you might say. "There are battles to fight, wars to win, Little League games to play, staff meetings to attend." Joshua could have easily said the same thing. But he realized that if we're not talking to our kids about the Word of God, then we're missing the mark completely.

And the stakes are getting higher because we're living in the last days. Dark will get darker and the dangers will become greater. Mom and Dad, if you care about your son or daughter, you will take this responsibility seriously. It is a big mistake to assume our kids know the Word. That's why Joshua said, "I know you're anxious to conquer the Land. I know you can't wait to drive out the enemy so you can settle in, grow your crops, and enjoy your family. But we're stopping here and now to go over the Word again."

The Word will be plastered on the wall of your soul and imprinted in your mind if you will take the time to review it time after time after time.

JANUARY 26

And the sun stood still, and the moon stayed, until the people had avenged themselves upon their enemies. Is not this written in the book of Jasher? So the sun stood still in the midst of heaven, and hasted not to go down about a whole day. And there was no day like that before it or after it, that the LORD hearkened unto the voice of a man: for the LORD fought for Israel.

Joshua 10:13-14

Do you ever come to the end of a day feeling frustrated, tense, or anxious because the day slipped away before you could accomplish even half of the things you intended to do? Does it ever seem to you like there's just not enough "day" in your day? There are so many obligations and responsibilities, opportunities and activities that the day seems to dissipate. And sometimes that can fill us with a great degree of frustration.

Such was not the case with Joshua. With the day elongated, he was able to do what the Lord commanded him to do. How? He spoke to the sun. We can do the same. In our world, to be busy is to be important. But such is not the case in God's economy. To Him, busyness is more of a curse than an asset. That is why Jesus says, "My burden is easy and My load is light. Come unto Me all that are weary and heavy laden, and I will give you rest. Learn of Me and you will find rest in your soul" (see Matthew 11:28-30). Therefore, if, like Joshua, you and I speak to the Son, things will stand still because He'll whisper in our ear, "Now that you've spent a bit of time with Me, talked things over, made confession of sin, read some Scripture, here's a couple things I want you to do today . . ."

We waste so much time trying to figure out what we should do next. And when we don't get to it, we feel condemned about it. In reality, the decision ought to have been made early in the day. I'm not saying there's no room for flexibility, but for the most part, I have discovered that the real key is to say early in the day, "Lord, what do You want me to do? By Your grace and with Your help, that's what I'll do."

And as I do those things, as I come to the end of the day, I realize the sun has indeed stood still. Therefore, like Jesus, I'm able to say, "Father, I've finished the work You gave me to do" (see John 17:4). The tensions disappear; the burdens dissipate; and I find myself living a life of serenity and tranquility to a much greater degree.

What God gives us to do is doable. Do what our Greater-than-Joshua did day by day. Before the day begins, find a quiet place and have a quiet time with a quiet heart. Let God direct your day: you will have fewer decisions to make and you'll be victorious in a whole new way.

JANUARY 27

Now Joshua was old and stricken in years; and the LORD said unto him, Thou art old and stricken in years, and there remaineth yet very much land to be possessed.

Joshua 13:1

In Joshua 11:23, we read that Joshua took the whole land and that the land rested from war. Here, we read that very much land remained to be possessed. Is this a contradiction? No, for although the victory was secure, there were still "mop-up operations" to complete in pockets of resistance where the enemy was holed up.

In our soul, there are pockets of resistance as well. However, in the Spirit-filled life we don't fight for victory because Jesus already was victorious on our behalf when He died on the Cross. The roaring lion has had his teeth kicked in. We don't fight for victory, but from victory. Positionally, we're the righteousness of God in Christ Jesus (2 Corinthians 5:21), but practically, there are still enemies lurking around my soul that need to be rooted out.

How do I root out the enemy? Here's the great news. Positionally, I enjoy the riches and inheritance because of Christ's death. Practically, I have victory over that which would make me miserable, ruin my testimony, and rob me eternally through Christ's resurrected life. You see, Jesus not only died to wash our sins away positionally, but He rose again on the third day to live within us practically. So when the Canaanites rise up, when the temptation threatens, the good news is that Christ is right there with you. The good news is that God will not allow you to be tempted above what you are able, but will always provide a way of escape, a way of victory - every single time (1 Corinthians 10:13). The Lord not only tells us what to do, but He sets up residence inside of us. Positionally, we're cleansed by His death. Practically, we're set free by His life.

JANUARY 28

Now therefore divide this land for an inheritance unto the nine tribes, and the half tribe of Manasseh, with whom the Reubenites and the Gadites have received their inheritance, which Moses gave them, beyond Jordan eastward, even as Moses the servant of the LORD gave them . . .

Joshua 13:7-8

Gad, Reuben, and half of the tribe of Manasseh were the ones who chose to remain on the east side of the Jordan rather than crossing with the rest of the tribes into the Promised Land. Their decision wasn't based upon God's best for their families but seemingly upon what was best for their cattle and bank accounts. History shows, however, that Reuben, Gad, and the half-tribe of Manasseh were the first ones to be carried away when the enemies of Israel attacked the nation.

The same thing happens to you and me. If you say, "I'm just going to hang out in the back," watch out. That is sure to be the most dangerous, most depressing place ultimately. God will not make me go in and go on in my walk with Him. The choice is up to me. He will take me as deep as I want to go - but He won't take me one step further than I want to go.

JANUARY 29

And these are the countries which the children of Israel inherited in the land of Canaan, which Eleazar the priest, and Joshua the son of Nun, and the heads of the fathers of the tribes of the children of Israel, distributed for inheritance to them.

Joshua 14:1

With Reuben, Gad, and the half-tribe of Manasseh remaining on the east side of the Jordan, the rest of the nine and a half tribes claimed their territory on the west side, in the Promised Land. Each tribe was given a certain region, described in chapters 13 through 21. These descriptions might seem tedious to us, but they were important and wonderful to the Israelites. Why? Because the descriptions were of their own inheritance.

So too, God has a wonderful plan for you. It might be boring to others, but for you, it's of utmost importance to know what territory God has given to you, where your place is in the Body of Christ, what God wants you to do. If your heart desires to know His will, be sure He will give the parameters to you. As time goes on, what you're to do will become clear to you.

"I am careful that I do not stretch myself beyond measure," Paul wisely declared (see 2 Corinthians 10:14-16). In other words, "I realize what God has called me to do and I want to take it all. But I'm not going to stretch myself beyond what He's called me to do and to be."

God has exacting boundaries for you. And it's our privilege and responsibility to explore, to pursue, to pray, to seek the Lord, to study, to wait on Him and say, "Lord, what territory have You mapped out as mine? Help me to stick to it and be faithful in it that I might take all the territory You have for me."

JANUARY 30

Then the children of Judah came unto Joshua in Gilgal: and Caleb the son of Jephunneh the Kenezite said unto him, Thou knowest the thing that the LORD said unto Moses the man of God concerning me and thee in Kadesh-barnea.

Joshua 14:6

Forty-five years before this account in Joshua 14, God had led His people to a place called Kadesh-barnea. Poised to go into the Promised Land, the people of Israel sent one man from each of the twelve tribes to check it out. The tribe of Ephraim was represented by Joshua, the tribe of Judah by Caleb. Ten of the spies returned, saying, "We can't go up against the people because they're stronger than us. Compared to them, we're just grasshoppers."

Joshua and Caleb, however, ripped their clothes in grief and said, "The land is an exceedingly good land. If the Lord delight in us, He will bring us into this land and give it to us. Do not fear the people of the land. For they are bread for us."

When others said, "We're going to get crunched and stomped on," Caleb said. "No, God's with us. And those giants are bread for us. We're going to eat them up" (see Numbers 14:9). And here, forty-five years later, an eighty-five year-old Caleb is about to claim the inheritance that Moses promised to give him (Deuteronomy 1:36).

Now, one would think that, at eighty-five, Caleb would say, "What I want is a condo on the beach on the Mediterranean seashore." Or perhaps, "Give me a cabin on the shore of the Sea of Galilee." But that's not what Caleb said. As we'll see, he asked for the land where the giants lived because he knew that the secret of strength lay not in taking it easy but in taking up a challenge. You see, God does not want us to fade away, to retire, or to pull back. Rather, He wants to take us from glory to greater glory (2 Corinthians 3:18). He wants us to become stronger and deeper, richer and better, year after year until the day He takes us to Heaven.

JANUARY 31

And now behold, the LORD hath kept me alive, as he said, these forty and five years, even since the LORD spake this word unto Moses, while the children of Israel wandered in the wilderness: and now lo, I am this day fourscore and five years old. As yet I am as strong this day as I was in the day that Moses sent me: as my strength was then, even so is my strength now, for war, both to go out, and to come in. Now therefore give me this mountain, whereof the LORD spake in that day; for thou heardest in that day how the Anakims were there, and that the cities were great and fenced: if so be the LORD will be with me, then I shall be able to drive them out, as the LORD said. And Joshua blessed him, and gave unto Caleb the son of Jephunneh Hebron for an inheritance.

Joshua 14:10-13

At eighty-five years old, Caleb said, "I want the Anakims. I want food. I don't want to kick back. I don't want an easier load. I don't want to retire. What I want, what's keeping me strong and vigorous is giants. I thrive on them" (see Numbers 14:9). Why would Caleb say this? Because he understood that what God's people need is not comfort but challenges, because it is the giant difficulty, the giant heartbreak, the giant heartache that brings them to Hebron. Hebron, the place Abraham first built an altar, means "Fellowship." That's what giant problems do - they bring me to the place where I cry out to the Lord, call on the Lord, and look to the Lord. They bring me to fellowship. When things are comfy and cozy, I can find myself pulling away from fellowship. I can find myself spiritually putting my feet up, kicking back, retiring.

And that makes me old, grumpy, cranky, diminished. Why? Because it's in the place where I'm battling heartbreak and heartache, where I'm doing battle in the spiritual realm that I am forced to be on my knees, forced to say, "Lord, I can't make it without You."

If God gives you a promise, He will keep you so you can receive it and part-take of it. (Health is from the Lord; He sustains.)

JANUARY / 37

And the Lord says, "That's why I've allowed these Anakims to come to you. They're bread for you. They actually make you stronger because they bring you into Hebron."

"Give us this day our daily bread," Jesus taught us to pray (Matthew 6:11). When I think of bread, I think of sourdough with butter and strawberry jam. Yet, while the Lord does indeed give us bread to sustain us physically, He also gives us the bread of giant problems to make us strong and energetic spiritually.

I want to be like Caleb. I want to say, "I'm strong like I was at my peak."

The Lord says, "Okay, then I'm going to send bread your way - Anakims that will force you to come to Hebron."

That's what Jesus did. Such an abundance of bread did He provide for the multitude that there were twelve baskets left over. If this meant each disciple was given his own basket, I can picture them enjoying their "leftovers" on the grassy hillside, overlooking the Sea of Galilee. That very evening, they were on the Sea of Galilee facing giant problems. "We're dying!" they cried, as they fought the storm hour after hour. Yet it was then - in the midst of a giant storm - that Jesus, the Bread of Life, came to them, walking on the water (Matthew 14:27).

When we're eating bread on the grassy hillside, we don't understand who Jesus is. But when the seas are angry and the wind is howling, when there are giants around us and everything seems to be going down, it's then we hear His voice and see His face. It's then that we understand that He is our Bread.

As believers, we're the luckiest people in the world because we are the only ones who can count it all joy when various trials come our way (James 1:2). We're the only ones who know that all things are working together for good (Romans 8:28). We're the only ones who can say, "There's a giant of a problem in my life - and I know it's bread for me."

How do I know that every storm the Lord sends my way will ultimately be good for me? Because the Bread of Life was broken on the Cross of Calvary to pay for my sins. Our Lord, our Joshua, our Jesus says to us, "I care about you deeply. I love you passionately. And anything that comes your way is

Wonder Bread. It will build your body, keep you young, and bring you into fellowship with Me."

FEBRUARY 1

So the children of Joseph, Manasseh and Ephraim, took their inheritance. And the border of the children of Ephraim according to their families was thus . . .

Joshua 16:4-5

Joshua 16 and 17 describe the inheritance given to Joseph's two sons, Ephraim and Manasseh. Although Manasseh was the older brother, Ephraim is mentioned first. And therein lies a story . . .

Hearing that his father was sick, Joseph brought his two sons to be blessed by their grandfather, carefully positioning them so that Manasseh was on Jacob's right side and Ephraim on his left. After pronouncing blessing upon Joseph, Jacob prepared to bless Joseph's sons by placing his right hand - the hand of priority - on Ephraim and his left on Manasseh. "Wait a minute, Dad," Joseph said. "You're confused. Manasseh is the firstborn. Therefore, your right hand should be on his head."

"I know what I'm doing," Jacob insisted. "Manasseh will be a great people - but Ephraim shall indeed be greater" (Genesis 48:19).

This is often the way of God . . .

It was Abel and not Cain who was blessed, even though Cain was the first-born. Jacob and Esau were twins, but Esau was older. Jacob, however, was the blessed one. Ishmael was Abraham's firstborn. Isaac, however, was the child of promise. Aaron was the elder son of Amram and Jochebed, yet it was their second-born son, Moses, who was called to deliver God's people. David was the youngest of Jesse's sons, yet it was he - a man after God's own heart - who was anointed king.

This pattern is seen throughout Scripture.

Why?

I suggest it shows you and me that God forgets about our firstborn and blesses our second born. Kids? No, our lives. That is, our first life is forgotten about. Our new life is what God focuses on and blesses.

"You must be born again," Jesus told Nicodemus (John 3).

"Therefore if any man be in Christ, he is a new creature: old things are passed away; behold, all things are become new," Paul told the Corinthians (2 Corinthians 5:17).

"Knowing this, that our old man is crucified with him, that the body of sin might be destroyed, that henceforth we should not serve sin," he told the Romans (Romans 6:6).

Ours is the God of the second-born - and the second chance.

And for that, I'm oh so grateful.

FEBRUARY 2

There was also a lot for the tribe of Manasseh; for he was the firstborn of Joseph . . .

Joshua 17:1

Joshua 16 detailed the inheritance given to Joseph's second son, Ephraim. Here in chapter 17, we see the inheritance given to Manasseh, his firstborn son.

The Book of Joshua illustrates what it means to move into and live out the Spirit-filled life. The people of Israel were set free from bondage in Egypt the night the blood was placed on the doorposts of their homes. So too, we were set free from bondage to the world by the blood of the Lamb on the doorposts of our hearts.

After they were set free, the people of Israel made their way to the Red Sea, where they were baptized when the waters parted (1 Corinthians 10:2). So too, the baptism of believers signifies death and resurrection to a whole new way of living.

When their faith faltered shortly thereafter, the Israelites found themselves wandering in the wilderness for an entire generation - approximately forty years.

That can happen to you and me as well. We're born again, baptized in water, but then we get distracted. Oh, we're still Christians, but we're wandering in the wilderness, swatting flies, and eating dust. Things are dry, not like they used to be, not like they're supposed to be. We wander and we wonder sometimes year after year until, like the Israelites, we come to a second baptism - the Jordan River, which speaks of the baptism in the Spirit.

A new generation came to those waters, and as they obeyed the command of the Lord to put the soles of their feet into the water, they entered into the Promised Land. So too, when you and I engage our souls and say, "Lord, I want to step out. I want to press in. I want to take hold of all You have for me," a new dimension of spiritual life begins. The baptism in the Spirit transforms those who were wandering and weak into those who are dynamic and fruitful.

Maybe you're at the point where you're saying, "Lord, I love You, but I'm tired of the dryness of my soul. I'm tired of wandering around aimlessly. I want You to take control. I want to see Your Spirit come upon me and flow through me. I'm going to do whatever You tell me to do. I'm going to step out. I'm going to take a risk and begin to press in to what You say is available for me this very day."

As you receive by faith the empowering of the Spirit, you enter into the Promised Land - a Land where there are battles to fight and where there are wars to wage - but also a Land of milk, honey, and grapes the size of bowling balls.

FEBRUARY 3

And there remained among the children of Israel seven tribes, which had not yet received their inheritance. And Joshua said unto the children of Israel, How long are ye slack to go to possess the land, which the LORD God of your fathers hath given you?

Joshua 18:2-3

It was evidently up to the leaders of the tribes to approach Joshua and say, "We're here to receive our lot, our inheritance." Yet at this point, seven of the twelve tribes had not yet done so. Why? I suggest it was that, without a specific region appropriated to them, they would have no battles to fight. They could be on the coast for a while and then go into the valley of Jezreel or on to Jerusalem. Whenever difficulties arose, they could simply pack up and move. And there are Christians who are just like them.

There are people who have left the wilderness of carnality and who have received the baptism of the Holy Spirit. They've entered the Promised Land of the Spirit-filled life, and are experiencing something of abundance - yet they don't want to be locked in to a specific territory, a specific congregation. "I want to attend this meeting over here and that church over there," they say - until the pastor makes them angry and they head in a different direction. "When the building project is complete, I'll be back," they say. Although people with this mindset might think they're being led by the Spirit, in reality, they are simply neither accountable to, nor responsible for, anyone. They're involved as long as it is comfortable for them, but if they're asked to do something that stretches them, they'll leave.

The majority of the tribes failed to claim their inheritance. And, sadly, Joshua's question still needs to be asked in our generation: "When are you going to quit floating around, sink some roots, put your hand to the plow, and claim territory for the Kingdom?"

FEBRUARY 4

And the men went and passed through the land, and described it by cities into seven parts in a book, and came again to Joshua to the host at Shiloh.

Joshua 18:9

The word "describe" seen here in verse 9 and previously in verse 4 literally means "to survey." Three men from each of the seven tribes who hadn't claimed their inheritance were sent to survey the land. Here's the question:

Where did they learn how to survey? Did they learn while wandering in the wilderness? I don't think so. Did they learn while fighting in the Promised Land? Not likely. I suggest they learned the art of surveying while in Egypt. Those who were twenty years of age when they left Egypt would have been involved in all kinds of construction projects requiring surveying skills.

Sometimes we wonder why we're in the occupation, the situation, or the position we're in when it doesn't seem to be advancing us in our plan for life. That's what these men must have thought as they surveyed Egyptian land for Egyptian building projects. Little did they know, however, that they would use the very skills they were learning there to lay the groundwork for their own inheritance in the Promised Land.

Be faithful, dear saint, in whatever position the Lord has placed you. Trust that He's preparing you in ways you might not be able to even imagine for the specific part you'll play, the unique role you'll fill in the days that might be too far down the road for you to see now, but which He knows all about.

FEBRUARY 5

The sixth lot came out to the children of Naphtali, even for the children of Naphtali according to their families.

Joshua 19:32

The inheritance of Zebulun and Naphtali is called "the Galilee of the Gentiles" in Matthew 4. Throughout Israel's history, Zebulun and Naphtali were always being beat up because the enemies of Israel - the Babylonians, the Assyrians, the Greeks, the Persians, and the Romans - came from the north. Consequently, Zebulun and Naphtali resided in "the Galilee of the Gentiles" because Gentiles resided there ultimately.

Isaiah prophesied that the land of Zebulun and Naphtali would see a great Light (Isaiah 9:1-2). Indeed, those who were depressed, in bondage, and under attack were those who saw a great Light because where did Jesus base His ministry? Where did He spend virtually all of His time except when He traveled to Jerusalem? Galilee. You might be in the dark today - depressed and beat up. If so, you're just the person the Lord especially wants to visit. If you're in a place of being wiped out, understand that it was the people who sat in great darkness who saw a great, great Light (Matthew 4:13-16).

FEBRUARY 6

And the coast of the children of Dan went out too little for them: therefore the children of Dan went up to fight against Leshem, and took it, and smote it with the edge of the sword, and possessed it, and dwelt therein, and called Leshem, Dan, after the name of Dan their father.

Joshua 19:47

Why did Dan go north? Because the southern region was too hard for them to control. They left the region to which they were assigned and went north because it was easier - or so they thought. In reality, they fell into idolatry, made a golden calf eventually, and were attacked constantly. Thus, by trying to avoid struggle, they found themselves in an infinitely worse situation. They were under attack to a greater degree and had a tough time throughout history because they didn't stay in the place the Lord knew would be best for them.

And oh, how often we have found the same to be true in our lives.

FEBRUARY 7

When they had made an end of dividing the land for inheritance by their coasts, the children of Israel gave an inheritance to Joshua the son of Nun among them: according to the word of the LORD they gave him the city which he asked, even Timnath-serah in mount Ephraim: and he built the city, and dwelt therein.

Joshua 19:49-50

It was only after everyone else had an assigned section that Joshua claimed his territory. Timnath-serah was hill country. It was similar to Caleb's territory - a tough assignment.

Philippians 2 tells us we're to have the same mind as Jesus, Who came in humility and gave up His rights and chose to die on the Cross in order to provide redemption for lost sinners like you and me.

Timnath-serah literally means "abundant portion" because abundance is always found when we lay down our rights. It's the hard stuff that brings abundance. It's when you have to roll up your sleeves and put your hand to the plow, it's when you get involved and engaged that you find abundant life. The abundant life is found in walking in the Spirit, seeking first the Kingdom, taking on the territory you've been assigned, and not giving up. Joshua claimed Timnath-serah as his own. Yet Jesus took on an infinitely tougher assignment when He took on my salvation.

FEBRUARY 8

And the children of Israel gave unto the Levites out of their inheritance, at the commandment of the LORD, these cities and their suburbs.

Joshua 21:3

Although the Levites were not given territory, as were the other tribes, they were given cities within the territories of the other tribes. The Levites were those who worked in the Tabernacle, those who cared for the spiritual life of the people of Israel. They were spread out over forty-eight cities. This meant that every Israelite was near to a Levitical community, near to men who knew the Scriptures and were dedicated to serving the Lord.

Along with Simeon, Levi was to have no inheritance due to his dealing with Shechem (Genesis 34, 49). Yet the curse on Levi was reversed and transformed into a major blessing when the Lord said, "Levi, I will be your inheritance. You'll be scattered everywhere in order to serve Me, and your cities will be protected by the rest of the nation." Simeon and Levi were both cursed, but God reversed the curse upon Levi. Why? I believe the answer lies in Exodus 32:28.

You see, the day Moses came down from Mount Sinai with the Ten Commandments in hand, the people were dancing around a golden calf. "Who is on the Lord's side?" Moses said. "Who will deal with this sin?" Only one tribe volunteered - the tribe of Levi. The Levites unsheathed their swords and went throughout the congregation dealing with their friends and relatives. It was painful, but they had to do it because the tribe of Levi knew, perhaps better than anyone, that sin cannot go unchecked.

So too, God can take our sin and turn it around for good. He can reverse the curse even today. Wherever you've been, whatever you've done, if you repent and say, "Lord, from here on out, I'm going Your way," He'll turn the mistakes you've made around for good. Oh, the scars will still be there. But God will open new doors and do wonderful things in your life. You'll be more blessed than you could have ever imagined if - and only if - you repent. It's all a matter of repentance, of changing directions.

FEBRUARY 9

And the LORD gave unto Israel all the land which he sware to give unto their fathers; and they possessed it, and dwelt therein.

Joshua 21:43

God gives a promise and then keeps it - but there is often a period of time between when the promise is given and the fulfillment of it is seen. Therefore, don't give up. Don't be cynical. Instead, keep to the course to which God has called you. Believe the promises He's given to you in the Word. And, with faith and patience, you'll inherit them.

I wonder how many people give up a month, a day, or an hour too soon and just miss God's blessing. In Hebrews 6:15, we read that it was after Abraham patiently endured that he obtained the promise. Abraham goes down in history and is celebrated throughout eternity as a man of faith. He heard the Word. He mixed it with faith. He patiently endured - and he obtained the promise.

Believing might have been simple for Abraham, perhaps you're thinking, but me? I don't have faith that God will bless my marriage, my kids, or my job. I can't believe because my faith is so weak. Are you sure? I suggest that your faith is huge, colossal, titanic in size. After all, you're in the hall of faith, in the company of Moses and Abraham, Sarah and Gideon . . .

> Through faith we understand that the worlds were framed by the word of God, so that things which are seen were not made of things which do appear.

Hebrews 11:3

Your belief that God created all things is itself an indication of the colossal size and strength of your faith. Believing God created the world out of nothing is the hardest thing to believe. Everything else is a piece of cake by comparison. The second biggest issue deals with the resurrection of Jesus Christ. "Blessed are those who have not seen and yet believe," Jesus said to Thomas after Thomas said he wouldn't believe Jesus was alive until he touched His wounds (John 20:29).

Do you believe Jesus rose from the dead? If so, I suggest with a sparkle in His eye and a grin on His face, Jesus would say, "Awesome! You haven't seen Me physically, but yet you believe in Me. You are a blessed person!"

Therefore, when the enemy whispers in your ear, "You're not going to see that happen. You're never going to see that work out because your faith is too weak," you need to say, "I believe creation was accomplished by my Father. I also believe Jesus rose from the dead. I couldn't believe either one of those things had not the Father given me huge, colossal-sized faith. He has given me faith for the big issues, and everything else - health, finances, relationships - is miniscule by comparison."

Mix the Word with faith. Patiently endure - and, like Abraham, you'll obtain every promise He has made to you.

FEBRUARY 10

And the children of Reuben and the children of Gad called the altar Ed: for it shall be a witness between us that the LORD is God.

Joshua 22:34

Ed means "witness." This altar was meant to be a witness to the unity of the twelve tribes. Jesus said that our *"ed"* - the witness of our unity as the Body of Christ - is love. The world will know we're believers not by our bumper stickers or the size of the Bible we carry. "They'll know you are My disciples," Jesus said, "by your love" (see John 13:35).

"Father, let them be one that the world might know that I am in You and You are in Me," Jesus prayed (see John 17:21).

Gang, we get to love people and love each other. Love is the key. Love is our witness. Where is unity found? At the altar of the Cross of Calvary. It is neither our eschatology nor our pneumatology - neither how we view the end times nor how we view the manifestations of the Holy Spirit - that make us one. We are one because we all believe in the same Lord. We eat of

His body. We drink of His blood. Unity is found at the foot of the Cross, at the altar called Calvary. Whether regarding division among family members, churches, or brothers and sisters in the congregation, unity is found only at the altar where the Lamb was slain for you and me.

The enemy wants to cause believers to wage war with each other. Be warned. Be wise. And just love people in Jesus' name.

FEBRUARY 11

> *And if it seem evil unto you to serve the LORD, choose you this day whom ye will serve; whether the gods which your fathers served that were on the other side of the flood, or the gods of the Amorites, in whose land ye dwell: but as for me and my house, we will serve the LORD.*

Joshua 24:15

"We will serve the Lord," said Joshua. "I expect this to be reality. My kids will serve the Lord right beside me."

The Bible says that without faith it is impossible to please God (Hebrews 11:6). Therefore, Dad, Husband, or Grandpa, you need to say, "I have faith that God will do what He's promised." What has God promised? He has promised that He Who has begun a good work will be faithful to perform it (Philippians 1:6), that He is able to keep that which is committed to Him (2 Timothy 1:12), that if you train up a child in the way he should go, even when he is old, he will not depart from it (Proverbs 22:6).

For ~~120 years~~ 100 years or less, Noah pounded away on the ark, preparing it not only for the animals, but for his wife, three sons, and their wives as well. What amazes me is that he prepared these rooms twenty years before his sons were even born. That's faith!

You can do the same thing. In faith, say, "I believe my family will indeed serve the Lord. I believe my kids won't be wiped out and washed away but that they'll be on the Ark of salvation." Have faith. Believe. It's important because without faith it's impossible to please Him.

"As for me and my house, we will serve the Lord."

Declare this for your own family. Expect it to be so. And realize it begins with you.

FEBRUARY 12

Now after the death of Joshua it came to pass, that the children of Israel asked the LORD, saying, Who shall go up for us against the Canaanites first, to fight against them?

Judges 1:1

In contrast to the Book of Joshua, which talks about entering into the Promised Land by faith, the Book of Judges deals with enjoying the Land by faithfulness. The application for us is that we have entered into the Land of our Heavenly inheritance apart from anything we've done or haven't done. We're received salvation as a free gift of God (Ephesians 2:8). Yet, if we are going to be a people who *enjoy* our salvation, we must be a people who walk in faithfulness to the Lord. While we enter the Kingdom simply by faith, we enjoy our presence in the Kingdom by our obedience and faithfulness to the Lord and to His Word.

If you're miserable today, if you feel as though life is a great big disappointment, it could very well be due to an area in your life where you are being disobedient, where you are not being faithful to the things God has shown you and to which He has called you. Take heart, dear saint, you're at the right place, for the Book of Judges is built on the premise that faithfulness and obedience are not only necessary for victory in the Land, but for enjoyment of the Kingdom.

Although the Israelites were in the Promised Land, pockets of Canaanites were there as well. Consequently, there was still much guerilla activity throughout the land of Israel.

The same is true of us. Our salvation is secure. Jesus won the war when He hung on the Cross and cried victoriously, "It is finished." But there's still work for us to do, still pockets of resistance in our flesh.

FEBRUARY 13

And the LORD said, Judah shall go up: behold, I have delivered the land into his hand.

Judges 1:2

"Where do we begin? What should we do first?" asked the children of Israel concerning the mop-up operation before them.

"Start with Judah," the Lord said.

Judah means "praise." Praise always has priority in warfare. On the Day of Pentecost, before Peter stood up to deliver the message in which three thousand would be saved, we first see the Holy Spirit inspiring the people of God to worship Him, magnify Him, and glorify Him as they spoke praise in other tongues (Acts 2:11). Something unique happens when we praise the Lord. Praise prepares the way, clears the air, sets the stage. Praise is powerful.

I need to be reminded of this a lot. Praise paves the way to victory. When you're discouraged and don't know what to do, call for Judah. Lift up your hands, bow your knees, express your heart energetically, and watch and see how the enemy is beaten back.

FEBRUARY 14

And Caleb said, He that smiteth Kirjath-sepher, and taketh it, to him will I give Achsah my daughter to wife. And Othniel the son of Kenaz, Caleb's younger brother, took it: and he gave him Achsah his daughter to wife.

Judges 1:12-13

This story reminds me of a similar situation in the life of David. King David was desiring to conquer Jerusalem and so he said to his men, "The first one of you guys who finds a way to break into the city shall be general of my army" (see 1 Chronicles 11:6).

Here, Caleb says, "The first one who takes the city of Debir (also called Kirjath-sepher) gets to marry my daughter" - who must have been quite a prize. As it so happened, Caleb's nephew was the first one to make it inside the city, and thus he was rewarded.

The principle in both the story of David and Caleb is that God blesses and honors the individual who is an initiator. Too often, people hold back and wait, thinking, "I really can't start a home Bible study," or "I can't disciple some junior high kids. Nobody has asked me." That's not the point. Perhaps no one will ask you to do anything, but the Holy Spirit will lay upon your heart certain things *He* desires you to do, and God will bless you as you initiate, instigate, and move out in those specific areas and visions.

This week, ask the Lord what Debir He has for you to conquer. If God is calling you to assemble an intercession group, don't call the church office and ask permission - just do it! If He is calling you to China, God bless you! I encourage and exhort you in the name of Jesus to respond to the varied, creative, needful avenues of ministry He will open before you via the promptings of the Holy Ghost.

FEBRUARY 15

*And the LORD was with Judah; and he drave out
the inhabitants of the mountain; but could not drive out the
inhabitants of the valley, because they had chariots of iron.*

Judges 1:19

Why couldn't Judah drive out the inhabitants of the valley? Because their
eyes were fixed on the iron chariots rather than on Almighty God. If your
eyes are fixed on the Lord, I care not how formidable your foe might be,
it can be overcome. But if your eyes are on the obstacle - if you're focused
on the problem, if you're in bondage to your past - you will not drive out
your enemy no matter how small it is. You've got to lift your eyes higher
and fix them on the Father. Yes, the enemies of Judah had chariots of iron,
but if Judah had lifted their eyes higher and focused upon the One who has
twenty thousand chariots at His command (Psalm 68:17), they would have
been victorious.

Judah was successful in the mountains, but they were discouraged and defeated in the valley. We sometimes tend to live in our past. We think that
because we've had problems with iron chariots previously, we need always
be fearful whenever we see them on the horizon. Not true. We need to be
a people who put the past behind us - past defeats, past discouragements,
past wounds, past failures, past sins.

"This one thing I do," said our brother, Paul, "forgetting those things which
are behind, and reaching forth unto those things which are before, I press
toward the mark for the prize of the high calling of God in Christ Jesus"
(Philippians 3:13-14). We need to put the past away and lift our eyes higher
- beyond the failure of the past, beyond the chariots of the present - to the
high calling of God Who enables us to do all that He asks of us.

FEBRUARY 16

And the man went into the land of the Hittites, and built
a city, and called the name thereof Luz: which is the name
thereof unto this day.

Judges 1:26

This man was spared and saved - but what did he do? Did he join the people of God? No. After experiencing deliverance, he went into an area of present-day northern Syria, and built another city called Luz - just like the city that had been destroyed.

The same thing happens today. When people go through hard times, they receive the blessing, mercy, and forgiveness of God. But then they soon find themselves going back to the old areas, rebuilding the old cities, and doing the old things once again. If the Lord has touched your life, if He has called you into His Kingdom, if He has brought you into His family, when things start getting easier, don't give in to the temptation of saying, "I don't have to be as intense any more. I can sort of kick back. I can go back up to northern Syria where I came from and kind of rebuild old ways."

Don't do it! That's what this man did. What happened to him? The Bible doesn't say. His name isn't mentioned; his deeds are not recorded from this point on. Thus, it seems his life didn't count for much in the economy of God.

FEBRUARY 17

*And the anger of the LORD was hot against Israel; and he
said, Because that this people hath transgressed my covenant
which I commanded their fathers, and have not hearkened
unto my voice; I also will not henceforth drive out any from
before them of the nations which Joshua left when he died:
that through them I may prove Israel, whether they will
keep the way of the LORD to walk therein, as their fathers
did keep it, or not. Therefore the LORD left those nations,
without driving them out hastily; neither delivered he them
into the hand of Joshua.*

Judges 2:20-23

Because the Israelites continually disobeyed Him, the Lord said, "I'm going
to allow their enemies to remain." Thus, the Canaanites, Hittites, Perizzites,
Jebusites, Girgashites, Ammonites, and the Amorites served as instruments
whereby the Lord could test His people. So too, 1 Corinthians talks about
the testings we face. You see, many of the problems we go through are the
result of our own stupidity. Many of the difficulties we encounter are the
direct result of our own disobedience. Yet the Lord will use those very difficulties and problems in order to test us, to prove us, to show us where we
stand.

You will be tested, gang, and it is during the time of testing - when fire
sweeps through your life, your marriage, your family - that you will discover
whether you have been building with wood, hay, and stubble, or with gold,
silver, and precious stones. If everything burns in the time of testing, then
you need to deal with it, saying, "Father, I have been building with the
wrong material. Correct me."

Whenever fire sweeps through your life, don't try to put the fire out. You'll
only get burned. Instead, let the fire go. Let it burn. And then when it's
over, come back and poke around. See in the midst of the ashes if there's
any gold, silver, or precious stones - and rebuild with them. I believe it is
crucial for us not to be those who try to put out fires in our church, in our
marriages, or at our jobs. Don't be one who puts out fires. It won't work.

Oh, you might delay the fire a bit. Or you might diffuse it somewhat - but only for a while. Instead, let the fire burn because you will never know what you're building with in life, in ministry, or in your occupation until the day of trial comes and the fire is unleashed.

That's why, as Christians, we must never be defensive. We must never answer accusations or protect ourselves in any area. We must welcome the fires that sweep through our lives, our families, our ministries, and our jobs in order that in the light of the flames, we might see clearly the true nature of our building materials.

Let the fire rage. Let the Canaanites - those who might be attacking you, misunderstanding you, or accusing you - stand, for through them, you'll be able to see exactly where you're at, how you're developing, how you're maturing.

That's what Jesus did. If there was ever anyone who would have been justified in getting tough and taking a stand, it would have been Him. If there was ever a time for someone to say, "This isn't right, and it must not happen," it was when His enemies accused and cursed Him. But He didn't. He submitted. He went to the Cross.

How can you stop a man who doesn't fight back? How can you stop a church who will embrace difficult times? How can you stop a family or a marriage that actually welcomes fires? How can you stop people like that?

You can't.

FEBRUARY 18

And the children of Israel did evil in the sight of the LORD, and forgat the LORD their God, and served Baalim and the groves. Therefore the anger of the LORD was hot against Israel, and he sold them into the hand of Chushan-rishathaim king of Mesopotamia: and the children of Israel served Chushan-rishathaim eight years. And when the children of Israel cried unto the LORD, the LORD raised up a deliverer to the children of Israel . . .

Judges 3:7-9 (a)

Chushan-rishathaim means "double darkness." And that's what the king of Mesopotamia was - a very evil, wicked ruler. The Lord used Chushan-rishathaim as an instrument of chastening, that through him the Israelites might come to their senses. So too, we're given over to double darkness when we don't destroy those things we know must go. Depression sets in. Confusion fills our thinking. We're in the dark about what we're supposed to do, where we should go, who we are. It's a double darkness. It's the reality of sin.

No doubt the Israelites prayed to the Lord all the while they were in bondage to Chushan-rishathaim. But it evidently took eight years for them to cry to the Lord, to reach a place of desperation and intensity in their prayer.

"Dear God," we pray, "it's really been (ho hum) a long day, so I don't have much energy to talk to You tonight (yawn), but I really need help with my car payment (zzzz)."

If the Lord responded to us in the same degree of intensity and passion that we talk to Him, He would say, "(Yawn) Really? It has been a long day (stretch). And maybe I can get to it, but I can't promise . . ." Then He would nod off.

This was not the way Elijah prayed. When he prayed for rain, Scripture says he put his head between his knees and prayed seven times (1 Kings 18:42-43). I suggest this was because this was the position of birthing in that culture. There was something being birthed by Elijah that day as he labored in prayer - once, again, a third time, four, five, six, seven times. And in answering his prayer, it is as if the Lord said, "I like that. In a world plagued by mediocrity, apathy, and laziness, it's good to see a man who knows it's dry in his soul or in his land and prays passionately and fervently for rain."

Do you find yourself in bondage today? Let me tell you what the answer is: Cry out to the Lord. I'm convinced that we, as Christians, do too much talking about the Lord, and not enough talking to Him. We are very ready, very eager to receive counsel, but very reluctant to cry out. The reason counseling offices are filled in Christendom today is because people do not bow their knee and call out to the Lord in fervency. Throughout Scripture, God is consistently seen responding to His people when they cry out. Truly, the effectual fervent prayer of a righteous man availeth much (James 5:16).

FEBRUARY 19

. . .who delivered them, even Othniel the son of Kenaz, Caleb's younger brother. And the Spirit of the LORD came upon him, and he judged Israel . . .

Judges 3:9 (b)-10 (a)

The first of the named judges was Othniel. What was his secret? The Spirit of the Lord came upon him. There is no substitute for the Spirit of God. Jesus said, "You shall receive power when the Holy Ghost comes upon you and you shall be My witnesses" (see Acts 1:8). We must be those who seek the fullness, the power, and the anointing of the Spirit if we are to be used effectively for the Kingdom; for while the Spirit indwells every believer at the moment of conversion, His "coming upon" ministry uniquely empowers every believer for service. Every believer has the Holy Spirit. The question is, Does the Holy Spirit have every believer?

How does the Spirit come upon us? When, like the Israelites, we cry out and say, "Father I need the power of the Spirit. I'm tired of being in bondage. I'm tired of the drought within. I want to be filled with You and used by You for Your glory." Jesus said, "If you, being evil, know how to give good gifts to your children, how much more will the Heavenly Father give the Holy Ghost to them that ask?" (see Luke 11:13).

FEBRUARY 20

And after him was Shamgar the son of Anath, which slew of the Philistines six hundred men with an ox goad: and he also delivered Israel.

Judges 3:31

Shamgar was an unlikely hero indeed. His name gives us insight into his personality, for in the Hebrew culture, names carried great significance and were given according to one's personality or prophecy concerning him. Shamgar's father was named Anath, or "Afflicted." Shamgar's own name means "The desolate dragged away one" - not a very likely name for a hero.

Shamgar is also an unknown hero, for there is no mention of him anywhere in Scripture except for this single verse. Consequently, we don't know about his past, nor do we know what happened to him after this incident took place.

Unlikely, unknown, and unsung - that's Shamgar. After all, how many of you proclaim the heroics of Shamgar? How many name him as one of their favorite Bible heroes? And yet, Shamgar was utilized in God's work and recorded in God's Word as one whom the Lord used mightily.

What did Shamgar do? This man - who was unknown, unlikely, and unsung - accomplished an incredible feat. He took on six hundred Philistines and whipped them single-handedly - six hundred Philistines who so oppressed the people of Israel that men were afraid to travel on the highways; six hundred Philistines who virtually brought village life to a standstill. The Philistines were brutal oppressors, yet Shamgar killed six hundred of them with only an ox goad.

Why did he use an ox goad? I believe it was because Shamgar was one who worked with oxen - a rancher, a herdsman. You see, the ox goad - a stick used to prod cattle - was a common instrument, easily accessible to anyone who worked with livestock.

I point this out to remind you that the Lord delights in using whatever is in your hand in order to bring about His purposes through your life. God has gifted you with talents, given you abilities, and placed within you certain desires and interests - and those are the very components He desires to utilize for the work of His Kingdom through you. Truly, He will use whatever is in your hand.

When God called Moses to go before Pharaoh, Moses balked, fearing no one would listen to him.

"What is that in your hand?" asked the Lord.

"A rod," answered Moses.

"Throw it down," said God.

As Moses threw the rod to the ground, it miraculously became a snake. And when he picked it up, it became a rod once again.

God used a common, ordinary, everyday shepherd's rod to accomplish His plan through Moses (Exodus 4).

David grew up slinging stones against trees, fence posts, and any other target he could find as he watched his father's flocks. So what did the Lord utilize in David's life to slay a giant? A simple sling and a few stones (1 Samuel 17:49).

I think of Peter and Andrew. What was in their hands when the Lord called them for service? They were casting fishing nets into the sea. Thus, Jesus said, "Follow Me, and I will make you fishers of men" (see Matthew 4:19).

Among five thousand hungry people on the hillside was a little boy. What did he have in his hand? Five loaves and two fish - which the Lord used to feed the entire crowd (John 6:9).

I am reminded of the Apostle Paul. What was in his hand when he was converted? A pen, for he was a scholar whose command of the

Greek language exceeded every other scholar in history. So what did God use most powerfully in Paul's life? A pen, as Paul authored one epistle after another.

Gang, the Lord can use whatever skills, interests, or abilities you have. He will use whatever is in your hand for His glory. He will give you insights and open doors. Great things will take place through you. The kingdom of darkness, the kingdom of selfishness, and the kingdom of greed will be beaten back as you take whatever ox goad is in your life and say, "Lord, use it for Your glory."

FEBRUARY 21

Curse ye Meroz, said the angel of the LORD, curse ye bitterly the inhabitants thereof; because they came not to the help of the LORD, to the help of the LORD against the mighty.

Judges 5:23

Although we don't know its exact location, Meroz was a city of Israel in the region of the battle that ensued between Israel and the Canaanite king, Jabin. The inhabitants of Meroz were cursed for their failure to get involved in the battle.

The same is still true. Cursed will be the man or woman who does not get involved in the battle, who does not get involved in service. You see, when we all stand before the judgment seat of Christ, those who didn't get involved - who sat back day after week after month after year after decade, missing opportunities in their own communities to be part of God's plan for the area - will weep. "Why did I waste my life?" they will cry. "What was I thinking? Why did I have time for this and that - but not to get involved in what God called me to do, in what He gave me the ability to do?"

God has things in store for us that are mind-blowing, gang, but this is the only opportunity we have to be able to be at the top or middle level - ruling ten or five cities. There will be many in Heaven who make it, "yet so as by fire" (1 Corinthians 3:15). They will be there, but they'll have no rewards because they buried the personality, intellectual ability, musical skill, or finances God entrusted to them. As a result, they'll curse themselves.

The way to be sad today is to not serve the Lord - to focus on your problems, your situation, your hurts, your needs, your life. Everything is discouraging when we live for ourselves. Instead of worrying about what shape you're in emotionally, financially, or physically, forget about yourself and start serving others. Jesus said, "The measure you give out will be the measure returned to you" (see Matthew 7:2). Start serving others and I guarantee you'll find yourself free from the curse of self-absorption today, and free from cursing yourself in the days to come.

FEBRUARY 22

And there came an angel of the LORD, and sat under an oak which was in Ophrah, that pertained unto Joash the Abiezrite: and his son Gideon threshed wheat by the winepress, to hide it from the Midianites. And the angel of the LORD appeared unto him, and said unto him, The LORD is with thee, thou mighty man of valour.

Judges 6:11-12

The threshing of wheat was usually done at a higher elevation in order to allow the wind to blow the chaff away. Gideon, however, realized that every time he threshed wheat, the Midianites would sweep in and rip him off. So he threshed wheat not on a mountaintop but in a winepress, a lower spot, a hidden area.

I love this! Here's Gideon, hiding from the Midianites, knees knocking, shaking with fright - yet the Lord calls him a mighty man of valor. Why? Because He sees His own not in their present problems, but as finished products. How do I know? Turn to Romans 8 . . .

And we know that all things work together for good to them that love God, to them who are the called according to his purpose. For whom he did foreknow, he also did predestinate to be conformed to the image of his Son, that he might be the firstborn among many brethren. Moreover whom he did predestinate, them he also called: and whom he called, them he also justified: and whom he justified, them he also glorified.

Romans 8:28-30

Please hang on to this. God is saying that you who are part of the elect were predestined by Him, called by Him, made just by Him, and glorified by Him. It doesn't say you *will be* glorified. It says you *are* glorified. That is why in Ephesians 5:27, Paul talks about the Church as being a glorious Church without spot or wrinkle. When we look at each other, we see lots of wrinkles and a whole bunch of spots. But God transcends the time/space dimension and views us in our eternal state. Yes, He's aware of our present struggles, but He also sees us as glorified.

This is fabulous, folks, because I am one of the few who, throughout the history of humanity, have been selected, elected, and chosen by God to be part of His eternal family.

So are you.

FEBRUARY 23

And he said unto him, Oh my Lord, wherewith shall I save Israel? behold, my family is poor in Manasseh, and I am the least in my father's house. And the LORD said unto him, Surely I will be with thee, and thou shalt smite the Midianites as one man.

Judges 6:15-16

"Who am I?" Gideon asked in verse 15.

"That's not the issue," the Lord says in verse 16. "The question is: Who am *I*, for *I* will be with you. And that is all you need."

The key to service, to ministry, to being used by the Lord and being an instrument of the Lord is to say, "It's not who I am. It's who You are, Lord. And if You choose to use the foolish things of the world to confound the wise, if You choose the weak things to show Your strength, then I qualify. And if You choose to use me, You'll get all the glory because it's obvious I can do nothing on my own."

What has God called you to do? What's on your agenda this week? Is there something you know you should be engaged in, but don't feel capable to do? Through this story, God would say to you, "It's not about you. It's about Me. I'm with you."

FEBRUARY 24

And the LORD said unto him, Peace be unto thee; fear not: thou shalt not die. Then Gideon built an altar there unto the LORD, and called it Jehovah-shalom: unto this day it is yet in Ophrah of the Abi-ezrites.

Judges 6:23-24

After seeing the Lord, Gideon was an altered man. Therefore, it is only logical that he would build an altar. *Jehovah-shalom* means "the Lord is peace." About to face the fight of his life, Gideon didn't feel particularly courageous. Rather, he felt unqualified, uncertain, unsure, knowing he had been called to do something out of the realm of human possibility. Yet, in meeting with the Lord at the table, he had peace.

When the disciples were afraid because Jesus told them He would be betrayed, He said, "Don't let your heart be troubled. In My Father's house are many mansions. I go to prepare a place for you" (see John 14:1-2). What's the key to not being troubled? I believe, as this story portrays, it's to go to the Lord's Table and realize there will be peace beyond this present day, beyond this present problem. I can let my heart be troubled, or I can let my heart not be troubled. It's up to me. And I make that choice every day. By focusing on eternity - on Jehovah-shalom - Gideon left with peace in his heart and a new perspective on his mind.

FEBRUARY 25

And the LORD said unto Gideon, The people are yet too many; bring them down unto the water, and I will try them for thee there: and it shall be, that of whom I say unto thee, This shall go with thee, the same shall go with thee; and of whomsoever I say unto thee, This shall not go with thee, the same shall not go. So he brought down the people unto the water: and the LORD said unto Gideon, Every one that lappeth of the water with his tongue, as a dog lappeth, him shalt thou set by himself; likewise every one that boweth down upon his knees to drink. And the number of them that lapped, putting their hand to their mouth, were three hundred men: but all the rest of the people bowed down upon their knees to drink water. And the LORD said unto Gideon, By the three hundred men that lapped will I save you, and deliver the Midianites into thine hand: and let all the other people go every man unto his place.

Judges 7:4-7

Why were these three hundred chosen? Possibly it was for the following reasons . . .

First, they were free from fear. Twenty-two thousand were sent home because fear and faith are mutually exclusive (Judges 7:3). Only ten thousand men were free from fear. Why did they have no fear? I suggest it was because they had an understanding of eternity. So too, as Christians, we know the reality of eternity. Therefore, we must not fear the difficulties or dangers of this life. Those with eternity's values in view are those who serve the Lord with abandon.

Second, the three hundred were chosen because they were men of humility. You see, in Israeli culture, the dog was despicable. To be called a dog, to look like a dog, to be associated with a dog was to be avoided. Yet here, the men who were chosen scooped up water with their hands and lapped it like dogs.

Third, the three hundred were men of priority. That is, they didn't spend unnecessary time doing necessary things. Yes, they needed to drink, but they never lost sight of the possibility of attack from the Midianites. So too, there are things in this life to which we must tend. There are chores and responsibilities to which each of us is obligated. But the man or woman used by God will not devote unnecessary time to doing necessary things. They will streamline their life as much as possible because they realize the battle is raging, the time is short, the calling is great.

Eternity, humility, priority - these were all characteristics held by the three hundred chosen men. Yet an equally possible scenario was that these three hundred guys were not necessarily depicting noble qualities at all. It could be that these were broken-down, fat guys who simply couldn't get into the water. It could be that their knees were bad and their backs were out. It could be that in choosing the men who couldn't put their faces in the water, God was saying, "I want to use the old fat guys - guys the world would laugh at, ignore, or discard."

The three hundred may have lacked the ability to lay down and drink from the stream, but the one thing they had was availability - and that's the one ability that matters most.

FEBRUARY 26

So the people took victuals in their hand, and their trumpets:
and he sent all the rest of Israel every man unto his tent, and
retained those three hundred men: and the host of Midian
was beneath him in the valley.

Judges 7:8

The odds went from 4:1 to 14:1 to 450:1 as only three hundred men were allowed to move with Gideon into battle against the Midianites. We read of those same odds in 1 Kings 18, where Elijah alone was victorious against 450 prophets of Baal.

Maybe today you feel as though the odds are stacked terribly against you, that your circumstances look impossible. Rejoice! Be glad! God has set you up to bring you through and to show Himself strong. That's His intention, that's His purpose for you - to put you in an impossible situation so He can show you and those around you just how strong, how wonderful, and how glorious He is.

FEBRUARY 27

And he said unto them, Look on me, and do likewise . . .

Judges 7:17 (a)

"Look on me and do likewise," said Gideon.

"Follow me as I follow Christ," echoed Paul (1 Corinthians 11:1).

Gideon was a man of action. He was a doer, not simply a talker. He sought the Lord, selected 300 troops out of 32,000, risked his life by sneaking into the Midianite camp, surveyed the situation, overheard a conversation, came back, developed a strategy, supplied his troops, and then did battle. No committees, no dialogues, no discussions. He was a doer. He made things happen. And that's the kind of men God is looking for today - men who see the need and fill it, men who go for it. Gideon was a man who understood that leadership was not about lecturing, but simply about leading; not saying, "You go," but saying, "*Let's* go."

I like Gideon. He didn't say, "Listen to me." He said, "Look on me." This is real leadership. Whether in a marriage, family, ministry, or on the job site, the key is to say what Paul and Gideon said: Watch me. Do what I do.

That's my prayer for us.

FEBRUARY 28

And he divided the three hundred men into three companies, and he put a trumpet in every man's hand, with empty pitchers, and lamps within the pitchers. And he said unto them, Look on me, and do likewise: and, behold, when I come to the outside of the camp, it shall be that, as I do, so shall ye do. When I blow with a trumpet, I and all that are with me, then blow ye the trumpets also on every side of all the camp, and say, The sword of the LORD, and of Gideon. So Gideon, and the hundred men that were with him, came unto the outside of the camp in the beginning of the middle watch; and they had but newly set the watch: and they blew the trumpets, and brake the pitchers that were in their hands.

Judges 7:16-19

We live in a world oppressed by Midianites, dominated by Midianites, controlled by Midianites. I'm not speaking of an external race of people, but of an internal struggle within people. The dominion of Satan, the control of self, and the oppression of sin is within the heart of every human being, for, like David, we are all born into sin (Psalm 51:5). We have all been tainted by sin; we have all succumbed to sin. But praise be to God, we can be liberated. We can be rescued. We can be free. God has called us into His glorious Gospel - the good news that Jesus Christ died for our sins, paid the price for all of our iniquity, rose from the dead, and wants to set up residence within our hearts, to free us, to liberate us, to lead us into life that is both abundant and eternal. That's the Gospel.

And we who have come into this saving knowledge of Jesus are to trumpet this Gospel to all who are still dominated, controlled, and oppressed by the Midianites of sin, Satan, and self. We have the answer. The Light of the world, Jesus Christ, dwells within us. His light is inside of us - but it is also to be radiating from us. And there's the rub.

You see, most of us understand that Jesus is the Light because most of us have walked in His light - and yet all too often His light remains inside, all bottled up. The Lord wants to release the light of Jesus which He has placed in you. He wants His light to shine out from you in order that others can be saved and freed and satisfied. How does this happen? Only by breaking - for just as the light of the torch was hidden within the earthen vessel until the pitcher was broken, so too, if our lives are going to be a blessing, there must first be a breaking. The light is *in* the earthen vessel. But the light cannot shine forth *from* the vessel until there is a breaking *of* the vessel.

Gang, you cannot be a blessing until you first go through breaking. Why? Because we live in a broken world. The baby in his playpen cries over a broken toy. The little boy is upset because of his broken bike. The junior higher is in agony over a broken arm. The high school sophomore is in pain because of a broken heart. The young wife is crying because of broken marriage vows. The businessman is in despair because of broken hopes. The middle-aged man is hurting because of broken health. Wherever you look, wherever you observe people, you see hurts. People are broken. People are in tough situations. And we who have the Light and Life of Jesus Christ can only touch them to the degree that we are able to relate to them.

FEBRUARY 29

Then the men of Israel said unto Gideon, Rule thou over us, both thou, and thy son, and thy son's son also: for thou hast delivered us from the hand of Midian. And Gideon said unto them, I will not rule over you, neither shall my son rule over you: the LORD shall rule over you.

Judges 8:22-23

Amen! I love it! The people came to Gideon and said, "You're a hero. Rule over us."

"No way," said Gideon. "I will not rule over you; my son will not rule over you. The Lord is the One who will rule over you."

Please let that sink in, precious people. You see, the Lord is the One who is to rule over you - not men, not elders, not pastors, not apostles, not people. People who are in ministry are to serve and to assist others, not to rule over them (2 Corinthians 1:24). Why do I say this? Because there's a tendency in the heart of each of us to want to look to a man to give us direction. Why? Because it's easier to go to someone and say, "Tell me what I should do," rather than to seek the Lord and say, "Father, what is Your desire and intention for me in this matter?"

How important it is that we learn to seek the Lord and to seek His face.

MARCH 1

And after Abimelech there arose to defend Israel Tola the son
of Puah, the son of Dodo, a man of Issachar; and he dwelt
in Shamir in mount Ephraim. And he judged Israel twenty
and three years, and died, and was buried in Shamir.

Judges 10:1-2

Tola's dad's name, *Puah,* means "splendid." His grandfather's name, *Dodo,* means "beloved one." Tola's name, however, meant neither "splendid" nor "beloved," but "worm." This being the case, Tola was probably as obscure in his own time as he is today. He was a man of Issachar who dwelt in Ephraim. That is, he wasn't dwelling among his own people.

Jesus is depicted here. Not only did He leave His home in Heaven to dwell among people who wouldn't receive Him (John 1:11), but in Psalm 22:6, He says, prophetically, "I am a worm and not a man."

The Hebrew word, *tola* - the plural of which is *tolaath* - is translated two ways in the Bible: as either "scarlet" or "worm." Why would the same word be used for both "scarlet" and "worm"? Because in Bible days, when people needed scarlet cloth, they would grind worms into a pasty, blood-red substance that would be used as a dye.

Why would Jesus say, "I am a worm"? Because, to reproduce, the *tola* would climb the trunk of a tree and fasten on a limb. Then the worm would lay the larva and cover the eggs with its body. Although the eggs would hatch, the worm wouldn't budge. So the larva would begin to feed on the body of the one who had given them life. As the *tola* gave its life for its young, its blood would leave a scarlet mark on the tree. After the dead worm fell, the bloody spot left on the limb of the tree would dry after three days, becoming a white, flaky substance that would fall to the ground like snow.

"Though your sins be as scarlet - *tola* - they shall be white as snow," Isaiah declares (see 1:18). Fastened to the tree of the Cross of Calvary, Jesus wouldn't budge until the work was finished. What work? The work that would allow you and me to be "hatched," to be born again. "Eat of My

Body," He says. "Drink of My blood. I give My life for you. And though your sins be as scarlet, they shall be white as snow" (see Mark 14:22-24).

By His blood, Jesus not only saved us, but, like Tola in the text before us, He is the Judge who defends us. You see, Revelation 12:10 tells us that Satan accuses us day and night, going before the throne of the Father, saying, "Look at him. Look at her. They've blown it here. They've messed up there." But the Bible says the accuser was overcome by the blood of the Lamb and the word of their testimony (Revelation 12:11).

"If any man sin, we have an Advocate, a Defender with the Father - that is, Jesus Christ the righteous," John declares (see 1 John 2:1). This means that when we sin, although Satan will be at the throne of God pointing out our failures and shortcomings, we have a Defender - the Tola, the scarlet Worm, Jesus - who says, "Father, she has eaten of My body. He has tasted of My blood. They are clean."

Hearing the accusations of the prosecuting attorney, and listening to the defense of His Son, the Father hits the gavel in the courtroom of Heaven and says, "Case dismissed for lack of evidence."

And celebration breaks forth.

MARCH 2

Now Jephthah the Gileadite was a mighty man of valour, and he was the son of a harlot: and Gilead begat Jephthah.

Judges 11:1

Talk about an unlikely hero! Jephthah was the result of his father's relations with a harlot. In Jephthah's time and culture, being born illegitimately carried a terrible social stigma. Wherever he went, he would be the butt of jokes, teased and taunted. Yet in Hebrews 11, Jephthah's name is recorded for all eternity as one of the giants of faith, one of the heroes of God's people.

Dear brother, precious sister - regardless of your past, no matter your reputation, if God used Jephthah, He can use you - for God loves to use the most unlikely, unqualified people.

"Look to the rock from which you were hewn and to the hole of the pit from which you were dug," declares the Lord (see Isaiah 51:1). In other words, "Consider where you've come from. And upon the basis of what I have already done in your life, look forward to how I will bless you and make your life fruitful in the future."

Every one of us was brought out of the pit, gang. There are no exceptions.

> Look at Abraham. Even after he was called by God, even after he was ordained to be the father of faith, he still wavered, foundered, and fell. Fearing Pharaoh, he lied not once, but twice about his wife in order to save his own skin (Genesis 12 and 20).

> Look at Moses. After he was called into ministry, he murdered a man, buried him in the sand, and ran for his life to the desert (Exodus 2).

> Look at Jonah. He was called by God to usher in the world's greatest revival. But when the Ninevites began to acknowledge God and repent, Jonah was totally discouraged, wishing the Ninevites would have been blasted instead of blessed (Jonah 3 and 4).

> Look at Peter. After spending three years with Jesus, watching His miracles, hearing His teaching, sharing meals with Him, conversing constantly with Him, he stood by the fire of the enemy and denied ever knowing Him (John 18).

> Look at Paul. He was a man so cruel and callous, so barbaric and brutal that when he finally did get saved, the early Church initially refused to believe it (Acts 9).

> Look at John Mark. After receiving a call to the mission field, he got homesick and hightailed it back home (Acts 15:38).

No matter where you look in the Word, you will find individuals who were once in the pit, but brought out of the pit by the One who had no fault whatsoever - Jesus Christ Himself.

Knowing this allows me to move on. I can say, "Lord, in spite of my failures, I'm still moving on in You according to Your grace, mercy, and love." Second, it allows me to reach out. When other people fail and fall, instead of coming down on them, talking about them, or finding fault with them, I'm free to reach out in love to them.

Folks, that tough guy, who seems so hopeless and so out of it to you, might be the next Jephthah in a future move of God. That fellow you think is bizarre, raunchy, or rude just might be the man God is tapping on the shoulder to lead the next revival.

MARCH 3

Then went Samson down, and his father and his mother, to Timnath, and came to the vineyards of Timnath: and behold, a young lion roared against him. And the Spirit of the LORD came mightily upon him, and he rent him as he would have rent a kid, and he had nothing in his hand . . .

Judges 14:5-6 (a)

A Nazarite was to stay away from grapes. Watch out, Samson!

First Peter 5:8 says Satan is a roaring lion, seeking whom he may devour. Here, in a place where he shouldn't have been, Samson comes face to face with just such a lion.

Satan tempted Jesus three times in the wilderness with heavy-duty temptations (Matthew 4). But Jesus was victorious because the Spirit of God had already descended upon Him (Matthew 3:16). Apart from the Spirit, you and I will get eaten up, munched on, wiped out. Satan is sneaky, subtle, and strong. Don't underestimate him. But the Spirit of God upon your life will give you victory as you seek His anointing daily, as you call upon Him in the morning hours. And when Satan comes later on in the day, even if, like Samson, you're by a vineyard where you shouldn't be, God's Spirit will give you power to do battle against him.

Truly, this is the only way to deal with the adversary. Satan is a roaring lion who cannot be dealt with in our own strength.

MARCH 4

And when he came unto Lehi, the Philistines shouted against him: and the Spirit of the LORD came mightily upon him, and the cords that were upon his arms became as flax that was burnt with fire, and his bands loosed from off his hands. And he found a new jawbone of an ass, and put forth his hand, and took it, and slew a thousand men therewith.

Judges 15:14-15

Here's Samson - tied up by the men of Judah, turned over to the Philistines - when suddenly, the Spirit of God comes upon him. He pops the ropes and starts swinging the jawbone of a donkey. When he's done, one thousand Philistines lay dead.

This cracks me up. I mean, the Philistines had the most advanced weapon's system of their day. But in Judges 3, Shamgar killed six hundred of them with an ox goad. And here, twelve chapters later, one thousand more are beaten with the jawbone of a donkey. Later on, Goliath - the greatest Philistine of them all - will be beaten with a stone and a sling. Isn't that just like the Lord to use the foolish things of the world to confound the wise, the weak to show up the strong? Look at us - we're ox goads, jawbones, stones. We're perfect examples of the foolish things of the world confounding the wise (1 Corinthians 1:27).

In your own personal battles, God can use whatever is in your hand. "That's nothing," the world will scoff. But with the Spirit of God - it becomes something mighty.

March 5

And she said, The Philistines be upon thee, Samson. And he awoke out of his sleep, and said, I will go out as at other times before, and shake myself. And he wist not that the LORD was departed from him.

Judges 16:20

This verse is the most tragic in the entire book. "How could Samson be so stupid?" we wonder. I suggest he knew Delilah was no good, that he knew Delilah was setting him up. I mean, he had already seen that three times previously. He wasn't dumb. But I believe what was happening in his mind was the same thing that happens in ours. You see, God had told him that, as a Nazarite, he must not touch grapes, must not touch carcasses, and must not cut his hair. He touched grapes - and nothing happened. He touched a carcass - and nothing happened. So, he must have thought that if he cut his hair nothing would happen.

So too, we think "Maybe the Bible isn't really as strict as it sounds. Maybe it doesn't really matter if I compromise a little here and a little there. Maybe I can get away with it. Maybe it's okay." But it's not, and we won't, for it doesn't work that way.

What a shock it must have been to Samson when he suddenly found himself weak, helpless, wiped out.

Although Samson missed a fantastic opportunity, we read in Hebrews 11 that he is one of the few men who were inducted into God's "Hall of Faith." This means that, although in our estimation, Samson might be described as mediocre, God saw something in Samson which placed him in a very select group that made him a giant in God's economy.

I suggest to you that Samson plays a monumental role in God's economy because he portrays the Person of Jesus Christ in a most wonderful way.

"How can this be?" you ask. "Samson ignored the counsel of his godly parents. He was ensnared with Philistine women. He was proud and arrogant. How can it be that he is a picture of Jesus?"

In Matthew 12:40, Jesus reached back to the story of a mediocre man named Jonah and said, "As Jonah was in the belly of the whale for three days and nights, so will the Son of Man be in the center of the earth, buried. And even as Jonah was spewed out, so will I rise again." In other words, Jesus was able to reach back to Jonah and say, "This guy pictures My resurrection." And I suggest He could do the same with Samson.

I suggest He could say, "Samson pictures Me - not My resurrection, but My death. As he stood with his hands outstretched, pushing against the pillars, saying, 'Let me die that the enemies of Israel might perish,' so too, with arms outstretched, I died that the hordes of hell might be beaten back."

MARCH 6

Now it came to pass in the days when the judges ruled, that there was a famine in the land. And a certain man of Beth-lehem-judah went to sojourn in the country of Moab, he, and his wife, and his two sons. And the name of the man was Elimelech, and the name of his wife Naomi, and the name of his two sons Mahlon and Chilion, Ephrathites of Beth-lehem-judah.

Ruth 1:1-2 (a)

In chapter 1, we are introduced to a happy Hebrew family residing in the country of Judah, in the city of Bethlehem.

How do I know they were happy?

Check out their names. *Elimelech* means, "God is my King;" *Naomi* means "pleasant;" and, according to *Our Nearest Kinsman* by Roy Hession, *Mahlon* means "song;" while *Chilion* means "satisfaction."

This family was one where God was King; where there was pleasantness, song, and satisfaction. Why? Because they resided in the city of Bethlehem.

Bethlehem means, "House of Bread," and it is the city where Jesus, the Bread of Life, would be born centuries later. No wonder there was satisfaction and pleasantness in Elimelech's family. No wonder there were songs and happiness. God was their King and they were living in the House of Bread.

Gang, we will always be a happy, blessed, successful people if we dwell in the House of Bread, which is the Word of God. When we eat of Heavenly manna, we will experience earthly happiness.

How do I know this?

Psalm 1 declares that the man who meditates in the Word and who delights in the Law of the Lord will be like a tree whose leaf does not wither, a tree which prospers in whatever it does. Picture, if you would, a strong oak tree. What is an oak tree? An oak tree is simply a little nut that refused to give ground. I like that! Because that's what we are. We're all little nuts, and all a little nutty. But if we refuse to give ground, and plant our roots in the Word of God - if we study it, meditate on it, devour it, and make it top priority in our lives - we will find ourselves growing in strength and stability. We will find ourselves experiencing God's blessing.

MARCH 7

And they came into the country of Moab, and continued there.

Ruth 1:2 (b)

Elimelech and his family left Bethlehem-judah when famine came to the land. "I don't get it," you say. "How could a famine inflict the House of Bread, the Place of Praise?"

In 2 Chronicles 7, God told His people that if they turned from Him and began to serve other gods, He would send famine to their land. Evidently that is what happened here. Oh, it might have been subtle, even imperceptible at first, but there was nonetheless a turning away from the Lord. The result? Dry times.

Amos wrote about a famine not of food, but of hearing the Word of the Lord (Amos 8:11). Maybe you can relate to that. Perhaps you no longer feel like you're hearing from God or are in communion with God. There was a time when every time you opened the Word, God seemed to speak to you. There was a time when coming to Bible study was the most exciting thing for you. But not now. There is famine in your land. The days are dry, dreary, and difficult.

Precious people, I don't care who you are or how close to God you might be; you can bet your bottom dollar that there will come into your walk seasons of dryness and times of difficulty. The question is not whether times of famine will come. The question is: Where will you go when they do?

Second Chronicles 7 teaches that the cure for famine is to remain where you are and call upon God. But Elimelech and his family went to Moab instead.

This is a fundamental mistake we often make. In the Book of Isaiah, the Lord declared that He would go with us *through* the fire (Isaiah 43:2). But so often we want to *avoid* the fire. We want to change our circumstances. We want to run from the difficulties.

So, when famine came, Elimelech, upon the prodding of his wife Naomi, decided that instead of praying it through and remaining in the land until God graciously blessed again, they would make a move, a short sojourn in Moab, where they heard there was plenty of food and an abundance of water. It seemed to be the chance of a lifetime. In reality, it was a death march toward the grave.

MARCH 8

And Mahlon and Chilion died also both of them; and the woman was left of her two sons and her husband.

Ruth 1:5

When God is no longer my King, it is only a matter of time before the song on my lips ceases to exist. Whereas at one time, there was a beautiful flow of praise and adoration to the Lord - there is now cynicism and sourness, murmuring and complaining because Mahlon is dead.

Chilion was the next to die. Have you ever thought, "What's wrong with me? Why has the satisfaction which was once so sweet to me departed?" Could it be that you left the House of Bread and the Place of Praise?

You see, Naomi's experience is a perfect picture of exactly what takes place when we leave the House of Bread and the Place of Praise: First, God is no longer our King; then the song departs from our heart; finally, satisfaction leaves our soul. It's an order that is absolute and irrefutable. And we have all experienced it to some degree.

MARCH 9

Then she arose with her daughters in law, that she might return from the country of Moab: for she had heard in the country of Moab how that the LORD had visited his people in giving them bread.

Ruth 1:6

This intrigues me because it was Naomi's loss that led her to listen. Please keep this in mind: This story is not to show God punishing Naomi for wandering off into Moab. Her loss was not punitive - it was corrective. Its purpose was to get her back on track - back to Bethlehem, the House of Bread; back to Judah, the Place of Praise.

So too, in your life and in mine, when there is loss, it is not for punishment. Why? Because the punishment for our sin could never be severe enough. I know you; you're like me. We all deserve to be totally consumed. Whatever God could send our way could never be punishment enough for our sin. The punishment which should have come upon us was poured out upon

Jesus Christ, Who died in our place. Therefore, His work in our lives is not punitive, it's corrective.

If you have been in a place of loss - materially or internally, vocationally or relationally - know this: You are experiencing loss not because God is mad at you, angry with you, or disappointed in you, but because He wants to speak to you. And He knows that sometimes the only time we will listen is when we are at a place of loss where we can do nothing else.

MARCH 10

Wherefore she went forth out of the place where she was, and her two daughters in law with her; and they went on the way to return unto the land of Judah.

Ruth 1:7

Naomi, the prodigal daughter, goes back home. And I am reminded of Luke 15 . . .

When the prodigal son - after leaving his father's house, going to a far country, and spending his father's fortune on wine, women, and song - finally came to his senses, he realized he was sitting in a pigpen eating pig slop.

The difference between a prodigal and a pig is that although the prodigal might spend some time in the pigpen, he doesn't make it his home. If the pigpen is your home today, you need to seriously evaluate your relationship to your Father. But if you find yourself in the pigpen today, wanting desperately to get out - take hope. Take the first step back home toward your Father, and like the prodigal son, you will see Him running to meet you.

The only time in the Bible when God is seen to be in a hurry is in the person of the prodigal son's father, who hitched up his robes and ran down the road with abandon to meet his son. What a beautiful picture of restoration and redemption, renewal and revival. That's our Father.

MARCH 11

And they lifted up their voice, and wept again: and Orpah kissed her mother in law; but Ruth clave unto her.

Ruth 1:14

In this verse we see Naomi grieving, Orpah leaving, and Ruth cleaving.

Orpah, whose name means "youthful" or "immature," shows the reaction of an immature believer - much emotion, but no devotion; conviction, but no commitment. Jesus talked about this in the parable of the sower (Mark 4) . . .

Some hear the Word and spring up quickly, but when the hot sun comes out, they dry up and wither away because they have no roots.

So too, some believers get totally excited when they hear a sermon or a testimony or a concert - but their roots are not grounded in the Word of God. There is no devotional life, simply an emotional hype. And when the hard times come - when there's a price to pay to follow Jesus - like Orpah, they turn away.

Ruth, on the other hand, cleaves to Naomi.

The same remains true today, for there are those who kiss with emotion, but others who cleave with devotion. The Bible indicates that God isn't impressed with how high we jump, but how straight we walk. Ruth stayed with Naomi. She walked the walk.

MARCH 12

And Ruth said, Intreat me not to leave thee, or to return
from following after thee: for whither thou goest, I will go;
and where thou lodgest, I will lodge: thy people shall be my
people, and thy God my God: where thou diest, will I die,
and there will I be buried: the LORD do so to me, and more
also, if ought but death part thee and me.

Ruth 1:16-17

"Even if God's hand is against you, Naomi," Ruth said, "the worst God gives is better than the best the world offers." What a sentiment expressed by Ruth! This intrigues me because it means that Ruth saw in a broken, embittered Naomi a spiritual reality that superseded anything she had seen in Moab.

I say this to encourage you who perhaps have been in Moab recently. You may be like Naomi - coming back *to* nothing, and coming back *with* nothing. But, like Ruth, there will be those who will see your brokenness and repentance and follow you right into the Kingdom.

Why?

Because "good people" usually do not draw sinners. Naomi realized she herself needed to get back to the Lord - and that is the person with whom the sinner feels most inclined to travel.

If you have been in a place where you know you haven't been what you should be, or doing what you should do, you still have the opportunity, like Naomi, to bring someone back with you.

MARCH 13

I went out full, and the LORD hath brought me home again empty . . .

Ruth 1:21 (a)

Would you please underline this verse in your Bible and underscore it in your mind? This is the reason backsliding is so ridiculous. When you leave Bethlehem-judah - the House of Bread, the Place of Praise - and wander off to sojourn in Moab, you will always leave full, but come back empty. Sin always brings sorrow and sadness. Be not deceived; God is not mocked: for whatsoever a man sows, that shall he also reap (Galatians 6:7).

Naomi went through ten years of proverbial hell on earth and would carry scars for the rest of her life because she left the land of the true and living God.

Gang, the mathematics of sin are always the same, for sin adds to your sorrows, subtracts from your energy, multiplies your troubles, and divides your loyalty.

Naomi went out full, but returned empty. But praise be to our Lord - the remaining three chapters of the Book of Ruth chronicle Naomi's refilling and recharging as the Lord renews and revives her. Naomi's story is truly one of the interesting subplots of this magnificent little book.

Even if you have sojourned in Moab for a long season, even though you left full and are now coming back empty, know this: First of all, God can and will refill and revive you. Second, if you will extol His grace and His goodness, He will actually use you to bring a whole lot of Ruths back with you.

MARCH 14

So Naomi returned, and Ruth the Moabitess, her daughter in law, with her, which returned out of the country of Moab and they came to Bethlehem . . .

Ruth 1:22

Often, when you and I backslide, the tragedy is that we take others with us.

"I'm going fishing," Peter said. "I'm not good enough. I'm not worthy enough to follow Jesus Christ any longer" (see John 21:3).

What did the other disciples say?

"We'll go with you," they said, as they boarded the boat of backsliding together.

But here is Naomi coming back, returning to the place of blessing, and look, she is bringing Ruth with her - Ruth who will be so instrumental in the very genealogy of Jesus Christ; Ruth, who is herself an illustration of the Body of Christ. Ruth is brought into the Land of Promise by a broken Naomi.

When was Ruth brought into the place of blessing? It wasn't when she was impressed with Naomi's pleasantness and perfectness. It was when she saw Naomi's brokenness and bitterness.

Precious people, I am convinced that very often our friends, family, colleagues, and neighbors are not getting saved and not responding to the Gospel because they look at us and see the life we are presenting to them as being totally together, and they say, "God is the God of the together person, the perfect person - which is fine for you because you're together and you're perfect. But I'm not. Therefore He could not be my God."

Why is it we try so hard to present ourselves as perfect? We know we're not. Who are we kidding? We all know we have problems and weaknesses, temptations and difficulties. And yet we carefully cultivate an impeccable image to present to the world. I suggest to you that people are touched and moved not when you and I preach from the pulpit of perfection, but rather when we share from the place of brokenness and humility - not pointing to our togetherness, but to God's graciousness.

Marrying into Naomi's happy Hebrew family did not convert Ruth. You see, it was not until Naomi - Miss Pleasant - became humble and confessed freely that the Lord had dealt bitterly with her that Ruth said, "Your God shall be my God because I can relate to a God like that."

MARCH 15

And Naomi had a kinsman of her husband's, a mighty man of wealth, of the family of Elimelech; and his name was Boaz.

Ruth 2:1

The word translated "kinsman" is *goel* in Hebrew. *Goel* means "redeemer" and has its roots in the 25th chapter of Leviticus wherein God outlined a plan to prevent capitalism from getting out of hand. Every fifty years, in the Year of Jubilee, all properties purchased by corporations or wealthy individuals due to bankruptcy were to revert back to the original owner. In the Year of Jubilee, all debts were canceled. It was the Father's safeguard against the greed which causes such disparity between rich and poor.

As gracious as the Year of Jubilee was, however, fifty years is a long time to be without your land - especially if you're a farmer. So the Lord made another provision: The closest kinsman had the right at any time to buy back property which had been lost through bankruptcy, poor business practices, or mismanagement. That is why the word *goel* is translated both "kinsman" and "redeemer."

This is an important concept because Jesus Christ is our *Goel*. We're bankrupt. We're out of it. Like Ruth and Naomi, we have nothing. But there is One who is wealthy. There is One who stands in strength. He is our Kinsman Redeemer, Jesus Christ.

Boaz is about to redeem Ruth and bring her under his covering - even as Jesus Christ has redeemed us and brought us under His covering.

MARCH 16

And Ruth the Moabitess said unto Naomi, Let me now go to the field, and glean ears of corn after him in whose sight I shall find grace. And she said unto her, Go, my daughter. And she went, and came, and gleaned in the field after the reapers: and her hap was to light on a part of the field belonging unto Boaz, who was of the kindred of Elimelech.

Ruth 2:2-3

In Deuteronomy 24:18-20, the Father provided another compassionate law which stated that a poor person could go into the fields during the time of harvest and gather whatever was left behind by the reapers - a "work-fare" system. Familiar with Old Testament Law, perhaps through conversations with Naomi, Ruth said "Let me go glean for us. It's better than starving."

Her "hap" was to end up in the field of Boaz. I like that! Although Ruth certainly didn't know that this wealthy, strong landowner was a kinsman of Elimelech, the Lord had directed her steps. Nothing just happens. God is at work. There's a grand plan coming into play.

Ruth is a picture of you and me, as we shall see. We're the Bride of Christ. But we were lost, impoverished, hungry - and it just so "happened" that we found ourselves in His field. One day, someone invited us to church, to Bible study. It is all part of God's grand plan to send people your way, allowing you to come into contact with our Boaz - Jesus Christ.

MARCH 17

And Boaz answered and said unto her, It hath fully been shewed me, all that thou hast done unto thy mother in law since the death of thine husband: and how thou hast left thy father and thy mother, and the land of thy nativity, and art come unto a people which thou knewest not heretofore. The LORD recompense thy work, and a full reward be given thee of the LORD God of Israel, under whose wings thou art come to trust.

Ruth 2:11-12

Boaz said, "I know you, Ruth. I've heard about you."

The same is true of us. We fall before our Greater-than-Boaz and say, "Why have I found grace in Your sight?"

And He answers, "I know you."

Romans 8 declares, "whom He did foreknow, He predestined; whom He predestined, He called; whom He called, He justified; whom He justified, He glorified." It all begins with the foreknowledge of God. He says, "'I know you guys. I see your hearts. And I'm choosing you. I'm electing you. I've chosen to be gracious unto you."

I can't help but think of Nathanael . . .

When Philip came to him in John 1, saying he had found the Messiah, Nathanael cynically said, "Can any good thing come out of Nazareth?"

"Come and see," Philip said.

When Jesus later saw Nathanael coming, He said, "Behold an Israelite in whom there is no guile - one who is not easily tricked."

I like that! Jesus could have condemned Nathanael for his cynicism. Instead, he commended him for his caution.

"How do you know me?" asked Nathanael.

"Before Philip came to you, I saw you sitting under the fig tree," Jesus answered (see John 1:48).

The Lord sees us. The Lord knows us. And the Lord has chosen to show grace unto us. I don't understand it. I don't deserve it. But I am so grateful for it.

Good news, gang. The Lord does not condemn you. He commends you. He doesn't focus on your sin. He hears your sigh. He hears your heart saying, "I want more of You, Lord. Even though I am a Moabite, even though I have problems, I want to be right in Your sight." And He responds with grace.

MARCH 18

So she kept fast by the maidens of Boaz to glean unto the end of barley harvest and of wheat harvest; and dwelt with her mother in law.

Ruth 2:23

Ruth listened to the counsel of her elders. Boaz, an older man, said, "Stay with the maidens."

Naomi, her mother-in-law, said the same thing. And Ruth was wise enough to listen.

As I read the Scriptures more and more, I see a linkage of elders and youth, of young and old. Young people have zeal, but it is often without knowledge. Older people have wisdom, but often lack vision. The two are needed together. Thus, we see Moses with Joshua, Elijah with Elisha, Eli with Samuel.

There's a need for young and old - for vision and wisdom, for energy and experience - to work together.

We need each other!

March 19

And he said, Blessed be thou of the LORD, my daughter: for thou hast shewed more kindness in the latter end than at the beginning, inasmuch as thou followedst not young men, whether poor or rich.

Ruth 3:10

"You have showed more kindness in the latter end than at the beginning." This is what our Greater-than-Boaz says to you.

"When you came into My field, that was a blessing. When you showed up at church, when you had morning devotions, when you came into the field to glean the wheat of My Word, you blessed Me. I know you could have gone water skiing. I know you could have stayed home. I know you could have slept in, but you came into My field and you blessed Me.

"And now you're blessing Me even more by wanting Me to cover you, to redeem you, to rescue you. It's not an obligation to Me - it's an elation for Me. You could have sought some young man, some new fad, some exciting trip, but you sought Me - the Ancient of Days. You put aside other alluring pursuits and you sought Me to cover you. You've blessed Me."

Boaz had strength and wealth, pedigree and prosperity. He had everything - except one upon which to pour out his love.

Jesus Christ is the Creator of all things. He, too, has it all. But what He desires is a Bride. And guess what we are! Anyone who will fall before His nail-pierced feet and say, "Cover me," He will in no wise cast out (John 6:37).

MARCH 20

So Boaz took Ruth, and she was his wife: and when he went in unto her, the LORD gave her conception, and she bare a son. And the women said unto Naomi, Blessed be the LORD, which hath not left thee this day without a kinsman, that his name may be famous in Israel. And he shall be unto thee a restorer of thy life, and a nourisher of thine old age: for thy daughter in law, which loveth thee, which is better to thee than seven sons, hath born him. And Naomi took the child, and laid it in her bosom, and became nurse unto it.

Ruth 4:13-16

You left full, Naomi. You came back empty. And now God is blessing you once again. The women told Naomi that Ruth was better than seven sons, seven being the number of perfection. Their words were prophetic indeed, for out of Ruth's line would come forth not only King David, but the Perfect One - Jesus Christ.

Naomi, this prodigal daughter of the Old Testament, came back to Bethlehem, where God rebuilt, rebirthed, restored, and renewed her.

And that's what He'll do with us - if we'll just come back to Him.

MARCH 21

And she vowed a vow, and said, O LORD of hosts, if thou wilt indeed look on the affliction of thine handmaid, and remember me, and not forget thine handmaid, but wilt give unto thine handmaid a man child, then I will give him unto the LORD all the days of his life, and there shall no rasor come upon his head.

1 Samuel 1:11

"Lord, if You give me a son," Hannah prays, "he'll be Yours." No doubt Hannah had prayed countless times about her situation. But now her prayer would be answered. This doesn't mean God didn't hear her before, for every time she prayed she was heard (Psalm 34:17, 69:33, Proverbs 15:29, Jeremiah 33:3, John 9:31).

God can say "Yes" to our requests. He can say "No." Or He can say "Wait." If He says "No," that's just as much an answer as if He said "Yes." If He says "Wait," that's okay because that is exactly what was happening to Hannah. Here, she prayed, "Lord give me a son, and I'll give him to You." And that's what God was waiting for. Previously, she wanted a son to give to her husband. God, however, wanted a prophet to give to a nation. God had something much bigger and bolder, greater and grander in mind than Hannah did.

If you've prayed about your "barren" condition, if you're weeping bitterly, that is okay. It might be that God is simply waiting to get you into harmony with His heart, which means He wants to do something larger than your prayer. This is really encouraging to me because I've discovered that my "unanswered" prayers grow larger for those people or situations I'm forced to bring before the Lord over a long period of time. And I'm reminded once again that prayer is not about getting God to do my will, but about getting me in line with what He wants to do in and through me.

MARCH 22

And they rose up in the morning early, and worshipped before the LORD, and returned, and came to their house to Ramah: and Elkanah knew Hannah his wife; and the LORD remembered her. Wherefore it came to pass, when the time was come about after Hannah had conceived, that she bare a son, and called his name Samuel, saying, Because I have asked him of the LORD.

1 Samuel 1:19-20

Samuel means "asked of God." In naming her baby, Hannah remembered that his delivery was in response to her prayer made nine months earlier. I'm convinced the biggest problem in our prayer lives is forgetting what we prayed for. When the answer to our prayer comes nine days, months, or years after we asked, we say, "Wonderful!" but forget it is in answer to what we were praying for previously.

Forgetting what I prayed for previously causes me to think God is not responding to my prayers presently. For example, in a moment of honesty before the Lord, I pray, "Lord, there are things in me that need to be changed. Make me a man who is broken before You and totally dependent on You. Lord, change me." And He begins that process. But then, three weeks later, I pray, "Lord, I need a raise desperately." But the raise doesn't come. Why? Because God is still answering my prayer that I be dependent on Him. Since we don't remember what we pray for, we often end up offering contradictory prayers.

When I look back over my journals, inevitably I hear myself saying, "No wonder I'm going through this now. I prayed for it way back then." Forgetting what we pray for is a problem most of us have that keeps us from being men and women of prayer. Such was not the case with Hannah.

MARCH 23

> *Also before they burnt the fat, the priest's servant came, and said to the man that sacrificed, Give flesh to roast for the priest; for he will not have sodden flesh of thee, but raw. And if any man said unto him, Let them not fail to burn the fat presently, and then take as much as thy soul desireth; then he would answer him, Nay; but thou shalt give it me now: and if not, I will take it by force.*

1 Samuel 2:15-16

In Leviticus chapters 3 through 9, God declared that the fat of the sacrifice was to be completely burned on the altar, signifying the offering of it to

Him. In Old Testament times, the fat was considered to be the best part of the meat. Therefore, God could have been accused of keeping the best part for Himself. We now know that the fat is actually the worst part of the meat. Therefore, God was protecting His people from that which would have harmed them.

That's always the way it is with God. We say, "Why can't I have that? Why can't I go there? Why can't I do that? God must be keeping something good from me."

But the Lord would say, "I'm not going to explain what I'm doing because I want you to trust Me. But as time goes on, you'll see that the things, people, or places I withheld from you would have been harmful to you."

MARCH 24

And the child Samuel grew on, and was in favour both with the LORD, and also with men.

1 Samuel 2:26

Samuel kept growing in God. And what happened? He not only found favor in the eyes of the Lord, but also in the eyes of men. Our kids sometimes have the mistaken idea that if they stand for the Lord and walk with Him, they'll be put down or left out. Not true. Yes, there will be a certain degree of persecution in the Christian walk, but notice what happened to Samuel. He found favor in the eyes of God and of men too.

Blessed is the man who doesn't walk with the ungodly and sit in the seat of the scornful, but whose delight is in the Law of the Lord. Whatever he does will prosper (Psalm 1). As parents, we need to remind our kids that the real key to having a prosperous, exciting life, the key to finding favor in the eyes of both God and men, is to do what Samuel did. He walked with the Lord, and God blessed him indeed.

MARCH 25

And the child Samuel ministered unto the LORD before Eli. And the word of the LORD was precious in those days; there was no open vision.

1 Samuel 3:1

The word of the Lord was precious - or rare. Speaking to believers in Revelation 3:20, Jesus says, "Behold, I stand at the door and knock. If any man hear My voice and open the door, I will come in and sup with him and he with Me." In other words, the question isn't whether Jesus is speaking. The question is: Are we listening?

There's no question God speaks. Psalm 29 tells us His voice is so powerful that it moves mountains and clears forests. The question is, are God's people tuning in? Are they able to perceive and receive the Word He speaks constantly? There are numerous voices speaking via radio and television waves traveling through any given location. The fact that we don't hear them is not because those voices aren't present, but because we're not tuned in to them. Our antenna isn't up, our TV sets aren't on. The same thing is true spiritually (John 10:27). Our Shepherd speaks constantly. The question is, are we tuned in to His frequency? Am I picking up and receiving what He's saying?

MARCH 26

And ere the lamp of God went out in the temple of the LORD, where the ark of God was, and Samuel was laid down to sleep; that the LORD called Samuel . . .

1 Samuel 3:3-4 (a)

Samuel was ministering to the Lord when God spoke to him. Ministering *to* the Lord is different from ministering *for* Him. Ministering *for* the

Lord is teaching a lesson, giving a sermon, helping someone in His name. Ministering *to* the Lord, on the other hand, is drawing near to Him personally and privately. Ministry *to* the Lord takes place not on stage, but in the pew. Ministry *to* the Lord is not about what others see us do, but what the Lord alone enjoys as we spend time with Him. Ministering *to* the Lord is the highest calling in life, and every single one of us can do it.

I love it when my wife makes a meal for me or irons my shirt. But those things can't begin to compare to the love I feel when she's ministering to me - being by my side, sharing with me, loving me. The same is true of the Lord. When you minister to Him, it's a far higher calling than ministering for Him (Ezekiel 44).

MARCH 27

> . . . *and he answered, Here am I. And he ran unto Eli, and said, Here am I; for thou calledst me. And he said, I called not; lie down again. And he went and lay down. And the LORD called yet again, Samuel. And Samuel arose and went to Eli, and said, Here am I; for thou didst call me. And he answered, I called not, my son; lie down again. Now Samuel did not yet know the LORD, neither was the word of the LORD yet revealed unto him.*

1 Samuel 3:4 (b)-7

Notice at this point, Samuel didn't know the Lord personally. He hadn't yet heard from the Lord audibly. But he knew about the Lord. Samuel knew that, as God, He deserved worship and affection. Samuel didn't yet know the Lord, but here he is, year after year, ministering to the Lord.

Ministering *to* the Lord before ministering *for* Him is also seen in the Book of Acts . . .

As they ministered to the Lord, and fasted, the Holy Ghost said, Separate me Barnabas and Saul for the work whereunto I have called them.

Acts 13:2

This verse should be noted by anyone who wants to be a servant of Jesus Christ, for it was as Paul and Barnabas ministered to the Lord that He separated them for ministry. Find ways you can minister to the Lord, where no one else sees what you're doing, but where you are pleasing the Lord simply because He's worthy.

MARCH 28

And the LORD said to Samuel, Behold, I will do a thing in Israel, at which both the ears of every one that heareth it shall tingle. In that day I will perform against Eli all things which I have spoken concerning his house: when I begin, I will also make an end. For I have told him that I will judge his house for ever for the iniquity which he knoweth; because his sons made themselves vile, and he restrained them not. And therefore I have sworn unto the house of Eli, that the iniquity of Eli's house shall not be purged with sacrifice nor offering for ever.

1 Samuel 3:11-14

God didn't speak to Eli. He spoke to Samuel. Why? I suggest it was because Samuel got out of bed. God talks to us in the middle of the night as well. But we think it's the pizza or our husband's snoring or the caffeine from the double latte we ordered earlier that keeps us up. I am convinced, however, that the Lord speaks to our souls at night because it's the only time our hearts are quiet enough to hear Him. The question is, "Will I respond?"

When I do, I hear Him say, "There's something I want to talk over with you. I have direction to give you. I have a word of correction for you." If you want your dreams to come true, gang, you've got to get out of bed! Four times in one night, Samuel got out of bed to check out what was going on. On the fourth time, he discovered it was the Lord all along. God interrupts your sleep or your life, your plans and your schedule, because He wants you to hear from Him.

MARCH 29

And Samuel lay until the morning, and opened the doors of the house of the LORD. And Samuel feared to shew Eli the vision. Then Eli called Samuel, and said, Samuel, my son. And he answered, Here am I. And he said, What is the thing that the LORD hath said unto thee? I pray thee hide it not from me: God do so to thee, and more also, if thou hide any thing from me of all the things that he said unto thee. And Samuel told him every whit, and hid nothing from him. And he said, It is the LORD: let him do what seemeth him good. And Samuel grew, and the LORD was with him, and did let none of his words fall to the ground. And all Israel from Dan even to Beer-sheba knew that Samuel was established to be a prophet of the LORD. And the LORD appeared again in Shiloh: for the LORD revealed himself to Samuel in Shiloh by the word of the LORD.

1 Samuel 3:15-21

God not only spoke to Samuel because of his responsiveness, but because of his tenderness. Samuel didn't want to say to Eli, "Eli, you're in trouble. You haven't disciplined your sons. Now judgment is coming to you and your family. And it's too late for any sacrifices to make up for what you've done."

Living in the Temple, Samuel no doubt observed Eli's sons and was aware of their immorality and problems. Therefore, he could have said, "Aha! At last these guys are getting what they deserve." But that wasn't the heart of Samuel. Nor was it the heart of Daniel.

Before Daniel gave Nebuchadnezzar the interpretation of his dream, he said, "I wish this dream applied to your worst enemy rather than to you, for you're going to go insane like an animal for seven years and eat grass like a cow in the fields" (see Daniel 4:19). Daniel could have said, "Great! It's about time God brings Nebuchadnezzar down a notch or two." But that wasn't the heart of Daniel, nor is it the heart of anyone who is in tune with God.

Whatever God speaks to you must be enveloped in tenderness and love. Even if the message is a difficult one, it's always to be delivered in humility and kindness.

MARCH 30

Woe unto us: who shall deliver us out of the hand of these mighty Gods? these are the Gods that smote the Egyptians with all the plagues in the wilderness. Be strong, and quit yourselves like men, O ye Philistines, that ye be not servants unto the Hebrews, as they have been to you: quit yourselves like men, and fight. And the Philistines fought, and Israel was smitten, and they fled every man into his tent: and there was a very great slaughter; for there fell of Israel thirty thousand footmen.

1 Samuel 4:8-10

Even though Israel had brought the Ark of the Covenant into their camp, thirty thousand men died. This was a horrible defeat; a brutal, bloody battle in which the Philistines butchered the people of Israel.

The same thing can happen to me. I bring the "Ark" into my camp. My boxes are all checked off on my spiritual "To Do" list; therefore, it's sure to be a great day. But I've discovered that sometimes when my boxes are all checked off, the day goes horribly. "Lord," I cry, "I checked my boxes. I read my Bible, prayed, and went to church. I even tithed eleven percent last week! Why don't I have victory?"

And the Lord would say to me, "It's not about bringing a box into your camp or checking a box off on a list. Only a relationship with Me will bring victory as I guide you step by step, day by day."

Reading two chapters a day or attending church two times a week won't guarantee victory any more than bringing the box into the camp brought victory to the Israelites. God doesn't work that way. If, however, reading two chapters a day or attending church two times a week is done for the purpose of meeting Him, of learning more about Him, of spending time with Him, He has promised to meet us there (James 4:8).

MARCH 31

When the Philistines took the ark of God, they brought it into the house of Dagon, and set it by Dagon. And when they of Ashdod arose early on the morrow, behold, Dagon was fallen upon his face to the earth before the ark of the LORD. And they took Dagon, and set him in his place again.

1 Samuel 5:2-3

Half fish and half man, Dagon was the god of the Philistines. Also worshipped by the Assyrians, he was considered by the people in the region of Canaan to be the father of Baal.

I once talked to a man who desperately wanted to be free from a certain addiction. Although he had tried numerous programs and counseling sessions, nothing worked. This story of Dagon proved to be a key for him. Dagon could not stand in the presence of the Lord. Therefore, I told this man that if he tried to get victory over the "Dagon" of his addiction in his own power, he would only become obsessed with it all the more. "Forget about Dagon," I said. "Instead, bring in the Ark. Bring in the presence of the Lord. Spend time in His Word, in prayer, in fellowship with Him - and Dagon will fall." And that's exactly what happened.

The key to overcoming darkness is not to curse, cajole, or karate chop the darkness. The key is simply to turn on the Light. Bring the Ark into any situation and watch Dagon go down because darkness and light are mutually exclusive. Light always eventually wins (1 John 1:5).

APRIL 1

And the men of Israel went out of Mizpeh, and pursued the Philistines, and smote them, until they came under Beth-car. Then Samuel took a stone, and set it between Mizpeh and Shen, and called the name of it Eben-ezer, saying, Hitherto hath the LORD helped us.

1 Samuel 7:11-12

Ebenezer means "stone of help." In setting up this stone, Samuel was saying, "Up to this point, the Lord has helped us."

Why is this important to do? Because sometimes we think, "Oh, no. Things will never work out. My marriage is on the rocks. My finances are down the drain. Everything looks grim." What we need in times like this is an "Ebenezer stone," which reminds us that God has never failed us, that what we fear doesn't come to pass. Yes, there are definite challenges that come our way - but in those challenges, God always shows Himself strong. He's always there for us.

I have found journaling to be a wonderful "Ebenezer stone." Reading through my journals, I am reminded again and again that God has never let me down in the past, which gives me confidence that He won't let me down in the future. Whether through journaling or songwriting, letters or pictures, I encourage you to put your own "Ebenezer stone" in place, where you can be reminded of God's faithfulness in the past, draw strength for the present, and hope for the future.

APRIL 2

But the thing displeased Samuel, when they said, Give us a king to judge us. And Samuel prayed unto the LORD.

1 Samuel 8:6

Instead of lashing out at the people, Samuel looked up to the Lord - a wise thing to do because the wrath of man never works the righteousness of God (James 1:20). Instead of coming down on the people, Samuel simply prayed.

When you feel frustration churn in your stomach, it's always a good thing to slip away to a quiet spot and talk it over with the Lord. When you return, you'll have an entirely different perspective, countenance, and attitude - and the outcome will be entirely different. When I don't do this - when I blow my top, let off steam, or give someone a piece of my mind - I never fail to regret it.

APRIL 3

And the LORD said to Samuel, Hearken unto their voice, and make them a king. And Samuel said unto the men of Israel, Go ye every man unto his city.

1 Samuel 8:22

Although it was not His plan for them, God gave His people what they wanted.

> O Israel, thou hast destroyed thyself; but in me is thine help. I will be thy king: where is any other that may save thee in all thy cities? And thy judges of whom thou saidst, Give me a king and princes? I gave thee a king in mine anger, and took him away in my wrath.
>
> Hosea 13:9-11

God can give us what we ask for. This is one of the real dangers of the "Name it and claim it" school of thought. God is the King. He knows what's best for me. He knows what will make me happy. I think I do - but I'm almost always wrong. I believe this is where the radical faith movement is in grave error. The assumption there is, "God, I know this thing, that person, or that career is perfect for me, so I claim it in faith." In so doing, people become their own king, using God to bring about their own demands.

I have discovered that it is infinitely wiser to say, "Lord, here's the way I see it. Here are my thoughts about this. But, Lord, You see what I don't. You know what I can't. So I gladly, happily defer to Your perfect plan for me."

The old adage remains true: God always gives His best to those who leave the choice with Him. Always.

APRIL 4

To morrow about this time I will send thee a man out of the land of Benjamin, and thou shalt anoint him to be captain over my people Israel, that he may save my people out of the hand of the Philistines: for I have looked upon my people, because their cry is come unto me.

1 Samuel 9:16

The day previously, Samuel heard the Lord say, "Tomorrow a man is going to come - the one I have chosen to be the captain, the king of the nation." I find it interesting that the Lord whispered in Samuel's ear the day before this event took place - to let him know what was ahead. In 1 Samuel 8:21, we read that Samuel heard all the words of the people and he rehearsed them in the ears of the Lord. Those who whisper in the ears of the Lord will hear the Word whispered in their ear as well. I'm convinced that many times I don't hear what the Lord wants to say in my ear because I haven't first spoken in His ear. Samuel was a man who understood what it meant to pray without ceasing. As a result, the Lord whispered in his ear, telling him the man who would be king was on his way.

APRIL 5

Then Samuel took a vial of oil, and poured it upon his head, and kissed him, and said, Is it not because the LORD hath anointed thee to be captain over his inheritance? When thou art departed from me to day, then thou shalt find two men by Rachel's sepulchre in the border of Benjamin at Zelzah; and they will say unto thee, The asses which thou wentest to seek are found: and, lo, thy father hath left the care of the asses, and sorroweth for you, saying, What shall I do for my son?

1 Samuel 10:1-2

I like what Samuel says because there are times when we, too, lose our donkeys - when we feel very real burdens, tensions, and anxieties. And as He did to Saul, God says, "I want to help you with that."

As a seer, Samuel is a type of the Holy Spirit, who searches out the deep things of God (1 Corinthians 2:10). "You've come to the right place," Samuel said. "But before I give you information about your lost donkeys, I want you to sit at the table with me."

Saul could have said, "My dad is worried. I have a job to do. Thanks, but no thanks. I can't take time to sit at the table." But Saul didn't do that. To his credit, he heard what the seer said, and sat down. I suggest that a practical picture is painted in this vignette. That is, like Saul, we're worried about stuff that is ultimately not all that important. God will take care of it - but there's a bigger calling, a grander picture. There's a big plan for us. There's a Divine design for our lives. Therefore, when you feel overwhelmed by problems and tensions, burdens and frustrations, slow down. Come to the Table. Come to Communion. Come and dine. Wait on the Lord. It's not about your problem. It's not about the donkeys. It's about your being anointed as royalty to be used by God eternally.

If Saul had said, "Sorry, I don't have time. I've got to get home," I suggest he would never have been king. I wonder who of us has missed out because we were worried about our donkeys, failing to realize the Lord was simply using them to call us away to commune with Him. When you're uptight or upset, come to the Lord's Table and dine with Him. Go to the top of the house - get above the situation - and say, "Lord, what do You want to say to me?" As it was to Saul, His answer will most likely be different than you thought, and bigger than what you could imagine.

APRIL 6

If ye will fear the LORD, and serve him, and obey his voice, and not rebel against the commandment of the LORD, then shall both ye and also the king that reigneth over you continue following the LORD your God: but if ye will not obey the voice of the LORD, but rebel against the commandment of the LORD, then shall the hand of the LORD be against you, as it was against your fathers.

1 Samuel 12:14-15

God is unbelievably gracious. He says, "If you choose to obey Me, I'll reign over you. But if you rebel, My hand will be against you."

The Bible says whom the Lord loves, He chastens (Hebrews 12:6). Therefore, God's chastening hand is a sign of His love. In one way or another, all of us have rebelled. But the great news is that, on the basis of this text, God says, "Even though you've rebelled against Me or ignored Me, if you'll obey what I say and fear again today, I'll be with you. If you don't, I'll chasten you because I am still your Father, and I still love you."

Many people who know they married the wrong person, made a wrong move, or took a wrong turn feel that there's no hope from that point on. God, however, says otherwise. "You wanted him. You got him. You wanted that job. It's yours. But I'm still here, and I always will be. If you choose to turn to Me today, and if you choose to once again obey, I'll reign over you."

That's grace, gang. God doesn't give up on Israel - and He won't give up on you.

APRIL 7

Moreover as for me, God forbid that I should sin against the LORD in ceasing to pray for you: but I will teach you the good and the right way . . .

1 Samuel 12:23

When the people asked him to pray for them, Samuel said, "God forbid that I should sin against the Lord in ceasing to pray for you." Prayerlessness is the epitome of selfishness because my failure to intercede for others means I am withholding that which would so greatly bless them. That is why Samuel was shocked at the suggestion that he wouldn't pray.

Prayer is the proof of love, and love is the product of prayer. If I love someone, I will pray for him. And if I pray for him, I will love him. That's why Jesus told us to pray for our enemies. If you pray for someone - even someone you don't like - something happens within you. You find your heart knit to those for whom you pray.

Intercession is the common denominator of all godly men and women. Whether it's in the Bible or in biographies, you'll notice that, without exception, the people who have really left a mark for the Lord and have made a difference in this world are men and women given to intercession.

Note that Samuel said he would pray before he said he would teach. If you're one who aspires to be used in Christian service, understand that it is not teaching, counseling, discipling, or even witnessing that is the priority of true ministry. It's prayer. The apostles who were setting the pace and leading the way in ministry said, "It is not reasonable that we should leave the ministry of prayer and the Word to tend to the practical needs in the church in Jerusalem" (Acts 6). What came first? Prayer.

Many believers know this theoretically, but they don't understand it practically. May we be the exception. Greatness awaits the man or woman who will make prayer a priority. Therefore, let us be people given to prayer.

APRIL 8

And it came to pass, that as soon as he had made an end of offering the burnt offering, behold, Samuel came; and Saul went out to meet him, that he might salute him.

1 Samuel 13:10

Samuel had told Saul to wait seven days before engaging in battle against the Philistines. When seven days had come and almost gone and Samuel hadn't shown up, Saul said, "My troops are leaving. I've got to do something." So he assumed the role of priest and offered a sacrifice himself rather than waiting for Samuel so that he could engage in battle.

No sooner had Saul finished offering the sacrifice than Samuel showed up. This is so often the way of God. So often the Lord waits until the last moment to step in. Why? It's not to tease us, but to test us. He takes us right down to the wire, not to taunt us, but to train us in order that we might have endurance (James 1:3). You see, the race we run as believers isn't a sprint. It's a marathon. And God knows how desperately we need endurance. The only way to get endurance is to go through testing that will force us to wait on Him in order that we might not panic, not run off the track, not throw in the towel. C. H. Spurgeon said the snails made it safely to the ark because they had endurance. You might be a snail. I might be a slug. We might move very, very slowly - but we will make it to the Ark if we simply endure.

"Time is running out!" we cry. "We've got to do something!"

Do we? I can give you all kinds of advice and recommendations, but it's only when God steps in that there will be a real solution. The sage was right when he said that the brave man is not braver than any other, but simply braver for ten minutes longer. Who is the brave man? Who is the mature brother, the wise sister, the deep Christian among us? It's not one who is necessarily super-spiritual. It's simply one who has learned to wait and not panic.

Has God promised to show up? Has God promised you that He is going to work all things for good? Has God promised you that He will take the cares you cast on Him? Has God promised you that He will give a peace deep within? Has God promised that the desires deep within your heart will come to pass? If He has, wait for Him. Don't panic, dear people. Be brave. Saul thought he waited seven days - but seven days hadn't completely passed. He didn't wait the full course.

"Lord, make me a man of God," we pray. "Produce in me depth of character and wisdom."

"Okay," God says. "I'm going to take you through some experiences in which you will have the choice either to panic and try to solve the problem by sacrificing this or looking to them - or to trust Me."

April 9

> *Now there was no smith found throughout all the land of Israel: for the Philistines said, Lest the Hebrews make them swords or spears: but all the Israelites went down to the Philistines, to sharpen every man his share, and his coulter, and his axe, and his mattock. Yet they had a file for the mattocks, and for the coulters, and for the forks, and for the axes, and to sharpen the goads.*

1 Samuel 13:19-21

When the Philistines controlled the country, they would not allow the men of Israel to have swords. So to sharpen their plows and other implements of farming, the Israelites had to go to the Philistines.

It is always the way of the enemy to take away your Sword. "You can still farm. You can still do your work. I'll give you tools," Satan says. "I'll help you financially or educationally. I'll give you the instruments you need to succeed. But I don't want you to have the Sword." Self-help and advice books fill the shelves of many who won't open the Sword of the Word because Satan has tricked them into thinking they don't need it. I suggest, however, that the sixty-six book library you hold in your hand contains enough material to keep you busy studying for the rest of your life.

I truly thought that by this point in my life I would have a much better handle on this Book than I do. I know the Word not nearly like I ought to, not nearly like I want to. I don't have Zephaniah down like I ought to. I don't have passages in Romans memorized like I wanted to. I'm still sketchy on the flow of certain sections of Revelation. Time is running out. My memory is fading and I need to give myself to the Sword. I am more and more convinced that everything I need to know is in this Book - about parenting and grandparenting, about finances and family, about faith and the future. It's all right here. Satan will try to give us other tools - but it is the Sword that we need.

APRIL 10

And Jonathan said to the young man that bare his armour, Come, and let us go over unto the garrison of these uncircumcised: it may be that the LORD will work for us: for there is no restraint to the LORD to save by many or by few.

1 Samuel 14:6

Deuteronomy 32:30 tells us that one with the Lord will put to flight one thousand and two with the Lord will put to flight ten thousand. I like the Lord's mathematics because if one would put to flight one thousand you would think that two would put to flight two thousand. But God's economy is exponential and explosive, allowing two to have victory over ten times as many as one would.

Daniel 11:32 says that those who know their God shall do great exploits. In other words, the more I know about the Lord, the more faith I'll have to do great things for Him. William Carey, famous missionary of generations past, said, "Attempt great things for God and expect great things from God." Every believer ought to be involved in something so big that, unless

God is in it, it's doomed to fail. Go in over your head. Do something that is so much bigger than you are, that unless God is in it, it can't work. Jonathan models this mindset.

APRIL 11

Then said Jonathan, Behold, we will pass over unto these men, and we will discover ourselves unto them. If they say thus unto us, Tarry until we come to you; then we will stand still in our place, and will not go up unto them. But if they say thus, Come up unto us; then we will go up: for the LORD hath delivered them into our hand: and this shall be a sign unto us.

1 Samuel 14:8-10

Although Jonathan and his armor-bearer said, "Let's step out and see what the Lord might want to do," they weren't being presumptuous because they said, "If the Lord doesn't want us to go, we're not going to plunge ahead." In this, I see a wonderful balance.

A lot of people wait for something to happen - but they wait at a great distance. They say, "Lord, if You want to do something with me, You have my number." I think a better way is to do what Jonathan did. He stood on the edge. He was at the door. He wasn't going to force it, but he was in place to storm through it.

Perhaps you're in a place vocationally, relationally, or in ministry where the Lord is telling you to step up, move out, and get ready.

"But what if it doesn't work out?" you ask.

The Lord has promised to close doors no man can open and to open doors no man can shut (Revelation 3:7), but you can't see the door from a long distance. You've got to be there. That's what Jonathan did.

APRIL 12

And the people flew upon the spoil, and took sheep, and oxen, and calves, and slew them on the ground: and the people did eat them with the blood.

1 Samuel 14:32

So hungry were the people from the battle that they ate the food before them - the food of the enemy. It was unclean. It wasn't kosher. It wasn't prepared properly.

The same thing happens to me. If I don't partake of the meat of the Word, I'll end up eating the unclean meat of the world. If I've worked hard, focused like a laser, done battle - but haven't taken time to dip into the honey of the Word, when the day is over, I'll dive into a scoop of ice cream or two or a gallon. Then I'll turn on the TV and watch a political debate where political analysts scream at each other for two hours. By that time, I'll think I need a bowl of cereal. And before I know it, it's two in the morning and I'm still hungry. But when I open the Bible, the most amazing thing happens. My eyes are enlightened. My soul is satiated. Suddenly I'm talking with the Lord and hearing from Him. And it's wonderful - for it's what I wanted all along.

Eat the honey before you get so discouraged and weary that you dive into carnal stuff. The best thing you can do to remain healthy and happy is to eat of the honey regularly. It will keep you from eating the unclean meat of the world. Pack a pocket New Testament instead of a calorie counter in your purse or pocket. Always keep at least a section of Scripture close at hand.

APRIL 13

Then Samuel went to Ramah; and Saul went up to his house to Gibeah of Saul. And Samuel came no more to see Saul until the day of his death: nevertheless Samuel mourned for Saul: and the LORD repented that he had made Saul king over Israel.

1 Samuel 15:34-35

In verse 29, we read that the Lord is not a man that he should repent. The word "repent" can mean "to change direction," or it can mean - as it does forty-one times in the Old Testament - "to regret." God is simply regretting that the people demanded a king. In Deuteronomy 17:15, provision is made for a king. But the people got ahead of God because the king He intended for them was David.

Perhaps that's a word for some of us. "Delight yourself in the Lord, and He will give you the desires of your heart," Psalm 37:4 tells us. We cling to and claim this verse, as well we should, but not apart from its context, for three verses later, David tells us to wait patiently for God. God has a plan for our lives - and no small part of it requires patience. If we get ahead of God, we end up with Ishmael instead of Isaac, with Saul instead of David. It's a recurring lesson throughout Scripture (Psalm 27:14; Proverbs 20:22; Isaiah 40:31; Jeremiah 14:22; Lamentations 3:26; Hosea 12:6; Micah 7:7; Habakkuk 2:3; Zephaniah 3:8; Acts 1:4; Romans 8:25; 1 Thessalonians 1:10). Wait, wait, wait on the Lord.

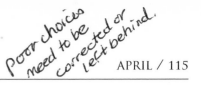
APRIL 14

And the LORD said unto Samuel, How long wilt thou
mourn for Saul, seeing I have rejected him from reigning
over Israel? fill thine horn with oil, and go, I will send thee
to Jesse the Beth-lehemite: for I have provided me a king
among his sons.

1 Samuel 16:1

"Quit your mourning and moaning, Samuel, there's work to do," God said.

"But I have reason to mourn. My heart is broken," Samuel could have said.

"I regret it, too, but I've moved on," God might have answered.

We need to move on, gang. Yes, there are incidents in our lives that are hurtful, even regrettable - sad things, hard times, raw deals; pain, problems, and disappointments. But we must move on. Why? Because we serve a God Who is on the move (Genesis 1:2). If I remain in the past problem or the past disappointment, I will miss the present move of God.

APRIL 15

And it came to pass, when he had made an end of speaking
unto Saul, that the soul of Jonathan was knit with the soul
of David, and Jonathan loved him as his own soul. And
Saul took him that day, and would let him go no more
home to his father's house. Then Jonathan and David made
a covenant, because he loved him as his own soul. And
Jonathan stripped himself of the robe that was upon him,
and gave it to David, and his garments, even to his sword,
and to his bow, and to his girdle.

1 Samuel 18:1-4

Jonathan - the crown prince, the next in line to the throne - looks at this unlikely hero, stripped himself of the robe he was wearing and the weapons he was carrying, and gave them to David. Jonathan was a hero in his own right. He could have looked at David as competition. But he didn't. Instead, he gave up his power and prestige to ally himself with this one-time shepherd boy from Bethlehem.

You might have a program, a plan, a passion. But the Lord would say to you today, "Let go. Give Me your robe and your weapons. Knit your soul with Mine, and what you'll find is freedom and fulfillment like you've never known."

Saul was determined to remain on the throne and in control. Jonathan does just the opposite. Saul goes down in infamy; Jonathan is exalted eternally. When you talk to people at work, on the campus, or in the neighborhood, the issue is always the same: Are you willing to get off the throne of your life? Are you willing to give control to the God Who loves you so much that He became the Good Shepherd who gave His life for you?

This is a daily issue for those of us who know the Lord as well. Who will be on the throne today? Will I give up my abilities and appearance to follow the One who gave up the throne of Heaven to die for me?

APRIL 16

And Saul saw and knew that the LORD was with David, and that Michal Saul's daughter loved him. And Saul was yet the more afraid of David; and Saul became David's enemy continually. Then the princes of the Philistines went forth: and it came to pass, after they went forth, that David behaved himself more wisely than all the servants of Saul; so that his name was much set by.

1 Samuel 18:28-30

The more David was exalted, the more jealous Saul became. Jonathan, however, had an even greater right to be jealous of David because they were of the same generation. But Jonathan is free from jealousy because he decided to help David accomplish his goal rather than to stand against him. Thus, in helping David, Jonathan is free from jealousy, goes down in history as a great man, and is rewarded eternally.

I guarantee there has been or will be a situation in your life similar to this. You'll have a choice to feel threatened and to throw spears - or to rejoice and help others excel. If you try to keep someone else down, you will spiral downward yourself. But if you help someone else go higher, you will inevitably be on an upward path as well. On a daily basis, let go of the spear, and pick up the harp.

APRIL 17

So Michal let David down through a window: and he went,
and fled, and escaped.

1 Samuel 19:12

God protected David through a bride who saved his life. "There are men who will ambush you," Michal told her husband. "Go out the back window and I'll cover for you."

It was David's bride who saved his life. So too, the people in the Body of Christ are the Bride of Christ - and they are the ones who will save your life. You might think people in the church are liars. That's okay, so was Michal. You might think the people in the church are idolators. That's okay, so was Michal. On a practical level, we are a blemished Bride indeed. But in God's eyes, because we have been washed in the blood of the Lamb and robed in the righteousness of our Lord, we are a glorious Church without spot or wrinkle, a holy priesthood, a spotless Bride (Ephesians 5:27; 1 Peter 2:5; Revelation 19:8).

I have discovered that when I go through valleys, difficulties, and tragedies, it's the Body of Christ I'm most thankful for. When the enemy is out to destroy you, it's the blemished Bride of Christ Who will rescue you.

APRIL 18

Then Jonathan said to David, To morrow is the new moon: and thou shalt be missed, because thy seat will be empty. And when thou hast stayed three days, then thou shalt go down quickly, and come to the place where thou didst hide thyself when the business was in hand, and shalt remain by the stone Ezel.

1 Samuel 20:18-19

Ezel means "the rock that shows the way." Therefore, David was to stay by the rock that shows the way. Like David, you might be at a crossroads, worried you won't figure out where you're supposed to go. I have great news for you: God will direct you. All you have to do is stay close to "the Rock that shows the way." That is, all you have to do is stay in touch with Jesus day by day by day. Even if your devotional life isn't what it should be, even if there are struggles with which you wrestle continually, even if you feel like you missed the boat previously, God is faithful. God blesses us in spite of ourselves if we simply plop ourselves by the Rock that shows the way.

As a father of five, I don't direct my kids on the basis of how they're doing. That is, I don't say to one, "Since you're being good, I'm going to give you lots of direction," and to another, "I can't direct you because you're struggling with this or dealing with that." No, I direct my kids wherever they're at. I want to give them as much direction, help, and assistance as they'll allow me to give them. The same is true of our Heavenly Father. He sees our needs and is aware of our frailty. Yet even when we are faithless, He is faithful still (2 Timothy 2:13).

APRIL 19

David therefore departed thence, and escaped to the cave Adullam: and when his brethren and all his father's house heard it, they went down thither to him. And every one that was in distress, and every one that was in debt, and every one that was discontented, gathered themselves unto him; and he became a captain over them: and there were with him about four hundred men.

1 Samuel 22:1-2

A cave is not an easy place to be. It's dark and discouraging. But Psalms 57 and 142, written while David was in the cave at Adullam, show a deep work going on in his soul . . .

> Be thou exalted, O God, above the heavens; let thy glory be above all the earth. They have prepared a net for my steps; my soul is bowed down: they have digged a pit before me, into the midst whereof they are fallen themselves. Selah. My heart is fixed, O God, my heart is fixed: I will sing and give praise. Awake up, my glory; awake, psaltery and harp: I myself will awake early. I will praise thee, O Lord, among the people: I will sing unto thee among the nations. For thy mercy is great unto the heavens, and thy truth unto the clouds. Be thou exalted, O God, above the heavens: let thy glory be above all the earth.

Psalm 57:5-11

When my spirit was overwhelmed within me, then thou knewest my path. In the way wherein I walked have they privily laid a snare for me. I looked on my right hand, and beheld, but there was no man that would know me: refuge failed me; no man cared for my soul. I cried unto thee, O LORD: I said, Thou art my refuge and my portion in the land of the living. Attend unto my cry; for I am brought very low: deliver me from my persecutors; for they are stronger than I. Bring my soul out of prison, that I may praise thy name: the righteous shall compass me about; for thou shalt deal bountifully with me.

Psalm 142:3-7

We want to be comfortable - but God knows that our souls do not grow in times of comfort (Romans 5:3-5). Therefore, He puts us in places where His work can be done, where His Word takes root. If you're in a cave today, you're in good company because God does deep work in hard places.

The group of four hundred men who were in debt, distressed, and discontented eventually became David's mighty men, an elite fighting unit. David was flawed indeed, yet more is written of him than any other man in Scripture because he was a man after God's heart - a man who pursued God. And as these four hundred men spent time with him, they became like him.

Like David's men, we too are in debt, distressed, and often discontented. But as we hang around the Son of David, Jesus Christ, an amazing thing happens: we become like Him (2 Corinthians 3:18). The key to greatness is to hang around Jesus constantly. Choose to make Jesus your identity and your passion; and slowly, but surely, you'll be conformed into the image of the One captivating your heart.

APRIL 20

Then David and his men, which were about six hundred, arose and departed out of Keilah, and went whithersoever they could go. And it was told Saul that David was escaped from Keilah; and he forbare to go forth. And David abode in the wilderness in strong holds, and remained in a mountain in the wilderness of Ziph. And Saul sought him every day . . .

1 Samuel 23:13-14 (a)

Ziph literally means "refining place." What a great place for David to go - a place where God will refine him. In the refining process, a smelter would heat ore to the point that it became liquid, with all of the impurities burned away. The smelter would know the process was complete when he could look in the pot of liquid ore and see his own face. So too, the Lord says, "I'm going to allow the heat to be turned up a bit, to burn out the impurities in you so that people might see something of Me in your life."

C. H. Spurgeon said that affliction is the tuner of the harp and the sanctifier of the son. I like that. How did David have such intimacy with the Lord, such passion for the Lord, such understanding of the Lord that He could write the psalms he wrote? His passion, wisdom, and understanding came from places like Ziph and Keilah - where people were chasing him down, where he was betrayed by people he had helped, where he would feel forsaken and alone - where God could deal with him.

How long does the process of affliction or refining go on? Longer than you might think. It takes awhile for the impurities to be burnt off, for the reflection of His face to be seen from my life or yours.

APRIL 21

David also rose afterward, and went out of the cave, and cried after Saul, saying, My lord the king. And when Saul looked behind him, David stooped with his face to the earth, and bowed himself.

1 Samuel 24:8

David's insights into the Lord, his dependence upon the Lord, his passion for the Lord are revealed in the Psalms he wrote during the time he was fleeing from Saul because the man who had nothing but anger toward him was God's instrument to make him into the man he desired to be.

The same is true with us. "Lord, change me," I pray. "I'm tired of the smallness of my soul, the hardness of my heart. Make me different than I am."

"Okay," the Lord says. "I'll send you an anointed instrument to help accomplish this change."

"Good!" I say, thinking it will be an anointed teacher, a Christian book, a close friend.

But He sends a Saul or two throwing spears at me.

Who has the Lord allowed to be in your life who throws spears at you, who brings grief to you? That person is the anointed instrument of God to work in you the love, kindness, and tenderness you long for. There's no other way for the Lord to change you but to send a Saul or two your way. The question is, what will you do? Will you cut the fringe?

I doubt that the blind man in John 9 would have washed in the pool of Siloam - or literally "sent one" - had there not been mud in his eyes. Why does God allow people we think are mud to get in our face? The reason is to cause us to go to the true Sent One and wash again. When everything is going well, I have a tendency to cruise on automatic pilot. But when there's mud thrown at me, I make my way to the Lord in desperation. I pour out my heart to the Lord and get into the water of the Word once again.

David said to Saul, "The Lord will judge between you and me. The Lord will work things out. The Lord will deal with you eventually. But I'm not to touch you because you are God's anointed instrument in my life."

What about that person who breaks your heart? Are you going to take them down a peg or two - or, like David, will you wisely choose not to touch the Lord's anointed?

APRIL 22

And David said in his heart, I shall now perish one day by the hand of Saul . . .

1 Samuel 27:1 (a)

David was a lover of God Who talked to the Lord constantly and wrote Psalms about the Lord very expressively. In this situation, however, we see him not talking to the Lord, but talking to his heart. The Hebrew phrase translated "in his heart" literally means David talked to himself. And in so doing, he got mixed up. He came to wrong conclusions. He fell into depression. He ends up living in enemy territory for almost a year and a half because he talked to himself rather than talking to the Lord.

I can do the same thing oh, so easily. I talk to myself and convince myself of all kinds of things that are completely untrue. As I drive home from church, I overhear myself saying,

"Now, Jon, what do you think about that?"

"I think what he said was unfair."

"I do too!"

"I think she could have been a little kinder. What do you think, Jon?"

"I completely agree. I don't know what's gotten into her."

"I've been wondering the same thing! It seems like they used to be so nice and so pleasant, but something's wrong with them now."

"I concur! You need to do something about them. You need to yell at them."

"You're right, Jon. Excellent advice!"

I think a lot of us talk to ourselves from time to time. Driving to church, walking the dog, mowing the lawn, we convince ourselves that we're right. We build up a case that's airtight. We become our own best ally. We feel more justified with each passing moment as we talk to ourselves.

But here's the danger with talking to yourself, with talking to your heart: According to Jeremiah 17:9, the heart is deceitful and desperately wicked. This means that when you're having a good "heart to heart" talk with yourself, you're getting counsel that is desperately wicked.

What are we to do? Philippians 4 says, "Be anxious for nothing. But in everything with prayer and supplication with thanksgiving, let your requests be made known" - not to yourself, not to your pastor, not to your spouse - "unto God. And the peace of God will keep your hearts and minds in Christ Jesus."

Imagine two stopwatches in your hands. One starts every time you talk to yourself or to others about a situation. The other starts every time you talk to your Father about the matter, communicating in articulate, intelligent, understandable prayer. After three days, what would these clocks look like? How much time would have been spent talking to yourself? How much time would have been spent talking to your Father?

There are some people with whom spending time is a joy. Why? Because their hearts and minds are at peace. Why? Because they're people of prayer. They have no fish to fry, no axes to grind, no battles to fight, no points to prove because they have learned to say, "Father, I don't know what to do about this. I'm tired of mulling it over in my mind or talking to people round about me. I'm just going to talk to You."

The only way to have this peace is to pray. If you talk to yourself more than you talk to your Father, you'll make big mistakes. But if you choose to talk to the Father, there will be a genuine peace about you that is winsome and attractive, pleasant and contagious. Bend your knee, open your heart, and wait on Him.

APRIL 23

And it came to pass, when David and his men were come to Ziklag on the third day, that the Amalekites had invaded the south, and Ziklag, and smitten Ziklag, and burnt it with fire; and had taken the women captives, that were therein: they slew not any, either great or small, but carried them away, and went on their way.

1 Samuel 30:1-2

Ziklag means "winding road." Life is like that. You think you have things all straightened out, all your ducks in the proverbial row, with nothing but smooth sailing ahead - until you come to a curve you weren't counting on, a pothole you didn't see. That's the way it will always be this side of Heaven. But one day, when we're called away, the streets will be straight (Isaiah 40:4) and paved with gold (Revelation 21:21) - no more winding roads, no more potholes.

David finds a curve he wasn't counting on. He and his boys make it back to Ziklag to reunite with their families only to discover that the Amalekites had invaded the town, burned down their homes, and carried their families away. It was a brutal, devastating, heartbreaking situation.

Amalekite means "dweller in the valley." Each time the Amalekites are seen in Scripture, they're an illustration of the flesh, warring against the people of God. That is why God said to Moses, "You shall war against Amalek from generation to generation" (see Exodus 17:16).

Whether it's due to the fleshly tendencies within us or to external enemies that seek to pull us down, you can count on a fight from Amalek. Right when you think you have things all figured out, another generation of Amalekites will rise up and war against you. Knowing this, aren't you thankful that He Who is within you is greater than any Amalekite who comes against you? (1 John 4:4).

APRIL 24

. . . but David encouraged himself in the LORD his God.

1 Samuel 30:6 (b)

David encouraged himself in the Lord. This is where it starts. This is what we must do to get back all that's been ripped off by the enemy. David couldn't depend on his men. They were angry with him. There was no one to pat him on the back and say, "It'll be okay." There was no one to wipe away his tears. But that's the way it usually is. Don't wait for a pastor to come, a friend to show up, a neighbor to drop by when you're depressed. If you do, you might have a long wait. David knew what he had to do. Everything looked grim. But he chose to encourage himself in the Lord.

How?

We see the answer in Psalm 42 . . .

Why art thou cast down, O my soul? and why art thou disquieted in me? Hope thou in God: for I shall yet praise him for the help of his countenance.

Psalm 42:5

I can be depressed, discouraged, despairing continually, or I can say, "Why are you this way, soul? Hope in God. Give praise to Him. Offer thanks to Him."

When I receive news that my city has been burned down, the first thing I must do is encourage myself in the Lord by thanking Him for the ways He has been so faithful time and time again. I reflect and remember - and begin to talk to the Lord audibly, giving Him thanks for what He has done.

> Little Tommy didn't understand this. When his mommy said, "You're going to have a baby brother or a baby sister," he was so thrilled that he told his kindergarten teacher. He told her again the next day. In fact, every day without fail he told her that he was going to have a baby brother or a baby sister.
>
> One day, his mother said, "Tommy, come here." As she placed his hand on her stomach, she said, "Feel that? That's your baby brother or sister kicking!"
>
> Tommy smiled faintly and walked away.
>
> The next day when he went to school he didn't tell his teacher he was going to have a baby brother or a baby sister. He didn't bring it up the second, third, or fifth day, either. Finally, after a couple of weeks, his teacher said, "Tommy, you haven't talked about the baby that's coming."
>
> Tommy burst into tears. "The baby's not coming," he cried. "My mommy ate it!"

Like Tommy, we don't understand things very well. Oh, this is awful, we think - failing to realize that God is up to something wonderful.

APRIL 25

And David said to Abiathar the priest, Ahimelech's son, I pray thee, bring me hither the ephod. And Abiathar brought thither the ephod to David. And David inquired at the LORD, saying, Shall I pursue after this troop? shall I overtake them? And he answered him, Pursue: for thou shalt surely overtake them, and without fail recover all.

1 Samuel 30:7-8

After encouraging himself in the Lord, *David inquired of the Lord.* "What do You want me to do, Lord?" The Lord answered him directly and quickly. And God will do the same with you.

It doesn't take as much as you think. Satan will say, "So you want to hear from the Lord? That's going to require three hours of constant prayer, three days of fasting, three weeks of getting away. You only have thirty minutes? God's not going to hear you. Ten minutes? Forget about it. Three minutes? You've got to be kidding. God's not going to give you direction in a three minute prayer."

I challenge that. Ask Peter. He was on the Sea of Galilee. He had been walking on the water, but now he's sinking quickly. He didn't pray for three days, three months, three hours, or even three minutes. He prayed three words: "Lord, save me." And the Lord grabbed him by the hand and pulled him out of the water (Matthew 14:30).

Satan will say, "It takes a lot more. That's not enough."

But Jesus said, "Do not think you're going to be heard because of your much speaking, your long praying. That's a heathen concept. When you pray, be simple" (see Matthew 6:7-8).

APRIL 26

So David went, he and the six hundred men that were with him, and came to the brook Besor, where those that were left behind stayed. But David pursued, he and four hundred men . . .

1 Samuel 30:9-10 (a)

Third, *David was engaged with the Lord.* Following praise and prayer, we see pursuit. Many times, people sit back and say, "Lord, if You want good things to come my way, bring them to me."

The Lord, however, says, "Take a step of faith. I'll be with you. I'll fight for you. But I want you to be engaged with Me. I don't want you passive because I want to prepare you for eternity."

To Elijah - another man who was depressed and holed up in a cave - God said, "Why are you in this cave of depression? You know better than this. I want you to go to Syria. I want you to anoint a new king. I want you to go to Israel and raise up a leader. I want you to find a young man named Elisha and mentor him. I have work for you to do" (1 Kings 19).

The Lord says the same thing to us. "Why are you in this cave? You know better than that." Do what you know, and you'll know what to do.

APRIL 27

And when the inhabitants of Jabesh-gilead heard of that which the Philistines had done to Saul, all the valiant men arose, and went all night, and took the body of Saul and the bodies of his sons from the wall of Beth-shan, and came to Jabesh, and burnt them there. And they took their bones, and buried them under a tree at Jabesh, and fasted seven days.

1 Samuel 31:11-13

When the men of Jabesh-gilead received word that Saul's corpse was pinned to the wall of a Philistine city, their hearts were stirred with compassion. Marching all night, the men of Jabesh-gilead risked their lives to recover the bodies of Saul and his sons. The bodies were so mutilated that they eventually had to burn them. But they buried their bones under a tree in their own city.

What moved these men? Why would they risk their lives, outnumbered and outmanned, to recover the headless corpse of a judged king?

I suggest it's because of something that happened forty years previously, when Saul was presented to Israel as her king (1 Samuel 10-11). Certain people applauded. "Long live the king," they said. But others said, "We're not going to have this farmer from the tribe of Benjamin rule over us." And Saul realized that the opinion about him was divided. So he went back to his farm and plowed away - until word reached him that the men of Jabesh-gilead were in trouble.

When Nahash the Ammonite threatened to wage war against the men of Jabesh-gilead, Saul was moved with compassion and rallied the men of Israel. With the 330,000 men who answered his call, Saul marched all night to rescue the inhabitants of Jabesh-gilead. And the men of Jabesh-gilead never forgot it. And forty years later, when he was naked and humiliated, the men to whom Saul had shown mercy returned the favor.

In Luke 6:38, when Jesus said, "Whatever is measured out will be measured back to you," He was talking about mercy. If we are those who learn mercy (Matthew 9:13), if we are those who love mercy (Micah 6:8), mercy will be shown to us. It might not happen for forty years - but when we need it most, it will be there (Matthew 5:7).

There was another King Whose body was pinned - not to a wall, but to a Cross. The agony was unbelievable; the humiliation, unspeakable. He was spiritually decapitated as well, for He was the Head - but where was His body? Except for John, all of His disciples had fled. He was burned in the fire of God's righteous indignation poured out upon Him. Yet, His bones were not broken.

And so we come to His Table day after day to say, "I remember what You did for me. We were about to be done in by the enemy, but You came from

Heaven to rescue us. Others might not remember. Others might not care. But we of Jabesh-gilead remember what You did when You marched all night and came to this world to save us."

APRIL 28

And he said unto me, Who art thou? And I answered him, I am an Amalekite. He said unto me again, Stand, I pray thee, upon me, and slay me: for anguish is come upon me, because my life is yet whole in me. So I stood upon him, and slew him, because I was sure that he could not live after that he was fallen . . .

2 Samuel 1:8-10 (a)

Twenty-five years earlier, God said to Saul, "I want you to kill every Amalekite" (1 Samuel 15). Why? The Amalekites were a constant problem for the people of Israel. As the Israelites made their way to the Promised Land, the Amalekites would attack the back of the pack - where the older folks, mothers with babies, and the sick and feeble would walk. Therefore, because they showed no mercy, God declared to Moses that he would war against the Amalekites from generation to generation (Exodus 17).

In 1 Samuel, God reiterated his charge against the Amalekites when he told Saul to destroy them - every man, woman, child, and all that they owned. Saul dutifully led the Israelite army in war against the Amalekites. When the battle was over, he said to Samuel, "Blessed be the Lord. We have obeyed what the Lord told us to do. We have been victorious over the Amalekites."

"If that's true," said Samuel, "what's the bleating I hear in my ear?"

"Oh," said Saul, "we saved a few of the sheep to sacrifice to the Lord."

"Who's that?" Samuel asked.

"Him? Oh, that's Agag, king of the Amalekites," Saul answered. "I brought him back here as a trophy."

Samuel then said to Saul, "Because you have not obeyed the Lord, the kingdom has been taken from you. You have lost your authority, opportunity, and ministry. You were supposed to kill every Amalekite, but because you compromised, because you did things your way, you're in trouble."

At the end of Saul's life, who finally did him in? Ironically, it was an Amalekite.

APRIL 29

And David lamented with this lamentation over Saul and over Jonathan his son: (also he bade them teach the children of Judah the use of the bow: behold, it is written in the book of Jasher.)

2 Samuel 1:17-18

During this period of lamentation and mourning for Saul and Jonathan, David says, "We need to teach the young people to be archers." Why would he say this at that time? 1 Samuel 13 tells us that the Philistines had taken away all weapons and instruments of iron from the Israelites to ensure their own military advantage as they ruled the region. It would seem that it was Jonathan and Saul who introduced the bow and arrow to the people of Israel. The arrows would be tipped with stone, thus eliminating the need for iron.

The lesson for us is simple and practical. That is, if there's been a loss in your life, a hurt in your heart, an ache in your soul, here's the key: Get back in the battle. Wage war against the enemy. Serve the Lord with new intensity. Give Him more than you have ever given previously. If you don't, you will remain in a state of depression and heaviness.

David showed great insight here. His call to arms would provide both a fitting commemoration of Saul and Jonathan, and needed restoration to the nation.

APRIL 30

And it came to pass after this, that David inquired of the LORD, saying, Shall I go up into any of the cities of Judah? And the LORD said unto him, Go up. And David said, Whither shall I go up? And he said, Unto Hebron.

2 Samuel 2:1

Here we see a real secret of David's success - why it was that he was used so effectively, why his life had so great an impact that we study him to this day. David was a man who inquired of the Lord.

"Is this the right time to go into the cities of Judah?" David asked.

"Yes," the Lord answered.

"Where should I go?" David asked.

"Go to Hebron," the Lord answered.

When David asked if it was time for him to go into the cities of Judah, God could have said, "Yes. Go to Hebron first." But He didn't do that. He gave David the specific information David asked for and waited until David asked for more.

The Lord does the same with us. He isn't reluctant to give guidance, but there's something more important than guidance. It's called intimacy. If you've prayed repeatedly for direction concerning a given situation but still aren't sure what the Lord would have you do, perhaps it's because He loves you so much that He wants to keep hearing from you. He wants you to come into His presence time and again. He wants you to feel the embrace of His grace.

Corrie Ten Boom asked this pointed question: "Is prayer your steering wheel, or is it your spare tire?" Many of us pull prayer out of the trunk when we're feeling flat or when there's a blowout. However, prayer ought to be the steering wheel guiding us through the day, keeping us out of the ruts and ditches of life. Some days I act like I can get through my day without prayer. How dumb of me. Prayer is the highest, most important calling of any believer. It will keep you out of the ditches of depression, the ruts of predictability, the snares of seduction. At the outset of his reign, David models the absolute necessity of prayer.

MAY 1

*Now there was long war between the house of Saul and the
house of David: but David waxed stronger and stronger,
and the house of Saul waxed weaker and weaker.*

2 Samuel 3:1

At this time, David is ruling over Judah. At war against Abner and the
household of Saul, there are battles raging, but Saul's forces are growing
weaker and weaker. David, on the other hand, grows stronger.

Spiritually, Saul is a symbol of sin and self; David, a symbol of our Savior.
There's a war going on in my soul that will last for a lifetime. But the house
of Saul - the house of self, the house of sin - grows weaker and weaker,
while the Kingdom of God grows stronger. Sure, there are setbacks along
the way. There are defeats we have on certain days. But as I look back and
chart the course, I can see that He Who has begun a good work in me is
indeed being faithful to complete it (Philippians 1:6). And because the One
who resides in you is greater than the one who comes against you (1 John
4:4), even though you might have discouraging days, you can be sure that
David becomes stronger as Saul grows weaker.

MAY 2

*And the fourth, Adonijah the son of Haggith; and the fifth,
Shephatiah the son of Abital; and the sixth, Ithream, by
Eglah David's wife. These were born to David in Hebron.*

2 Samuel 3:4-5

David already had three wives, but as he adds more and more, the story
gets worse and worse. According to Deuteronomy 17:17, kings were not to
multiply horses, store gold, or multiply wives. Knowing the Word, David
knows this.

David is very flawed. He has a propensity to lie. He's tempted by women. He has an ego that we'll see in the next part of the chapter. And yet overarching, he has a passion for God. We can have a tendency to say, "Sure, I sin. But I don't sin nearly to the degree David did." But that's the wrong perspective entirely. Don't measure your sins against David's. Instead, measure your virtues against his. David killed a giant. David danced before the Lord with passion. David wrote psalms. David was a lover of God. David was given to prayer. David praised God continually.

Am I a giant killer? Am I laying down everything for my Lord? Am I a poet and a prophet, a singer, dancer, and warrior for God? Are you? How strong is my passion for God? Can I truly say, "Only one thing have I desired of the Lord, and that will I seek after - to behold the beauty of the Lord and to inquire in His temple?" (see Psalm 27:4).

Where did David get this passion for God? It was developed in the pastures as he watched his sheep and in the caves as he fled from Saul. It was developed through prayer, through spending time with God.

Maybe the Lord is whispering in your ear, "I see in you the same potential."

"How can this be?" you ask.

"Because I put David in that place," He answers. "I gave David that kind of grace. All He did was respond to My tugging and whispering."

The path to passion is not mysterious or even mystical. It's very simple and practical. When the Lord says, "Get up and pray," you say, "Okay." When He tells you to take on that giant and share your faith, say "Yes." When He inspires you to write a love letter to Him, grab your pen. It is not up to us to generate the fire of passion. Our job is simply to stir the coals through faithfulness and obedience (2 Timothy 1:6).

MAY 3

And they buried Abner in Hebron: and the king lifted up his voice, and wept at the grave of Abner; and all the people wept. And the king lamented over Abner, and said, Died Abner as a fool dieth? Thy hands were not bound, nor thy feet put into fetters: as a man falleth before wicked men, so fellest thou. And all the people wept again over him.

2 Samuel 3:32-34

"What happened to Abner is not right," David said at Abner's funeral service. "He didn't deserve to die like he did. He wasn't imprisoned because of some wrong he had committed. He died foolishly because he was seduced, tricked, lured out of the city."

You see, in Old Testament times, if a man killed someone unintentionally - as Abner had done - he could find protection from his victim's avengers by running to one of six cities of refuge located throughout Israel. If, however, he stepped outside of the gate of the city, he would no longer be protected. Hebron was a city of refuge. That is why Joab had to meet with Abner at the gate (verse 27) in order to kill him.

Jesus Christ is our refuge. Don't be lured away from Him, gang, or else you'll lose the safety, security, satisfaction, and protection He offers to you. Abner was a great warrior, a true leader, loyal to a fault, a wise man - but he died as a fool because he stepped away from the city of refuge. Don't let this happen to you. Stay within the city of refuge, under the shadow of the wings of Jesus (Luke 13:34).

MAY 4

And David said on that day, Whosoever getteth up to the gutter, and smiteth the Jebusites, and the lame and the blind, that are hated of David's soul, he shall be chief and captain. Wherefore they said, The blind and the lame shall not come into the house.

2 Samuel 5:8

David wanted the city of Jerusalem for both spiritual and strategic reasons. So he said to his men, "The first guy who can find a way into the walled city of Zion will be my general." The fact that Jerusalem was surrounded by valleys on three sides and a mountain on the fourth made David's challenge seem impossible. Yet, with no water source on the inside, David knew that, because the Jebusites couldn't survive without water, there had to be a camouflaged shaft descending seventy-five feet to the Kidron River below.

First Chronicles 11 tells us the name of the man who found the shaft was Joab. As we have seen, Joab was not the most upstanding man. But one thing he did do: He found a way to get into the city. Joab's example is vital for us. You see, we serve a Greater-than-David - the Son of David - Jesus Christ. Like David, Jesus desires to take cities. But He also desires to take countries, families, and individuals. He wants to beat back the spiritual Jebusites who keep people in bondage. So what does He do? He comes to people like you and me and says, "I want to talk to him; I want to see her saved; I want to touch them. And the first person who will shimmy up the shaft will be My man." Like Joab, we might not be the greatest, the most worthy, or the most spiritual. But if we are simply willing to shimmy up the shaft, He'll use us mightily.

There are desires the Lord places on your heart, thoughts He puts in your mind, things you know the Lord would want you to do - to talk to your neighbor, to teach a Bible study, to reach your co-workers. But as sure as you feel that tug on the strings of your soul, you hear the taunting of the enemy saying, "You're blind. You're lame. There's no way you can make an impact." If that's the way you see yourself, you are in a perfect position to be blessed, for it was especially the blind and lame whom Jesus healed (Matthew 21:14).

William Carey, the great missionary who opened the continent of India for the Gospel, said, "Attempt great things for God and expect great things from God." In other words - "Shimmy up the shaft."

The Jebusites will say you don't have a prayer. Jesus, however, says, "I've healed your blind eyes and lame feet. Now look to Me and step out because there are people, families, and cities I want to claim through you."

MAY 5

And David went on, and grew great, and the LORD God of hosts was with him.

2 Samuel 5:10

David went on and grew great, or, literally in the Hebrew text, "David went going and growing." I like that. "Lord, let that be me. Help me to keep going and help me to keep growing." The Lord will take you as far as you want to go - but not one step further.

David was a man after God's heart. He wanted more of Him, wanted to be closer to Him, wanted to gain more knowledge about Him. What about you? Was there ever a time in your walk when you were closer to the Lord than you are now, when you felt His presence to a greater degree, when you were drawn to Him in greater intimacy? If so, I have great news for you. Right here, right now, you can say, "Lord, I'm here. I've been bogged down. But here I am. Take me deeper. Take me further. I want to keep going and I want to keep growing." And I guarantee He'll hear your prayer.

MAY 6

And when David inquired of the LORD, he said, Thou shalt not go up; but fetch a compass behind them, and come upon them over against the mulberry trees. And let it be, when thou hearest the sound of a going in the tops of the mulberry trees, that then thou shalt bestir thyself: for then shall the LORD go out before thee, to smite the host of the Philistines.

2 Samuel 5:23-24

Earlier, David went right into the valley and confronted the enemy head to head. Here, he's in the same valley, facing the same enemy, but the Lord gave him a different strategy. And in this, it's as if God says to us, "Forget about yesterday's strategy. It was good for then, but not for today. Stay in constant touch with Me."

The leaves of the mulberry trees in Israel are so light that even the slightest breeze will cause them to move. In fact, even an army would provide sufficient breeze to cause the mulberry leaves to move. If this massive Philistine army suddenly began to mobilize and move toward Jerusalem, that would indeed generate a large enough breeze to move the leaves - which would be a signal to David as to which direction they were marching.

In John 3:8, Jesus likened the Spirit to the wind. In Acts 2, the Spirit came with the sound of a mighty rushing wind. In other words, the work of the Spirit is supernaturally natural. "That's just soldiers on the move," the world says. But the believer who chooses to open his eyes will see God's hand behind everything.

Driving home today, I saw beautiful poppies blossoming beside the road. "Lord, this is so wonderful," I said. "Thank You for these bouquets."

And it was as if the Lord said, "These are for everyone and anyone who has eyes to see that I love them."

"What do you mean?" the cynic scoffs. "Those poppies are simply the result of seeds that fell or were blown there."

If that's how you choose to look at them, you can. But I chose to look at them as bouquets from God because every good and perfect gift is from above (James 1:17). If you cultivate this kind of mindset, you will see the work of the Spirit constantly. To live in the Spirit means you see everything as from God's hand - no matter what means He uses to bring it about.

MAY 7

And it was so, that when they that bare the ark of the LORD had gone six paces, he sacrificed oxen and fatlings.

2 Samuel 6:13

To sacrifice an animal required great energy and effort - yet David expended this energy and effort every six steps. The world places great value on efficiency. Moving the ark on a cart would have been vastly more efficient than carrying it and stopping every six steps. God, however, values effectiveness. Efficiency is doing things right. Effectiveness is doing the right thing. What's the right thing? Stopping every six steps.

You see, throughout Scripture, six is the number of man and the flesh. Therefore, offering sacrifice every six steps says, "Because I'm a man who deals with my flesh, I've got to stop every six steps, build an altar, and lay my dreams, my objectives, and my life down." Stopping every six steps says, "Lord, it's not about what I want to do. It's about what You want me to do. Therefore, I'm going to offer You the sacrifice of praise. I'm going to confess my fleshly tendencies every six steps throughout the day."

It's in stopping throughout the day to be "altared" that the *chabod*, the presence of God, will enter your city, your ministry, your family, your soul.

MAY 8

Which also king David did dedicate unto the LORD, with the silver and gold that he had dedicated of all nations which he subdued; Of Syria, and of Moab, and of the children of Ammon, and of the Philistines, and of Amalek, and of the spoil of Hadadezer, son of Rehob, king of Zobah.

2 Samuel 8:11-12

Here, David brought the spoil to Jerusalem and dedicated it to the Lord in order that it might eventually be used in the building of the Temple. You see, even though David could not build the Temple himself, he didn't pout. He didn't quit. He didn't get angry. He simply set to work, gathering all the necessary supplies for Solomon.

I point this out because sometimes people say, "If I can't be on the worship team, I'm not going to sing at all. If I can't be recognized or utilized in the way I think I ought to be, I won't do anything." David was used mightily because, even with all of his faults and failures, he served the Lord every way he could.

You might never be an evangelist, write a book, go to the mission field, or preach a sermon, but you can do what David did. You can work behind the scenes, providing the supplies through intercession and prayer. The Temple is known commonly as Solomon's Temple, but in reality, it was the heart of David behind it. And he will be credited eternally.

MAY 9

And the king said, Is there not yet any of the house of Saul, that I may shew the kindness of God unto him? And Ziba said unto the king, Jonathan hath yet a son, which is lame on his feet. And the king said unto him, Where is he? And Ziba said unto the king, Behold, he is in the house of Machir, the son of Ammiel, in Lo-debar. Then king David sent, and fetched him out of the house of Machir, the son of Ammiel, from Lo-debar.

2 Samuel 9:3-5

In Old Testament times, if a king from a different family than the previous one came to power, he would kill all of the relatives of the previous king in order to eliminate any rival. *Lo-debar* means "pasture-less place." Consisting of only rocks and sand, Lo-debar would have been a terrible place to live. Why did Mephibosheth live in such a desolate place? Because he no doubt feared the new king.

Mephibosheth means "shameful breath." This more than likely means that he had asthma, or some other breathing ailment. On top of that, he was lame. Second Samuel 4 tells us that when Saul and Jonathan died on Mount Gilboa, Mephibosheth was five years old. His nanny scooped him up to rush him to safety, but in her haste, she tripped. Mephibosheth fell to the ground, evidently injuring his spinal cord.

Here was Mephibosheth - hiding in a dry place, unable to breathe easily, and unable to walk at all. Perhaps that describes you or someone you know. Maybe you feel suffocated spiritually, in a dry place, unable to make any progress because you too were dropped . . .

"He told me he was going to marry me, and I gave myself to him completely. Then he dropped me. My heart is broken and now I'm crippled."

"My mom left my dad. She was a Christian, but she left and never came back. So here I am, hiding out in a desolate place."

"I thought I was the best baseball player on the team. But my coach cut me. That might not seem important to some, but to me, it's had a crippling effect."

"I was a good worker. I deserved better, but my boss dropped me to cut back on the budget."

There are countless stories of people who are crippled. I'm convinced that if we knew the secret stories of even our worst enemies, we would have nothing but compassion for them, nothing but love toward them.

There is One who does know their stories. And He knows yours as well. He's the King, the Son of David, calling out to those who are in pastureless places, to those with crippled feet. If you feel lame or crippled a bit, listen, and you'll hear the King calling - sending a messenger to you. Just as David sent messengers to the pastureless place, the King calls still.

MAY 10

Now when Mephibosheth, the son of Jonathan, the son of Saul, was come unto David, he fell on his face, and did reverence. And David said, Mephibosheth. And he answered, Behold thy servant. And David said unto him, Fear not: for I will surely shew thee kindness for Jonathan thy father's sake, and will restore thee all the land of Saul thy father; and thou shalt eat bread at my table continually.

2 Samuel 9:6-7

David spoke one word that changes the entire scene. He said Mephibosheth's name. And something in the way David spoke his name ministered to Mephibosheth's heart. I cannot help but think of Jesus at the Garden tomb. Mary was there weeping over the fact that His body was no longer in the tomb. In her turmoil she was conversing with a Man she thought to be the gardener. But when He said, "Mary," suddenly, in the very way He spoke her name, she identified Him as her Master (John 20:16).

John 10 declares that Jesus knows the names of His sheep. He knows your name, and He calls you individually. Do you hear His voice calling you today?

"It's okay," David said to Mephibosheth. "Don't be afraid. It's not what you think."

A lot of times it's not what we think. We think, "I'm so lame. I've been far from His pasture. And if the King is calling for me today, it's probably because He wants to lop off my head, or at least shake me up." But the next verse shows us that things are not always what we think.

Because Mephibosheth was linked to Jonathan, David would show him kindness in two ways. First, he would restore his land. You see, although Mephibosheth lived in a barren, desolate place, he was heir to the best land in all of the nation. Here, David promises to restore that inheritance to Mephibosheth. And He promises to do the same for us . . .

> And I will restore to you the years that the locust hath eaten, the cankerworm, and the caterpillar, and the palmerworm, my great army which I sent among you.
>
> Joel 2:25

What an amazing God we serve. He not only seeks and saves those who are lost, but makes up for their lost time as well.

In addition to restoring Mephibosheth's land, David promised to reserve his place - at the king's table. Historian Josephus tells us that a meal on King Solomon's table consisted of twenty-two thousand oxen, twenty thousand sheep, and fowl beyond description. In other words, there was plenty for everyone at the king's table.

The same is still true, for it is at the Table of our King that mercy abounds. The Lord would say to you today, "I've prepared a Table before you. Take. Eat. This is My body, broken for you. If any man hear My voice and open his heart, I will come in and sup with him. Come to the Table."

If your soul has been dry, it is to you especially that the Lord says, "Come and dine. And let Me restore all you've lost."

MAY 11

So Mephibosheth dwelt in Jerusalem: for he did eat continually at the king's table; and was lame on both his feet.

2 Samuel 9:13

Hearing the generous, gracious offer of the king, Mephibosheth didn't say, "Thanks, king. I'll see if I can drop in occasionally to have a bite with you now and then." No, he said, "King, I can't believe you would do this for a man like me. I will eat at your table continually."

When he came to David's table, did Mephibosheth walk straight? No. He was still lame in both his feet. He was still affected by the sin of the fall. So why is it that when Jesus says, "Come and dine," we say, "I can't. I'm too lame"? The Lord calls us just as we are to come and dine with Him. He calls you in the state you're in to receive the grace and abundance He has for you. The Table is set. And the Table is the only place where lame, twisted, crippled feet can't be seen.

Are you burdened because you're always looking at your flaws and your shortcomings - or are you blessed as you partake of the abundance of grace and mercy at the King's Table? I understand that many of us have been dropped brutally. But you must understand that you don't have to remain in your lame condition day after year after decade. Jesus was broken, that you might be healed. And His blood was shed to wash away the sin and the memory of that which haunts you. Come and dine, and you'll find yourself back in the land where you perhaps once were or where you long to be. Mephibosheth accepted the king's invitation. May we do the same.

MAY 12

And when all the kings that were servants to Hadarezer saw that they were smitten before Israel, they made peace with Israel, and served them.

2 Samuel 10:19 (a)

When was peace made with Israel? When the enemy was smitten. There has never been a successful peace treaty without a victory over the enemy - without a winner and a loser. David's dealing with the Ammonites began in kindness. But when his kindness was rejected, he became engaged in the battle and brought about a destruction of the enemy so complete that, rather than fighting him, they served him.

Our King, the Son of David, has commissioned you and me as servants to be communicators of kindness, messengers of mercy. It's so important to see that Mephibosheth received David's kindness. The Ammonite king, Hanun, didn't. Mephibosheth was poor, broken, lame, weak. Hanun was rich, proud, self-centered, and arrogant. As a servant of the King, I understand that those who are poor in spirit and meek, those who mourn their own sin, will receive the kind word I bring about the kindness of the King. But there will also be those who, like Hanun, will not receive the word we bring. Therefore, if you want to be fruitful in ministry, hang out with the people who are lame, the Mephibosheths. Spend your time with people who are weak, broken, and needy. Don't make your priority the millionaire athlete, the movie star, the political leader. It's not that they can't be saved - but that's not where the abundant harvest will be. David sent his servants to both Mephibosheth and Hanun. So too, we're to exclude no one, but we're to realize that the most fruit will be found not with the beautiful people, but with those who are crippled, with those who can't breathe right, with Mephibosheth.

MAY 13

And he wrote in the letter, saying, Set ye Uriah in the forefront of the hottest battle, and retire ye from him, that he may be smitten, and die.

2 Samuel 11:15

David had not only committed adultery, but now we see him committing murder. Remember, David was a man after God's own heart, a man who was singularly held up in the Old Testament as one of the greatest men of faith who ever lived. What's going on? It all started seemingly so simple. He neglected his duty to go to battle. Then his eyes wandered. His curiosity was aroused. He committed adultery, and now murder. David is stumbling badly. But that's the way sin is. Sin has a sneaky way of compounding itself. Before you know it, you're more deeply involved in it than you ever thought you would be. That is why it is absolutely essential to not give in at that first point of temptation. You cannot control the course of your destiny once you allow yourself to begin to flirt with sin. It will capture you. It will ensnare you. And ultimately it will destroy you. David once killed giants. Now this giant is killing him.

MAY 14

And when the wife of Uriah heard that Uriah her husband was dead, she mourned for her husband. And when the mourning was past, David sent and fetched her to his house, and she became his wife, and bare him a son. But the thing that David had done displeased the LORD.

2 Samuel 11:26-27

David no doubt thought he got away with his sin by cleverly covering his tracks. But God knew otherwise.

"Be sure your sin will find you out," we are warned (Numbers 32:23). No matter how well I think I've covered my tracks, the reality is that the sin will track me down. That's Satan's strategy. He sucks you into sin, and then he makes sure that the sin surfaces to expose you, to humiliate and condemn you. After nine or ten months of thinking he got away with this sin, David had to face up to its repercussions.

I pray that the Lord might remind us again that the most dangerous place to be in spiritual life is kicking back, pulling away, saying, "I taught Sunday school for years. I paid my dues. It's time for me to let someone else fight the battles and do the work." When that mentality creeps in, you're being set up to be taken down. The safest place to be is on the front lines, fully engaged in serving the Lord, in battling against the enemy. May God help us to truly learn the lessons we read about in His Word.

Through all of this, David goes down in history as one of the greatest of the greats because he had a heart for God. Yes, he failed miserably, but there was something about his heart that God loved. The Son of David said that the one who is forgiven much loves much (Luke 7:47). It is when we realize how sinful we are that we realize how merciful God is. And such realization causes us to love Him all the more.

God sees the heart. May He see in you a heart that is amazed by His mercy, grateful for His grace, a heart that loves Him passionately and loves to seek His face. If the choice is between a congregation that errs constantly but loves God passionately and a congregation of self-righteous Pharisees, I'll take the former. And, according to Jesus, so would God.

MAY 15

And the LORD sent Nathan unto David.

2 Samuel 12:1 (a)

God didn't send an enemy of David to talk to him about his sin. He sent a friend. This is most often the way of the Lord. When He has a word of correction to bring us, inevitably it will be by someone who has a heart for us. Conversely, unless your heart is filled with compassion for the person you are about to correct, it is probably not your responsibility to correct him.

As Jesus arrived at the Upper Room, He found His disciples arguing with each other concerning who was the greatest among them. He also noticed that their feet were dirty. Instead of chastising them for arguing, He girded Himself with a towel and washed their feet (John 13). Therefore, I have no right to point out the dirt on other peoples' feet unless I'm willing to wash them myself - time and again. Evidently, Nathan was such a man.

MAY 16

And David's anger was greatly kindled against the man; and he said to Nathan, As the LORD liveth, the man that hath done this thing shall surely die: and he shall restore the lamb fourfold, because he did this thing, and because he had no pity. And Nathan said to David, Thou art the man.

2 Samuel 12:5-7 (a)

Nathan told David of a rich man who killed his neighbor's one and only lamb in order to feed his friend. Upset that a rich man would steal from a poor man, David was right in saying the rich man should give four lambs to the poor man, for that was the restitution decreed in the Law (Exodus 22:1). The problem was that David didn't stop there. He went on to issue the death sentence upon the rich man. This was neither God's Word nor His heart. In David's awareness of his own sin, he was judging another harshly.

That's always the way it is. We will be harshest with the people who commit the same sin with which we struggle. My sins look terrible on someone else. The Master of mercy, the Model of grace was Jesus Christ. He stood up for the woman taken in adultery; He was tender with the woman living in sin. Why? Because He Himself was free of sin.

When Nathan told David the illustration was about him, suddenly David understood. Whenever there's a finger pointing at another, three are pointing back. This sobers me. We're all guilty. The Old Testament, as well as the Sermon on the Mount, drive us to the place where we say, "I'm a sinner. I need grace."

MAY 17

And David said unto Nathan, I have sinned against the LORD.

2 Samuel 12:13 (a)

David didn't defend himself or try to blame Bathsheba. He simply and succinctly said, "I've sinned against the Lord," period. No amplification, no raw emotion, just a simple declaration and honest confession.

"After murdering a man, stealing his wife, deceiving the country? All he can say is one sentence? That's not enough," we might protest. But that's a dangerous stance to take because we do not see a man's heart. A person can be crying on national TV and go out and do the same thing again and again. Someone else might not have a tear in his eye, but he can be sincere to the point where he never sins in that particular way again. David made a single statement. And that was enough.

In Psalm 51, we are given additional information concerning what was going on in David's heart . . .

> To the chief Musician, A Psalm of David, when Nathan the prophet came unto him, after he had gone in to Bathsheba.
>
> Have mercy upon me, O God, according to thy lovingkindness: according unto the multitude of thy tender mercies blot out my transgressions. Wash me throughly from mine iniquity, and cleanse

me from my sin. For I acknowledge my transgressions: and my sin is ever before me.

Psalm 51:1-3

David thought about his sin constantly . . .

> Behold, thou desirest truth in the inward parts: and in the hidden part thou shalt make me to know wisdom. Purge me with hyssop, and I shall be clean: wash me, and I shall be whiter than snow. Make me to hear joy and gladness; that the bones which thou hast broken may rejoice.

Psalm 51:6-8

As a former shepherd, David refers to a certain practice of Middle Eastern shepherds. That is, if a lamb continually wandered away, jeopardizing its own life by going into areas containing poisonous plants or wolves and foxes, the shepherd had no other recourse but to break its legs. Then he would reset the bones, splint them, and carry the lamb on his shoulders until the bone was healed. When the splint was taken off, the lamb would never leave the shepherd's side, so closely had it bonded with the shepherd.

So too, God declares that He will do whatever it takes to draw His children close to Him that they might understand how much His heart is for them, that they might not wander away and get beat up or poisoned unnecessarily.

> Hide thy face from my sins, and blot out all mine iniquities. Create in me a clean heart, O God; and renew a right spirit within me. Cast me not away from thy presence; and take not thy Holy Spirit from me. Restore unto me the joy of thy salvation; and uphold me with thy free spirit. Then will I teach transgressors thy ways; and sinners shall be converted unto thee.

Psalm 51:9-13

"Lord, I'll share what I found in You with others You send my way," David prays.

> Deliver me from bloodguiltiness, O God, thou God of my salvation: and my tongue shall sing aloud of thy righteousness. O Lord, open thou my lips; and my mouth shall shew forth thy praise. For thou desirest

not sacrifice; else would I give it: thou delightest not in burnt offering. The sacrifices of God are a broken spirit: a broken and a contrite heart, O God, thou wilt not despise.

Psalm 51:14-17

That which was happening in David's soul was real. We don't see a person's heart. Only God sees the heart. David said one simple sentence in 2 Samuel 12:13. Psalm 51, however, speaks volumes.

MAY 18

And David comforted Bath-sheba his wife, and went in unto her, and lay with her: and she bare a son, and he called his name Solomon: and the LORD loved him. And he sent by the hand of Nathan the prophet; and he called his name Jedidiah, because of the LORD.

2 Samuel 12:24-25

Solomon had two names. *Solomon* means "peaceful," which specifically speaks of the fact that David is at peace with God and with himself. *Jedidiah*, on the other hand, means "beloved of God." This encourages me because the Lord could have said, "I'm not going to honor your relationship with Bathsheba. You've blown it and nothing good is going to come out of that." But our God is the God of the second chance. Our God is the God Who exchanges beauty for ashes, the oil of joy for mourning (Isaiah 61:3). Our God turns that which is hurtful into something beautiful. David repented. He's been chastened. He's been forgiven. And now God would bless his relationship, for from this union would come Solomon.

Take hope, dear friend. Confess your sin. Turn to the Lord. He can turn a dark night into a bright morning if you'll simply come to Him.

MAY 19

And the king went forth, and all the people after him, and tarried in a place that was far off. And all his servants passed on beside him; and all the Cherethites, and all the Pelethites, and all the Gittites, six hundred men which came after him from Gath, passed on before the king.

2 Samuel 15:17-18

The six hundred men with David were part of the group we read about in 1 Samuel 22. When David was fleeing from Saul in the wilderness, men who were discontent, in debt, and distressed gathered around David. David used these rag-tag renegades as the base of his army. And this group is a perfect picture of us. We are in debt, distressed, and discontent - yet we find ourselves gathering around a Greater-than-David, the Son of David, Jesus Christ. These men were transformed into a crack unit of excellent troops. Because they were around David, they became like him. And because they endured real difficulties and tribulations with David, they formed into a tight group of loyal, capable soldiers.

We, too, gathering around our Greater-than-David, Jesus Christ, endure trials. But those very trials produce in us abilities and capabilities for service.

> Wherein ye greatly rejoice, though now for a season, if need be, ye are in heaviness through manifold temptations: that the trial of your faith, being much more precious than of gold that perisheth, though it be tried with fire, might be found unto praise and honour and glory at the appearing of Jesus Christ.
>
> 1 Peter 1:6-7

In Bible times, gold was purified by melting it to a liquid state. The smelter knew the purification process was complete when he looked into the liquid gold and saw his face. But until he could see his face, he kept the heat on. What's the Lord doing in our lives? He's keeping the heat on until we become a reflection of Him, until we are formed in the image of His likeness.

You might wonder why you've had some fiery, heavy trials. Know this: You're precious. You're gold. And the Lord says, "I'm going to purify you so that My reflection might be seen in you, so that when people see you, they'll see Me."

MAY 20

And when Ahithophel saw that his counsel was not followed, he saddled his ass, and arose, and gat him home to his house, to his city, and put his household in order, and hanged himself, and died, and was buried in the sepulchre of his father.

2 Samuel 17:23

When Ahithophel realized Absalom was not going to take his counsel, he knew David would eventually return to power - and that he would be hung as a traitor.

Why was Ahithophel so intent on bringing David down? In 2 Samuel 23:34, we read that Ahithophel had a son named Eliam. In 2 Samuel 11:3, we read that Eliam had a daughter named Bathsheba. This means Ahithophel was the grandfather of Bathsheba - the same Bathsheba whose husband Uriah was killed in battle by the order of David (2 Samuel 11:15). Now, it's eleven years later and evidently feelings of bitterness had been festering in Ahithophel's soul.

If I allow bitterness to be under the surface of the soil of my soul, it will eventually bear murderous fruit. It might take a month, a year, or eleven years to surface - but surface it will.

> Let all bitterness, and wrath, and anger, and clamour, and evil speaking, be put away from you, with all malice: And be ye kind one to another, tenderhearted, forgiving one another, even as God for Christ's sake hath forgiven you.

Ephesians 4:31-32

Was Ahithophel's anger justified? Yes. But although he had a reason to be angry, he couldn't afford the price, for his anger cost him his life.

"How many times shall my brother sin against me and I forgive him," asked Peter. "Seven times?" I'm sure Peter felt smug about this, for based on Amos 1:3, the rabbis taught one was required to forgive someone only three times. Jesus, however, told Peter he was to forgive not 7 times, but 490 times - more times than a person was able to keep track of (Matthew 18).

It has been said that bitterness is like swallowing a bottle of poison - and waiting for the other person to die. David doesn't die in this story. Ahithophel does.

Like Ahithophel, Jesus came to us with wise counsel. But, as collective humanity, we rejected His counsel. Ahithophel saddled a donkey. So did Jesus. Ahithophel rode into the city. So did Jesus. Ahithophel put his household in order. Jesus went to the Upper Room and gave instructions to His disciples. Ahithophel hanged himself. Jesus went willingly to the Cross, where He too hung for you and me. Ahithophel was buried in a sepulchre. Jesus was placed in a sepulchre. But, unlike Ahithophel, Jesus rose again.

I might have reason to be upset or bitter. But I can either be hung up by my bitterness - or I can see that Jesus took the reason for my bitterness upon Himself. We need not be bitter with anyone because Jesus understands our hurt - and it killed Him. Happy indeed is the man whose sins are forgiven (Romans 4:7) - not only the sins he's committed, but also the sins committed toward him. The Gospel frees us not only from our own sin, but also from the sin round about us. And I'm so glad.

MAY 21

Now therefore arise, go forth, and speak comfortably unto thy servants: for I swear by the LORD, if thou go not forth, there will not tarry one with thee this night: and that will be worse unto thee than all the evil that befell thee from thy youth until now.

2 Samuel 19:7

"Snap out of it," Joab said to David as David continued to mourn for his son, Absalom. "Don't you understand that your people placed their lives on the line for you - yet all they see is that you're moaning and groaning. If you don't wipe the tears from your eyes and wash your face, they will desert you by nightfall."

Our outlook affects others. Therefore, if you are a servant of Jesus Christ, if you are committed to the King, you must not allow yourself the pampered privilege of being discouraged.

When Aaron's sons Nadab and Abihu were killed, the Lord said to him, "Others may mourn, but you cannot, for you are anointed. You have a job to do" (Leviticus 10:6-7). And Aaron continued on in ministry.

If the anointing is on your life, you don't have the "right" to pout and whimper. Discouragement, depression, and defeat are instruments the enemy will seek to use to affect your family, friends, and community. It is the mature saint who says, "It's time for me to grow up and to cast my care not upon those around me, but upon the Lord solely" (see 1 Peter 5:7).

"I have learned in whatever state I am to be content," Paul said (Philippians 4:11). Contentment is the result of a decision you make with your mind rather than a feeling you have in your heart. God intervened on David's behalf. The rebels were defeated. The kingdom was spared. Yet all David could see was that his son was dead.

MAY 22

The LORD rewarded me according to my righteousness: according to the cleanness of my hands hath he recompensed me. For I have kept the ways of the LORD, and have not wickedly departed from my God.

2 Samuel 22:21-22

In this portion of a psalm also recorded in Psalm 18, David says, "The Lord has rewarded me because I have not violated His way." What? As I read the life of David, I see lies, adultery, and murder. What, then, is going on? In Psalms 38 and 51, we hear David acknowledge what a wretch he is, how he has failed the Lord. Before the Lord, he admits his sin. But here, in the presence of his enemies, he says he is righteous.

This is the way it must be. You see, the closer I get to God, the more I am aware of how far I am from Him, of attitudes that are amiss, of activities that are wrong. In the presence of my enemy, however - the accuser of the brethren who accuses me day and night - I say, "Back off. The Word of God says I am the righteousness of God in Christ Jesus" (see 2 Corinthians 5:21; Revelation 12:10).

You'll never be used by the Lord, you'll never develop a deep relationship with Him, until you learn that you are righteous in Christ Jesus. When He died on the Cross and said, "It is finished," it was finished indeed. The price for every sin you have ever committed or will commit has been paid.

Satan's favorite weapon is condemnation. Therefore, he will tell you that you can't be used, that you can't go on, but you can overcome him by the Word.

MAY 23

And the three mighty men brake through the host of the Philistines, and drew water out of the well of Bethlehem . . .

2 Samuel 23:16 (a)

It was hard to obtain the water from Bethlehem because Bethlehem was surrounded by Philistines.

"The words that I speak to you are spirit and life," Jesus said (see John 6:63). The Word of God is where you will draw from the well of the water of the Spirit. I guarantee that when you were most refreshed and doing the very best in the Lord was when you were spending time in the Word. But, like Bethlehem, the Word is surrounded by the enemy. I know the water of the Spirit is in it. But the Philistine of fatigue keeps me away. The Philistines of the phone, of chores, and of lethargy encamp around the Word.

How did the three mighty men break through to get water? The Bible doesn't say, because breaking through the Philistines that plague you is something that cannot be programmed or preached. It is up to each one of us to seek the Lord and say, "Father, how do I break through? Show me my schedule, my priorities, my obligations that stand between us." I guarantee that if you ask the Lord to show you how to rearrange your schedule in order to break through the Philistines, He will.

MAY 24

And Araunah said, Wherefore is my lord the king come to his servant? And David said, To buy the threshingfloor of thee, to build an altar unto the LORD, that the plague may be stayed from the people. And Araunah said unto David, Let my lord the king take and offer up what seemeth good unto him: behold, here be oxen for burnt sacrifice, and threshing instruments and other instruments of the oxen for wood. All these things did Araunah, as a king, give unto the king. And Araunah said unto the king, The LORD thy God accept thee. And the king said unto Araunah, Nay; but I will surely buy it of thee at a price: neither will I offer burnt offerings unto the LORD my God of that which doth cost me nothing. So David bought the threshingfloor and the oxen for fifty shekels of silver.

2 Samuel 24:21-24

In this passage, I think we are given understanding and insight into what made David so great. Why was he alone called a man after God's own heart (1 Samuel 13:14)? It certainly wasn't because he was sinless, for he had a series of failures that I dare say match or exceed any of ours. In fact, if he were on trial before the Christian community, I suggest the Christian community would have had a tendency to write him off long ago. Saul, on the other hand, would be applauded and approved. Saul, too, made mistakes. But not as seemingly blatant as David's. Therefore, I suggest that in the eyes of human understanding, Saul would be exalted, and David would be dismissed as one who wasted his potential.

But that wasn't God's verdict. Why? Because God looks at the heart, and David had a heart for God.

"Take the property," Araunah said. "Make your sacrifice so the plague might be stopped. It's free. It's yours."

"I will not give the Lord that which costs me nothing," David said.

Hear the heart of David. "I won't skimp," he said. "I won't cheat God. Yes, I failed Him in the past. But my heart is devoted to Him."

If you want to know the heart of David, read the Psalms. Saul never wrote a single psalm because Saul didn't have a heart for the Lord. Saul was outwardly impressive, but he used the things of God to exalt himself. David, on the other hand, used himself to exalt the things of God. When David penned the Psalms, he didn't know they would be preserved and studied for centuries. He was simply writing love letters. He just loved God.

What would you have done had Araunah come to you and said, "Take the property. Here's the wood for the sacrifice. Here's the oxen. Just take it"?

Would you have said, "Great! I can save a few shekels"? Or do you have a heart like David's, a heart that says, "I will give everything I have, everything I am to the One who gave His all for me"?

Many of us are skimpy and small. We give the Lord the leftovers of our time, of our energy. You might not be committing any moral sin. But God sees the heart (1 Samuel 16:7). He's looking for men and women who say, "I'm devoted to worshipping the Lord. I'm devoted to extolling and praising Him. I'm devoted to paying the full price."

Although severely chastened again - even at the end of his life - David is still to be exalted by the Lord and acknowledged throughout history as one of the very greatest of all men who ever lived. Why? Because he had a heart after God.

Do you?

MAY 25

And the days that David reigned over Israel were forty years: seven years reigned he in Hebron, and thirty and three years reigned he in Jerusalem.

1 Kings 2:11

Second Samuel 5:4 tells us David was thirty years old when he began his reign. Thirty is a significant number in Scripture. At thirty, the Levites assumed their ministry. At thirty, Joseph became prime minister of Egypt. At thirty, Ezekiel began making his powerful prophetic proclamations. At thirty, John the Baptist began to go throughout the countryside preaching preparation for the Kingdom. At thirty, Jesus began His public ministry. Thus, there seems to be something significant about the age of thirty. In God's economy, it would seem as though the years up to thirty are years of training and preparation.

David reigned over Israel for forty years and died at the age of seventy. Interestingly, Psalm 90, penned by Moses, says that the years of a man are seventy years. In other words, seventy years is a normal lifespan.

If you're under thirty, use the time to prepare wisely as you seek the Lord for what He has ahead for you. If you're over thirty, serve Him with maturity and wisdom. If you're under thirty, glean from your elders. If you're over thirty, set the pace for those looking to you. It has been said that the difference between a politician and a statesman is that a politician has his eyes on the next election, while a statesman has his eyes on the next generation. May God make us spiritual statesmen who have a heart for generations to follow.

MAY 26

In Gibeon the Lord appeared to Solomon in a dream by night: and God said, Ask what I shall give thee. And Solomon said . . .

1 Kings 3:5-6 (a)

Although the Lord appeared to Solomon in a dream, Solomon answered verbally. In this, I'm reminded of the account in Acts 12, where the Angel of the Lord came to Peter in prison, saying, "Follow me." Luke writes that Peter "went out, and followed him; and wist not that it was true which was done by the angel; but thought he saw a vision" (Acts 12:9). In other words, had Peter dismissed the Lord's words as having only ethereal, philosophical meaning, he would have eventually awakened on the hard floor of his prison cell. But, because he took the Lord at His Word and obeyed Him physically, Peter walked out of prison a free man.

Solomon could have taken the Lord's appearance as nothing more than an encouraging thought - but he didn't. He opened his mouth and spoke audible words that would result in incredible blessing.

Perhaps the Lord has been speaking to your heart about a certain matter but you have written it off as little more than a good idea. I encourage you to put feet to your faith, to do whatever it is He is asking of you and see if your physical action doesn't result in a physical response from Him, just as it would with Solomon.

MAY 27

Give therefore thy servant an understanding heart to judge thy people, that I may discern between good and bad: for who is able to judge this thy so great a people? And the speech pleased the Lord, that Solomon had asked this thing.

1 Kings 3:9-10

"Ask of Me anything," the Lord said. And Solomon asked for wisdom that he might be able to wisely lead the people God had placed under his leadership. The beginning of wisdom is truly to recognize the need for wisdom. You'll know you are becoming wiser when you say to the Lord, "I don't know as much as I used to think I knew."

> If any of you lack wisdom, let him ask of God, that giveth to all men liberally, and upbraideth not; and it shall be given him.
>
> James 1:5

The word "upbraideth" means that the Lord won't come down on, or get angry with those who ask for wisdom. On the contrary, God is pleased with such a request.

Jesus taught us that if we seek first His Kingdom and His righteousness, everything else we need would be added to us (Matthew 6:33). Solomon is proof of this. Consider the prayers you prayed today or this week. How many were for the good of the Kingdom? How many of your prayers were, "Lord, allow Your Kingdom to be expanded. Allow Your Name to be exalted," versus, "Lord, I need this . . . please help me with that"? Solomon didn't ask for himself. He asked for the kingdom. And the Lord was pleased.

MAY 28

And Solomon awoke; and behold, it was a dream. And he came to Jerusalem, and stood before the ark of the covenant of the LORD, and offered up burnt offerings, and offered peace offerings, and made a feast to all his servants.

1 Kings 3:15

Solomon awoke from his dream and immediately sacrificed to the Lord in Jerusalem. Again, Solomon is responding physically to a promise he would soon see fulfilled physically. At this point, however, his response is based solely on faith.

This combination reminds me of how we are saved . . .

> That if thou shalt confess with thy mouth the Lord Jesus, and shalt believe in thine heart that God hath raised him from the dead, thou shalt be saved. For with the heart man believeth unto righteousness; and with the mouth confession is made unto salvation.
>
> Romans 10:9-10

It is through the unseen belief of the heart coupled with the spoken word of the mouth that salvation is brought to the sinner. And the same is true throughout our Christian walk, for true faith is inevitably linked to outward manifestation.

MAY 29

And all Israel heard of the judgment which the king had judged; and they feared the king: for they saw that the wisdom of God was in him, to do judgment.

1 Kings 3:28

Two women who were harlots were living together and gave birth within three days of each other. When one child died in the night, the babies were switched, and suddenly, as one woman looked at the dead baby next to her, she realized it wasn't her baby at all. They came to Solomon to settle their dispute. There were no eyewitnesses to the crime, and because these women were harlots, the babies' fathers would not surface.

"Bring me a sword," Solomon declared, "and we will cut the living child in two, giving half to each woman."

Solomon's answer was absolutely brilliant for it was designed to unequivocally determine the rightful mother. You see, a true mother will never tolerate division. A true mother would sooner never see her baby again than to have it divided in any way. Thus, the true mother was immediately and indisputably identified as the one who was willing to give her child away. Be it in a marriage, a family, or a church body, division always leads either quickly or eventually to one thing: death. May we be as committed to unity as this mother was.

How wise of Solomon to call for a sword. The Word of God is quick and powerful, sharper than any two-edged sword (Hebrews 4:12). Therefore, if you're involved in counseling, sharing with friends or neighbors, or giving advice to people in need, the first words out of your mouth should be those of Solomon: "Bring me a Sword. Let's look in the Word."

MAY 30

And God gave Solomon wisdom and understanding exceeding much, and largeness of heart, even as the sand that is on the sea shore.

1 Kings 4:29

We are told that Solomon wrote three thousand proverbs and one thousand songs. He was also a dendrologist, a botanist, a zoologist, an ornithologist, an entomologist, and an ichthyologist. Solomon asked for wisdom and God certainly answered "above all he could ask or think" (see Ephesians 3:20). But He didn't stop there. He didn't limit His answer to giving Solomon only the gift of knowledge.

In 1 Corinthians 13, we are reminded that knowledge puffs up. Oftentimes, the more we know, the colder we can become. The more we know, the more cynical we can find ourselves. Not so with Solomon - for not only did he grow exceedingly great in understanding, but he was also given a correlating largeness of heart.

When we study the Word, I think we should pray, "Lord, allow me to not become cold or puffed up with knowledge. Give me the largeness of heart You gave Solomon" - for even if you know all things, if you don't have love, you have nothing at all.

MAY 31

And the house, when it was in building, was built of stone made ready before it was brought thither: so that there was neither hammer nor axe nor any tool of iron heard in the house, while it was in building.

1 Kings 6:7

All of the cutting and carving, all of the chipping and grinding was done in the quarry so that when the massive stones arrived at the Temple site, they fit together perfectly. What an amazing sight it must have been to watch the Temple going up silently.

We are living stones, gang (1 Peter 2:5). That makes this world the rock quarry. It's the place where we are chipped and cut, polished and ground so that when we get to Heaven, the clamor will cease, the work will be complete.

That means I'm going to be challenged by certain people I'd rather not be challenged by. God says, "They are the living stones next to you, so you better hang in there because they're My instruments to work on you, to shape you, to prepare you for what you're going to be throughout eternity. I'm building a temple for My habitation, and I've got to pound on you for a while. It's foundational."

Don't fight it, saint. Flow with it. Say, "Okay, Lord. If this is the boss You want me to work under, so be it. If this is the situation You want me to be stretched by, I submit to it." Thank the Lord for one another. Receive from each other, knowing God is building you for His glory.

JUNE 1

And the word of the LORD came to Solomon, saying, Concerning this house which thou art building, if thou wilt walk in my statutes, and execute my judgments, and keep all my commandments to walk in them; then will I perform my word with thee, which I spake unto David thy father.

1 Kings 6:11-12

Even while construction is going on, the Lord calls Solomon back to a very important reality. In the midst of this building project, He says, "Walk in My statutes. Execute My judgments. Keep My commandments; and I will perform My Word." In other words, the Lord was saying, "I'm not as concerned about building a building as I am about building you."

Dear friend, don't ever mistake activity and ministry for what is happening internally spiritually. You could be buzzing around doing all kinds of things for the Lord, but that doesn't necessarily mean you're doing well with Him. How is your relationship with the Lord? That's the issue. That's always the issue.

JUNE 2

But Solomon was building his own house thirteen years, and he finished all his house.

1 Kings 7:1

First Kings 6:38 tells us that Solomon spent seven years building the Temple. Here, we read he spent thirteen years building his own house. As we read through the chapter, we can gain some understanding of the immensity and expense of the house he constructed for himself. But I ask you to note something.

The Temple was a much more difficult project, yet his own house took him nearly twice as long to build. Why? I suggest it was because Solomon here is at the height of his personal piety, walking with the Lord more closely than he ever would. Thus, when it came to the Temple, he had a sense of urgency to complete the project, leaving the construction of his own house much farther toward the bottom of his list of priorities.

Later in Israel's history, the prophet Haggai will indict the people of Judah for being so concerned about building their own homes that they had neglected building the Temple of the Lord (1:6-8; 2:15-18). At this point, Solomon's priorities were correct. How about us? Are we like Solomon? As we look at ourselves and allow the Holy Spirit to shine the searchlight of His Word within our hearts, can we say, "Yes, Lord, I'm truly seeking Your Kingdom first"? Or are we building our own houses, tending our own needs? If you are doing the latter, you'll find yourself frustrated - for, as the Lord said through Haggai, your pockets will have holes and your stomach will be empty (1:6). Seek first the Kingdom, gang, and everything else you need will be added to you (Matthew 6:33).

JUNE 3

And he set up the pillars in the porch of the temple: and he set up the right pillar, and called the name thereof Jachin: and he set up the left pillar, and he called the name thereof Boaz. And upon the top of the pillars was lily work: so was the work of the pillars finished.

1 Kings 7:21-22

Jachin means "he shall establish." *Boaz* means "in it is strength." Jachin speaks of stability. Boaz speaks of strength. I like that. As you came into the Temple, you would see these two huge brass pillars named Stability and Strength. And yet on the top was lily work - beautiful, ornate carvings that were not seen except by someone looking down on them from above. This intrigues me because this beauty wasn't seen by the average person, not by those who would go in and out of the Temple. But as God, from His Heavenly perspective, looked down on these pillars - Strength and Stability - there was something beautiful for Him to behold.

As the temple of God, we too have some pillars in our midst - some men of strength, some women of stability - who are behind the scenes: prayer warriors, burden-bearers, Sunday school teachers, sacrificial givers. Some people receive honor right now. Others are pillars who may not be noticed by men, but whose lives are full of "lily work," who are beautiful to the Father and will one day be rewarded by Him.

JUNE 4

And he made a molten sea, ten cubits from the one brim to the other; it was round all about, and his height was five cubits; and a line of thirty cubits did compass it round about.

1 Kings 7:23

This bronze tank within the Temple was 7 ½ feet high, 15 feet across, and 45 feet in circumference. It was used by the priests to wash their hands and feet before they ministered to the Lord. In verses 27 through 29, we see that, not only was there this huge bronze tank that contained 14,000 gallons of water, but there were ten portable tanks six square feet in size that each held about 250 gallons of water for the priests to wash themselves whenever and wherever they had need.

The brass laver in the Tabernacle that preceded these lavers in the Temple was made from the mirrors of the Israelite women carried out of Egypt (Exodus 38:8). The image is perfect because we are cleansed by the water of the Word (John 15:3), which is also likened to a mirror in James 1:23. Therefore, I suggest that the laver in the Temple containing fourteen thousand gallons of water speaks of the full counsel of God (Acts 20:27), the Word in its entirety, while the smaller lavers speak of the smaller portions of the Word we carry in our hearts upon which we are to meditate throughout the day (Psalm 1:2; 119:105). As a "chosen generation, a royal priesthood" (1 Peter 2:9), we need both as we minister to the Lord and to people every day.

JUNE 5

There was nothing in the ark save the two tables of stone, which Moses put there at Horeb, when the LORD made a covenant with the children of Israel, when they came out of the land of Egypt.

1 Kings 8:9

Hebrews 9:4 tells us that the Ark contained the Ten Commandments, a pot of manna, and Aaron's rod. Here, however, we see only the Ten Commandments within the Ark. I believe the Holy Spirit included this information to help us to come to a very important understanding. That is, signs and wonders - budding rods and manna - as wonderful as they are, are not lasting. What lasts, what endures, what is absolutely essential is the Word of God.

According to Jesus, the greatest prophet who ever lived was neither Elijah, who called down fire from Heaven, nor Moses, who parted the Red Sea. The greatest prophet who ever lived was a man who did no miracles whatsoever. And yet all the things he spoke of Jesus were true. The greatest prophet who ever lived said, "I must decrease, but He must increase." The greatest prophet who ever lived was a man who simply pointed people to Jesus (Matthew 11:11; John 1:29). Like John the Baptist, you might not be one to perform signs, wonders, and miracles. But, like him, you can tell people about Jesus.

JUNE 6

But will God indeed dwell on the earth? behold, the heaven and heaven of heavens cannot contain thee; how much less this house that I have builded?

1 Kings 8:27

Solomon was right on when he said, "I realize this house I have built cannot possibly contain You, God." How big is God? The Milky Way galaxy we see overhead is one hundred thousand light-years long and ten thousand light-years wide. This means that, cruising at the speed of light, it would take you one hundred thousand years to travel from one end of it to the other. And yet Isaiah tells us God holds the heavens in the palm of His hand (40:12).

No wonder David asked, "What is man, that thou art mindful of him?" (Psalm 8:4). We're so puny. And yet this God Who is so huge has chosen to relate to us in the Person of Jesus Christ. I understand the heart of the Father, the grace, longsuffering, mercy, and tenderness of God because Jesus is the express image, the exact reflection of Him (Hebrews 1:3).

JUNE 7

And the king, and all Israel with him, offered sacrifice before the LORD. And Solomon offered a sacrifice of peace offerings, which he offered unto the LORD, two and twenty thousand oxen, and an hundred and twenty thousand sheep. So the king and all the children of Israel dedicated the house of the LORD.

1 Kings 8:62-63

Upon completion of the Temple, 22,000 oxen and 120,000 sheep were sacrificed. Not only was this expensive, but it required an incredible amount of effort and energy. But it was a delight to the Lord. As a New Testament priesthood, we are to offer the sacrifice of praise, the fruit of our lips, giving thanks to His name (Hebrews 13:15). What if the praises you offered to the Lord were recorded in Scripture? Would it be an impressive figure like this or would it be embarrassingly small?

I have recently re-enrolled in the school of praise, working through the Book of Psalms and learning the language of thanksgiving as I personalize the Psalms in my morning devotions. If you're finding it hard to verbalize praise, I would encourage you to enroll in this school as well. Work through the Psalms and make them yours. Put them in the first person. It's a wonderful tool and it will help you to become more expressive in offering praise and thanksgiving to our Lord.

JUNE 8

And it came to pass, when Solomon had finished the building of the house of the LORD, and the king's house, and all Solomon's desire which he was pleased to do, that the LORD appeared to Solomon the second time, as he had appeared unto him at Gibeon.

1 Kings 9:1-2

Twenty years earlier, the Lord appeared to Solomon the first time. Here, the Lord appears to him again. This reminds me that there can be great spans of time between the Lord's dealings with us. Therefore, I think it's dangerous to think we need to have a revelation from God or a miraculous experience every day or every week. Abraham went through years where he didn't hear from the Lord, and yet he is called the friend of God (James 2:23). Reading the Book of Acts, it's easy to assume that the early Church witnessed miracles daily if not hourly - until you remember that the Book of Acts covers a time span of thirty-eight *years*.

God is interested in developing us for eternity. To this end, He teaches us to walk by faith and not by sight. He wants us to develop discipline - to praise Him when we might not feel His presence, to study His Word even though we might not experience fresh revelation. God wants to develop and deepen you for what He has in store for you.

JUNE 9

And if thou wilt walk before me, as David thy father walked, in integrity of heart, and in uprightness, to do according to all that I have commanded thee, and wilt keep my statutes and my judgments: then I will establish the throne of thy kingdom upon Israel for ever, as I promised to David thy father, saying, There shall not fail thee a man upon the throne of Israel.

1 Kings 9:4-5

The Lord promised to establish Solomon's kingdom if he walked before Him with as much integrity as David had. The Hebrew word for integrity speaks of singleness. David had flaws and failures. He fell time after time. But one thing he had was integrity of heart. That is, he never left the Lord to follow false gods. He sinned. He strayed. He erred, to be sure. But his heart was always for the Lord, and it is the heart that matters (1 Samuel 16:7). That is why the Lord used David as a standard by which all other kings in Israel and Judah would be measured.

So too, regardless of your failing, folly, and faults, God looks at your heart. Therefore, be encouraged in the fact that, if your heart is toward Him and you're not leaving Him to serve other gods, He takes note.

In talking about Jesus, Isaiah was inspired by the Father to write . . .

Behold my servant, whom I uphold; mine elect, in whom my soul delighteth; I have put my spirit upon him: he shall bring forth judgment to the Gentiles. He shall not cry, nor lift up, nor cause his voice to be heard in the street. A bruised reed shall he not break, and the smoking flax shall he not quench: he shall bring forth judgment unto truth.

Isaiah 42:1-3

In my garden, if plants aren't looking good, out they go. If a campfire isn't providing heat, out it goes. Not so with the Lord. He's tender, compassionate, and exceedingly gracious. Therefore, I am increasingly convinced that, as Christians, we often expect more from each other than the Lord does. As Christians, we often expect more from ourselves than the Lord does. We picture the Lord as an angry God Who is out to quench the smoking flax and break the bruised reed. But that's not the way He is.

As I was thinking about a brother in the Lord, I prayed, "Lord, intensify his devotional life. Make him more fervent in his witness. Shake him out of his apathy. Wake him out of his lethargy." And the Lord impressed on my heart at that moment, quietly saying, "Be quiet. I'm happy with him. I've chosen him from eternity past. I saved his soul. I've embedded in his life a moral fabric that would have never been there apart from Me. I have a plan for him in eternity. He's doing just fine." And more and more, I'm beginning to see a different perspective. All too often, we punish ourselves and others, but that's not the heart of God. Allow the Lord to minister to you His thoughts concerning you. The Lord truly loves you. And if you simply walk in uprightness of heart, like David, you'll be established.

JUNE 10

And king Solomon gave unto the queen of Sheba all her desire, whatsoever she asked, beside that which Solomon gave her of his royal bounty. So she turned and went to her own country, she and her servants.

1 Kings 10:13

The queen of Sheba came, saw, and was saved. How do I know? Because Jesus said she will rise up in judgment against those who don't believe (Matthew 12:42). Because the queen of Sheba was a seeker of truth and sought out Solomon, ultimately she found the Greater-than-Solomon, Jesus Christ.

Solomon had the wisdom of God.
Jesus is the wisdom of God.

Solomon was a great king.
Jesus is the King of kings.

Solomon had great wealth.
Jesus has unsearchable riches.

Solomon spoke practically in proverbs.
Jesus spoke significantly in the Sermon on the Mount.

Solomon answered the queen of Sheba's questions.
Jesus is the answer to all questions.

Solomon revealed his riches to the queen of Sheba.
Jesus reveals His riches to any who seek His face.

Solomon loaded the queen of Sheba with a bounty.
Jesus does exceedingly abundantly above all we can ask or think.

How thankful I am for Jesus Christ - for the wisdom and perfection He embodies, for the riches and blessings He bestows.

JUNE 11

And the LORD was angry with Solomon, because his heart was turned from the LORD God of Israel, which had appeared unto him twice, and had commanded him concerning this thing, that he should not go after other gods: but he kept not that which the LORD commanded.

1 Kings 11:9-10

The issue is always the heart. Solomon's heart left the Lord and pursued other gods. The Lord makes mention of the fact that He appeared to Solomon twice. The Lord never appeared unto David. Yet Solomon heard from Him twice. This tells us that miraculous manifestations do not produce spiritual maturation. It's not miracles that produce maturity, it's the Word. David heard the Word of the Lord, responded to the Word of the Lord, and kept the Word of the Lord. David loved God deeply. If you're a lover of God, you're on good ground. If you love the Lord and appreciate Him and are thankful for what He's done in your life and Who He is to you, you're on good ground. But if your heart is not toward the Lord, you're on dangerous ground indeed.

Saul had no heart for the Lord. David had a whole heart for the Lord. Solomon had half a heart for the Lord. He began well but ended poorly, for his heart was turned.

JUNE 12

And Jeroboam and all the congregation of Israel came, and spake unto Rehoboam, saying, Thy father made our yoke grievous: now therefore make thou the grievous service of thy father, and his heavy yoke which he put upon us, lighter, and we will serve thee.

1 Kings 12:3 (b)-4

To complete his massive building projects, Solomon had taxed the people's wealth and strength. After his death, here at the outset of a new administration, the people asked his son to make their burden lighter. "Give me three days to consider your request," Rehoboam answered.

During that time, Rehoboam first consulted with his father's advisors. "If you will serve, encourage, and bless the people, you won't have a problem," they said. And they were right because, truly, the key to authority is humility.

The greatest Leader the world will ever know said, "Come unto Me all you who are weary and heavy laden, and I will give you rest. Take My yoke upon you and learn of Me, for My burden is easy and My yoke is light" (see Matthew 11:28-30).

The night before He was crucified, with His disciples arguing over who was the greatest, Jesus simply began to wash their dusty feet (John 13:5). How I love Jesus. There is no one like Him. Who else would tend and care for us even as we bicker and fight over who is the greatest? How we need to be more like Him.

JUNE 13

And Jeroboam said in his heart, Now shall the kingdom return to the house of David: If this people go up to do sacrifice in the house of the LORD at Jerusalem, then shall the heart of this people turn again unto their lord, even unto Rehoboam king of Judah . . .

1 Kings 12:26-27 (a)

Unfortunately, Rehoboam did not listen to the wise counsel of Solomon's advisers but instead followed the counsel of younger men who advised him to tax the people even more heavily than his father had. As a result, the ten northern tribes of Israel chose to follow another leader named Jeroboam. To keep his people from going south to Jerusalem to offer sacrifice in the Temple, Jeroboam made two golden calves and said, "These gods brought you out of Egypt." That should ring a bell, for when Moses was on Mt. Sinai receiving the Ten Commandments, Aaron made a golden calf and told the people it was the god who brought them out of Egypt. The implication in both cases was not that the golden calves replaced God, but that they simply represented Him. But, no matter how innocent it appears at the outset, trying to represent God with anything will eventually lead to idolatry.

Jeroboam is making a big mistake here. "Oh, no," he said. "If my people go down to Jerusalem to sacrifice there, their hearts will turn toward Judah and Rehoboam." Notice that Jeroboam didn't talk to the Lord about this. He talked to himself. Whenever I talk to myself, I get mixed up. And the same thing happened to Jeroboam. He went on to assign holy days and to appoint priests in an attempt to hold on to his kingdom.

May Jeroboam's sin be a warning to us, for how many compromises are we ready to make in an attempt to hold our own little kingdoms or agendas together? What problems are you facing today? Don't be like Jeroboam. Don't talk to yourself. Talk to the Lord. Seek His Kingdom, not your own.

JUNE 14

And it came to pass in the fifth year of king Rehoboam, that Shishak king of Egypt came up against Jerusalem: And he took away the treasures of the house of the Lord and the treasures of the king's house; he even took away all: and he took away all the shields of gold which Solomon had made. And king Rehoboam made in their stead brasen shields . . .

1 Kings 14:25-27 (a)

When Shishak, king of Egypt, came to do battle against Jerusalem, he plundered the gold shields that Solomon had made. What did Rehoboam, Solomon's son, do? He didn't have the resources to make more gold shields because the wealth and prosperity of the kingdom was falling rapidly. So, wanting to keep up appearances, he replaced them with brass shields.

Is the same thing happening in your life? Is the gold gone? Have the riches disappeared, yet you find yourself wanting to maintain appearances? Rather than do that, the Lord would give back to you the gold and silver you once had spiritually if you'll simply say, "Lord, I'm tired of playing games. I'm tired of putting up a front. I want to return my heart to You. I want to start walking with You once again."

The moment you do that, you can put away your brass shields because the riches and joy of the Lord will be restored to you.

JUNE 15

And Elijah the Tishbite, who was of the inhabitants of Gilead, said unto Ahab, As the LORD God of Israel liveth, before whom I stand, there shall not be dew nor rain these years, but according to my word.

1 Kings 17:1

Elijah means "Jehovah is my God." *Tishbite* means "stranger." Gilead is a rocky, rugged region that reaches heat of 120 degrees. This man of God from the rugged desert bursts on the scene and goes into the court of Ahab, saying, "The Lord God of Israel lives." Why did he say this? Because the kings of Israel thought God had died. That's why they turned to Baal, Ashteroth, and Mammon.

Proverbs 28:1 tells us that the righteous shall be as bold as a lion. Elijah was a lion-like man. In fact, all of the bold men of Scripture spent time in the desert. Paul spent three years. Moses spent forty years. David spent numerous years in the wilderness running from Saul. Are you in a desert experience tonight? Has it been four years or even forty years? Take heart, saint. You're being prepared and molded to be bold for the Kingdom.

Here were Ahab and Jezebel worshipping Baal, the god of rain, when Elijah burst in, saying, "The Lord lives and there won't be any rain."

As far as we know, Elijah wasn't commanded to do this. What gave him the audacity to make such a statement? First, he had a heart for God. He knew God's name was being blasphemed, or at best, ignored. Second, he knew the history of God. Deuteronomy 11 says if the people turned away from God and served idols, God would shut up the heavens. Third, Elijah was heard by God, for James tells us he prayed (5:17). So too, if we have a heart for God, know the history of God, and are being heard by God in prayer, we can move in great faith - and things will happen in our lives.

JUNE 16

And the word of the LORD came unto him, saying, Arise, get thee to Zarephath, which belongeth to Zidon, and dwell there: behold, I have commanded a widow woman there to sustain thee. So he arose and went to Zarephath. And when he came to the gate of the city, behold, the widow woman was there gathering of sticks: and he called to her, and said, Fetch me, I pray thee, a little water in a vessel, that I may drink.

1 Kings 17:8-10

This widow was a wonderful woman. I like her because she was industrious. She was down to a handful of meal and a little bit of oil. Yet she wasn't simply waiting for fate to run its course. She was working out in the field, gathering sticks, doing her best. As she gathered, she lifted her eyes and saw a man walking across her property in a dusty robe and with a sunburned face. "Give me some water," he said. And she did a wonderful thing - she went and got it for him. Water was scarce in that time. And yet she did something I would encourage us to learn: In the time of her trouble, trial, and difficulty, she gave what she could to someone else.

That's always the secret of life. Haven't you found that to be true? Get your eyes off your own little problems and see someone else crossing the property of this world who is hurting, thirsty, and dry. When you're feeling down yourself, look across the property of your life and you'll see someone with parched lips and sunburned face who is in greater need than you - and reach out to them.

JUNE 17

And she said, As the LORD thy God liveth, I have not a cake, but a handful of meal in a barrel, and a little oil in a cruse: and behold, I am gathering two sticks, that I may go in and dress it for me and my son, that we may eat it, and die. And Elijah said unto her, Fear not; go and do as thou hast said: but make me thereof a little cake first, and bring it unto me, and after make for thee and for thy son. For thus saith the LORD God of Israel, The barrel of meal shall not waste, neither shall the cruse of oil fail, until the day that the LORD sendeth rain upon the earth. And she went and did according to the saying of Elijah: and she, and he, and her house, did eat many days.

1 Kings 17:12-15

After receiving water, Elijah asked for cake, or bread, from the widow. When she told him she had only enough for the last meal for her and her son, Elijah said, "Don't worry. Make me the cake first - and afterwards, there will be a continual supply of meal and oil for you and your son."

I can almost see the widow's wheels turning. "Wait a minute," she must have thought, "why don't you fill the barrel and the oil jar first - then I'll be happy to give you a cake or two or three." But the Lord doesn't work that way.

True sacrifice is always out of survival, never out of surplus. We have a tendency to say, "Lord, if You bless me, then I'll give. If You bless us, then we'll move out." That's exactly backwards. You give first, then the blessing is released. Seek ye first the Kingdom of God and His righteousness - and *then* all these things shall be added unto you (Matthew 6:33). That's a hard one for us.

"Have the priests put their feet in the water," the Lord said to Joshua, "and the river will part."

Joshua could have said, "Lord, part the water first - then we'll be happy to step in." But he didn't. He obeyed - and the river parted (Joshua 3).

The Father is determined to make us men and women of faith. And He'll put us in situation after situation where faith must be exercised. It takes no faith to give out of surplus. It takes tremendous faith to give out of survival - when you just don't have it - whether it's time, finances, or love.

The widow believed. She stepped out in faith, and God blessed. Her needs were met. The Lord will not be a debtor to any man. If you are giving, sharing, sacrificing, He will never be in your debt. He'll more than make it up.

JUNE 18

(Now Obadiah feared the LORD greatly: For it was so, when Jezebel cut off the prophets of the LORD, that Obadiah took an hundred prophets, and hid them by fifty in a cave, and fed them with bread and water.)

1 Kings 18:3 (b)-4

Obadiah is an interesting character. His name means "servant of God," and yet he was working for a very wicked king - Ahab. Although some scholars question Obadiah's integrity, I'm not so sure we can judge him so easily. After all, in Philippians 4:22, rather than condemning the believers who were in Caesar's household, Paul greets them. Sometimes God plants believers in ungodly situations to be a light. Even though Obadiah was working under Ahab, even though he was not powerful like Elijah, even though he wasn't a prophet, he certainly was profitable to the prophets - for he hid them from murderous Jezebel.

So too, you might not be powerful like Elijah. But you can be profitable like Obadiah. When asked the secret of his spiritual strength, Spurgeon said, "I have people who pray for me." You might not be able to preach, but you can pray for those who do. You might not be able to cross the seas as a missionary, but you can pray for them. You might not be able to go door to door, witnessing, but you can pray. I believe that those who are Obadiahs - faithfully working behind the scenes - are not only profitable now, but will be greatly rewarded in Heaven.

JUNE 19

And Elijah went up to the top of Carmel; and he cast himself down upon the earth, and put his face between his knees, and said to his servant, Go up now, look toward the sea. And he went up, and looked, and said, There is nothing. And he said, Go again seven times. And it came to pass at the seventh time, that he said, Behold, there ariseth a little cloud out of the sea, like a man's hand. And he said, Go up, say unto Ahab, Prepare thy chariot, and get thee down, that the rain stop thee not. And it came to pass in the mean while, that the heaven was black with clouds and wind, and there was a great rain.

1 Kings 18:42 (b)-45 (a)

According to James 5:17, Elijah's secret was prayer. In public, his prayer was short. But here we see him praying in private, and his prayer takes on an entirely different dimension. He puts his head between his knees and prays. In Middle Eastern cultures, this was the birthing position. Here we see a man of prayer who prayed quickly in public - but in private he prayed with intensity and travail.

Do you know what it means to birth something in prayer? Have you experienced what it means to press in and pray through? Do you pray once or twice or three times and give up if nothing happens? That's too often my attitude. Not so with Elijah. He prayed until something was birthed. How I love to be around people who love to pray. It's hard work. Jesus prayed in Gethsemane with such birthing intensity that His face sweat blood. Do we even know what it means to keep asking, keep seeking, keep knocking? Elijah prayed and didn't give up.

Is your marriage a burden tonight? Have you prayed to the place of sweat? Are you experiencing tension over some situation? Have you prayed time and time again? Somehow, dear friend, the Lord teaching us to press in and pray is preparing us for the billions of years that lie beyond. He's not teasing you or making it hard on you. He's developing you and strengthening you.

The reason the Lord is stretching us in faith and teaching us in prayer and forcing us to mature is because He's training us for eternity.

Elijah saw a little cloud and said, "Tell Ahab to get moving. A storm's coming!"

"Wait a minute," we say. "A little cloud doesn't mean anything." Oh, but it does to a man of faith.

JUNE 20

And behold, the LORD passed by, and a great and strong wind rent the mountains, and brake in pieces the rocks before the LORD; but the LORD was not in the wind: and after the wind an earthquake; but the LORD was not in the earthquake: and after the earthquake a fire; but the LORD was not in the fire: and after the fire a still small voice.

1 Kings 19:11 (b)-12

Elijah was on the same mount upon which God had spoken to Moses through a burning bush and where He had given him the Law. Therefore, perhaps Elijah expected the Lord to work in big ways in his situation as well. Surely the Lord would do something to stop Ahab and Jezebel, he thought. Maybe He would zap Jezebel with lightning and swallow Ahab with an earthquake.

One of the reasons we get depressed is because the Lord doesn't seem to be doing something big. He's not shaking us up with experiences. He's not firing us up with the miraculous. "Lord, where are You?" we cry. "Why aren't You doing anything?"

As He did to Elijah, the Lord says to us, "I'm not in the wind, the earthquake, or the fire. I'm in the still, small voice, just whispering My will and My Word in your heart, leading you one step at a time, one day at a time, causing the circumstances in your life to work on you and direct you and guide you." Elijah had to learn that God was not necessarily going to work in the way, at the time, and in the manner he recommended. And so must we.

I am increasingly aware of the Lord working in still, small ways - that He's not panicking, that He's not frustrated, that He's not trying to bomb and blast; but that He just works in spite of me. Listen. God will speak to you as well. He will direct you through His still, small voice.

JUNE 21

Thus saith the LORD, Because the Syrians have said, The LORD is God of the hills, but he is not God of the valleys, therefore will I deliver all this great multitude into thine hand, and ye shall know that I am the LORD. And they pitched one over against the other seven days. And so it was, that in the seventh day the battle was joined: and the children of Israel slew of the Syrians an hundred thousand footmen in one day.

1 Kings 20:28 (b)-29

Even though this battle took place in the valley, the Israelites slew one hundred thousand Syrians in a single day. Why? Because the Syrians had said that the God of Israel was God only of the mountains. Satan said the same thing when he accused Job of only serving God because God had blessed him (Job 1:9-10).

And he says the same thing today. "Christians are happy as long as their spirits are high. Sure, they can sing and clap and enjoy the Lord as long as they're on the mountaintop. But put them in the valley, and once things don't go well at home or at work or with their finances, they'll be defeated and discouraged just like anyone else."

So God lets His people go through valleys to show the world that He is not the God of the mountaintops only, but also of the valley; that even in difficult days, dark times, and deep waters there will be a smile on the faces and a song in the hearts of His people. And that is when the world takes note.

Is your God the God of the valley? Or are you a Christian who only knows God as the God of the mountain - only rejoicing when things go the way you think they should? If God has privileged you to be in the valley, it's to show a watching world that you are not a mercenary - one who serves God only for your own prosperity - but that you are a lover of the Lord regardless of whether you're on the mountain or in the valley.

JUNE 22

And he took the mantle of Elijah that fell from him, and smote the waters, and said, Where is the LORD God of Elijah? and when he also had smitten the waters, they parted hither and thither: and Elisha went over.

2 Kings 2:14

Elisha struck the Jordan with Elijah's mantle - and the water parted. This interests me because the last miracle Elijah did was the same as the first miracle Elisha does.

Elisha watched what his master did, then duplicated it. What was the last miracle our Master did before going to the Cross? He healed Malchus' ear after Peter lopped it off with his sword (Luke 22:51). What is the miracle we should be doing? Healing those who have been hurt unnecessarily even by Christians who are wielding the sword upon each other. We must be people who heal, not people who hurt. "Be ye kind one to another," Paul would write, "tenderhearted, forgiving one another, even as God for Christ's sake hath forgiven you" (Ephesians 4:32). May the Lord help us to be healing, forgiving, redemptive people.

JUNE 23

And he said, Thus saith the LORD, Make this valley full of ditches.

2 Kings 3:16

In this dry and desert area, the word of the Lord was for the Israelites and Edomites to dig ditches. Only God could give the water, but it was up to them to trench the ground. This is such an important principle. You've got to dig the ditches in the dry times, in the hard times. You've got to daily dig the ditches and the Lord will fill them with water in His time. You might feel like your morning devotions are a rut, as dry as a desert. Dig the ditch anyway. And in the morning, in the Lord's timing, He will fill it with water.

It is a principle of God that is irrevocable and absolute. God will fill the ditch - but you must dig it. If the Israelites had only scratched the ground, that's all the water they would have received. The more you dig, the more you'll get. Sometimes it's just plain hard work - but whether it's Bible study, ministry, or prayer - you've got to dig the ditch first. Then the Lord will fill it in due time. May God help us to be those who dig in and prepare for mighty miracles.

JUNE 24

And it came to pass, when the vessels were full, that she said unto her son, Bring me yet a vessel. And he said unto her, There is not a vessel more. And the oil stayed.

2 Kings 4:6

This lady struck oil! She was in debt. With her two sons about to be carried away into slavery, she cried to Elisha. Elisha asked what she had. She told him she had but a little bit of oil. "Gather all the vessels you can find and start pouring," the prophet said. The lady did this - and a miracle took place, for as long as she kept pouring, the oil kept flowing.

Oil, of course, is a symbol of the Holy Spirit. The illustration here is an obvious one. The Lord will continue to flow through you as long as you are giving out to others. Maybe the Holy Spirit isn't flowing in your life. Could it be because there is no empty vessel in your house or in your life? Could it be because you haven't yet said, "I'm determined to minister to this person. I'm going to pour my life out for that person. I'm going to witness radically. I'm going to minister consistently"? Be like this woman. Gather around you empty vessels, empty people in need of the Lord. If you do, the Holy Spirit will fill you and flow from you perpetually. You too will strike oil.

JUNE 25

But as one was felling a beam, the axe head fell into the water: and he cried, and said, Alas, master, for it was borrowed. And the man of God said, Where fell it? And he shewed him the place.

2 Kings 6:5-6 (a)

As they were expanding their "dorm" in the school of ministry, one of the students found himself in a predicament. While he was doing the work of the ministry, the axe head he was using fell into the Jordan River. The axe head in this story is a symbol, a picture, of the cutting edge of power, of effectiveness. It speaks of the Holy Spirit.

The only way we'll ever build anything - be it ministry or marriage, families or friendships - is if we build in the power of the Holy Spirit. The psalmist declares that those who build apart from the Lord labor in vain (127:1). You can follow every principle of marriage, parenting, and ministry - and still fail if you are not doing it in the power of the Holy Ghost, for it is "'not by might, nor by power, but by My Spirit,' saith the Lord" (see Zechariah 4:6).

It was borrowed. Always remember that. The power upon your life is not your own. If you begin to think that the effectiveness of your ministry or the success of your marriage is because of who you are, one day you will wake up like Samson and stand to do battle - only to find, as he did, that the Spirit of the Lord has departed (Judges 16:20).

How did this man lose his axe head? He lost it in the process of service. He was trying to do what was right, but he became careless. You see, an axe head does not fall off suddenly. It becomes loose slowly.

At this point, all the young man had was a wooden axe handle. Wood in the Scriptures is symbolic of the flesh (1 Corinthians 3:12). Here's a young man, doing the work of the ministry, and suddenly, the power is gone, leaving him nothing but the wooden handle of the flesh. To his credit, he didn't say, "So what if the axe head is gone? Who cares if the power has departed? I'll just use this handle." That would have been ridiculous. And yet what do we do? So often, the cutting edge is gone, the power lost, yet we keep on ministering even though the anointing is not there.

This man said, "Alas, master." That is always the first step to reclaiming the cutting edge. Open and honest confession that you're not on the cutting edge like you once were is always the place where restoration begins.

Elisha asked one question: "Where did you lose it?" To the church at Ephesus, Jesus said, "I know your good works, your knowledge, your giving. But I have something against you, for you have left your first love. Remember from whence you are fallen and repent. And do your first works again" (see Revelation 2:1-5).

Was there a time when you loved the Lord radically, when you worshipped the Lord fervently, when you served the Lord consistently? Was there a time when you couldn't wait to get in the Word, when you found witnessing something that was natural? Was there a time in your life when you were more in love with Jesus and more fervent in serving Him than you are today?

If so, remember how it once was - and then repent. Say, "Lord, I admit to You, I confess before You that I'm not in the place I once was, in the place I long to be. And I repent." Then do your first works again. What were you doing when you loved the Lord? Did you get up early to pray? Do it again.

Did you open your house and share the Gospel with people? Do it again. Did you come consistently to Bible study and worship meetings? Do it again. It's so simple. Just go back to the place where you lost your cutting edge.

JUNE 26

And when the servant of the man of God was risen early, and gone forth, behold, a host compassed the city both with horses and chariots. And his servant said unto him, Alas, my master, how shall we do? And he answered, Fear not: for they that be with us are more than they that be with them. And Elisha prayed, and said, LORD, I pray thee, open his eyes, that he may see. And the LORD opened the eyes of the young man; and he saw: and behold, the mountain was full of horses and chariots of fire round about Elisha.

2 Kings 6:15-17

"Lord, open his eyes," Elisha prayed. And when his servant's eyes were fully open, he not only saw the problem, but he saw the solution. That is, he saw that the enemy which surrounded him was itself surrounded by angels and chariots far more powerful than any earthly army.

How I pray that, in every situation we face, we would not only see the problem but that we would see the solution - that the Lord is with us; that His angels are surrounding us; that His promises are applicable to us. He says He will never leave us or forsake us (Hebrews 13:5). He says He will complete the good work He began in us (Philippians 1:6). He says all things work together for good to them that love God (Romans 8:28). He says nothing separates us from His love (Romans 8:35-39). He says all of our needs will be met according to His riches (Philippians 4:19). He says He is the God Who heals us (Exodus 15:26). We need to see the reality of the spiritual forces surrounding the enemies who surround us.

Happy is the people whose God is the Lord (Psalm 144:15). The joy of the Lord is your strength (Nehemiah 8:10). Rejoice evermore (1 Thessalonians 5:16). Who is the person who is happy, who rejoices evermore? It's the one whose eyes are open to see the reality of spiritual promises and the presence of God. Who is the sad, depressed, discouraged, defeated one? The one who sees the problem but not the solution. May God give us eyes to see (Ephesians 1:18).

Even though you thought you were doomed, I suggest that you cannot even recall what you were worried about five years ago. Why? Because the promises of God stood. He is faithful. He promised to guide and provide - and He did. Maybe you know someone who thinks he's going down, going under. Do what Elisha did. First, speak a word of exhortation. Tell him to "fear not." Then pray a prayer of intercession. "Lord, open his eyes that he might see the sovereignty of God, the promises of Scripture, the reality of Jesus."

JUNE 27

Then spake Elisha unto the woman, whose son he had restored to life, saying, Arise, and go thou and thine household, and sojourn wheresoever thou canst sojourn: for the LORD hath called for a famine; and it shall also come upon the land seven years.

2 Kings 8:1

In the day of Elijah, God sent a terrible famine that lasted 3 ½ years. Here, in the day of Elisha, another famine will come - but it will last 7 years. That's the way the Lord works. He slowly but surely increases the pressure in our lives until we bow our knee and say, "Lord, *Your* will be done."

When Elisha told this woman whose son he restored to life that famine was coming, he didn't say, "Here's a miracle to see you through." He said, "You better do something practical. Go somewhere the famine is not going to hit." Sometimes the Lord does something miraculous. Other times,

He works very naturally. Elijah told the widow that if she made bread out of the ingredients she had, the Lord would continue to supply for her all the days of the famine (1 Kings 17). On the other hand, Elisha - who did even more miracles than Elijah - said to this woman, "I'm not promising a miracle. I'm telling you to do something practical: leave."

We can't box the Lord in. He works differently with different individuals in different times. You'll find nothing but frustration if you try to formulize God. God didn't write His Word like a manual. He didn't say, "Here's fifteen steps for healing the sick and ten steps for helping the hurting." I have often wished the Bible were written differently than it was. It seems there should be sections on Marriage, on Parenting, on Finances. Why did God write it this way? Because in His Word, we find general principles, but we must seek Him for specifics. Why? Because He wants to hear from us.

Dear saint, the Lord truly loves you and wants to spend time with you. The only difference between a strong believer and a weak one is responsiveness. The times you've been wakened in the night, thinking it was the pie you ate or the problems you face may have been the Lord, tapping you on the shoulder, saying, "I enjoy your company and I'd like to spend some time with you right now." The times you felt a stirring in your heart while you watched TV may have been the Lord calling you to spend a few moments with Him. God doesn't have favorites. He doesn't arbitrarily bless some more than others. No, the people who develop and mature in Him are simply those who have said, "I'll turn off the TV or roll out of bed in response to His call." And I guarantee not a one is disappointed.

JUNE 28

And Elisha died, and they buried him. And the bands of the Moabites invaded the land at the coming in of the year. And it came to pass, as they were burying a man, that behold, they spied a band of men; and they cast the man into the sepulchre of Elisha: and when the man was let down, and touched the bones of Elisha, he revived, and stood up on his feet.

2 Kings 13:20-21

In the heat of battle, a dead man was inadvertently thrown into Elisha's tomb. But when his body touched Elisha's bones, he immediately came back to life. Amazing!

Like the dead man in this passage, we must die to self if we are going to truly experience life. "If any man come after Me, let him deny himself, take up his Cross and follow Me," Jesus said (see Matthew 16:24). He did not say this to burden us but to liberate us because, as we have discovered, the more we think about ourselves and live for ourselves, the more miserable we become. But the more we die to self and take up the Cross, the more we spring to life.

If you want to be effective in ministering to other people, even as Elisha was dead, so too in ministry or in service, you've got to die to popularity. "If I please men, I cannot be the servant of God," Paul declared (see Galatians 1:10). If you take a stand for Jesus Christ and do what you believe is right for the Lord, there will be those who will misunderstand. That can be painful. But if you are going to minister, you've got to die in order that life might come forth. Jesus said he who lives for his own life will lose it, but if you give up your life, you'll find it (Matthew 10:39).

I have a hard time with this. I struggle on this point because when I sense that someone is unhappy with me or disappointed in me, my natural tendency is to keep from making waves or causing offense. But James said we offend in all things (3:2). The only solution is to live for the Lord and in such a way that you can say, "Father, I have finished the work which *Thou* hast given me and glorified Thy name (see John 17:4). I'm doing what

You're telling me to do to the best of my perception and abilities no matter the cost."

If you do that - if you die to self - life will spring forth. People will be touched. Lives will be changed.

Elisha was a man who, even after his death, still influenced and affected peoples' lives. How about you? What if the Lord took you home today? Oh, that we might live our lives in such a way that the memory of our lives - the words we spoke, the truth we shared, the love we showed, the example we set - might cause others to spring to life themselves.

JUNE 29

Now the rest of the acts of Jeroboam, and all that he did, and his might, how he warred, and how he recovered Damascus, and Hamath, which belonged to Judah, for Israel, are they not written in the book of the chronicles of the kings of Israel? And Jeroboam slept with his fathers, even with the kings of Israel; and Zachariah his son reigned in his stead.

2 Kings 14:28-29

Jeroboam was a wicked king, and yet the Lord used him powerfully. He had a long reign. He was prosperous. And yet he did not love the Lord. Oftentimes, we get confused on this issue. We see someone who is powerful and prosperous, who seems to get all the breaks, while we who love the Lord face one trial after another. Why is it that the evil people seem to do so well? Have you ever asked that question? Asaph did . . .

> Truly God is good to Israel, even to such as are of a clean heart. But as for me, my feet were almost gone; my steps had well nigh slipt. For I was envious at the foolish, when I saw the prosperity of the wicked . . . When I thought to know this, it was too painful for me; until I went into the sanctuary of God; then understood I their end. Surely thou didst set them in slippery places: thou castedst them down into destruction . . . Nevertheless I am continually with thee: thou hast

holden me by my right hand. Thou shalt guide me with thy counsel, and afterward receive me to glory.

Psalm 73:1-3, 17-18, 23-24

Asaph was confused and baffled - until he came into the house of the Lord. And suddenly his perspective was restored. I can't tell you how many times that has happened to me. Discouraged or confused, I have plopped into a pew - and when the Word was opened, it spoke exactly to me, and my vision was restored. That's why I love being in the house of the Lord. My perspective is always clarified once again. Let the Jeroboams have their success now. Ours is coming.

JUNE 30

Josiah was eight years old when he began to reign, and he reigned thirty and one years in Jerusalem. And his mother's name was Jedidah, the daughter of Adaiah of Boscath. And he did that which was right in the sight of the LORD, and walked in all the way of David his father, and turned not aside to the right hand or to the left.

2 Kings 22:1-2

A whitewater river guide once told me that the secret of whitewater canoeing is to stay in the "tongue," or the center, of the river because there are currents to the right and left that ultimately lead to a cracked canoe. That's what Josiah did. He didn't go to the right or the left. So often we, as Christians, can go off to the right. We can become very legalistic, thinking we alone are "right." The Pharisees veered off to the right. Or, we drift to the left and become so liberal in our theology that we stand for nothing. The Sadducees did this. That is why the Lord calls us, like Josiah, to remain in the center.

At this point, Judah will enter a period of peace and prosperity resulting from revival and reformation during the reign of Josiah. There were four great reformers, four great kings who ushered in revival in the country of Judah: Asa, Hezekiah, Jehoshaphat, and Josiah. But the reforms under Josiah went further and deeper than the reforms of any of the other reformers.

Revival is what every one of us longs for in some way. If your own heart is dry, you need a personal revival. If your children aren't walking with the Lord in the way you know they should, your family needs revival. If your workplace is an atmosphere of ungodliness and carnality, your colleagues need revival. Our God is the God of continual revival. And He *wants* to revive.

One eight year-old boy was totally in love with the Lord. And in him, the Lord had a base from which He could work. As you study history and read of revivals, you will find without exception that they begin with one individual excited about the Lord. All it takes is one.

"What difference can I make in my neighborhood or at my workplace?" we ask. "There are so many people, how could I affect that situation?" It only takes one . . .

In the late 1800s, there was a great evangelist named Gypsy Smith. He traveled the world, preaching on every continent. Wherever he preached, revival broke out. One day, a delegation of people came to him and said, "Reverend Smith, we desperately want to see revival in our area. It's so dry and dead. What can we do?"

Gypsy reportedly said, "Go home. Lock yourselves in your bedrooms. Take a piece of chalk. Draw a circle on the floor. Kneel in the circle and pray fervently that God would start a revival in that circle."

Revival doesn't begin by praying for your husband or wife, or praying for your boss. It begins when you get on your face before the Lord and say, "Let it begin with me."

JULY 1

And Jokim, and the men of Chozeba, and Joash, and Saraph, who had the dominion in Moab, and Jashubi-lehem. And these are ancient things. These were the potters, and those that dwelt among plants and hedges: there they dwelt with the king for his work.

1 Chronicles 4:22-23

I like this verse! It lists a group of men who were potters and gardeners. These were common jobs done by common workers. And yet here we read that they had a place in the palace. In other words, because they worked for the king, they dwelt with the king.

So too, if you're a potter or a gardener, a mechanic or a banker, a dishwasher or a teacher - and you're doing it as unto the King - you'll dwell with the King at that very place. Your occupation can become a real ministry if you'll do it as unto the King. For example, if you plant plants and say, "Lord, this is for You - a garden for Your glory;" if you give back change as a teller and say, "Lord, bless this person with wisdom on how they will use this money," you can make any occupation a ministry. And if you do it, you'll dwell with the King at that very point as you experience His presence in a powerful, practical way.

JULY 2

And this is the number of the mighty men whom David had; Jashobeam, a Hachmonite, the chief of the captains: he lift up his spear against three hundred slain by him at one time.

1 Chronicles 11:11

Jashobeam, also known as Adino in 2 Samuel 23:8, single-handedly took on three hundred enemies. This speaks to us very powerfully about the importance of lifting up our hands in prayer (1 Timothy 2:8). If you want to be a mighty man or woman of God, prerequisite number one is that you persist in prayer.

"But my hands are tired," you protest. "I've been praying about this issue for a long time and I'm getting worn out and beaten down." Do you recall what Moses did? He was on the mountaintop praying for the Israelites while the battle was raging with the Amalekites. When his hands were in the air, the Israelites would advance, but when his hands grew weary and began to fall, the Amalekites gained momentum. Finally, observing what was happening, Aaron stood on one side of him and Hur on the other to prop Moses' hands up until victory was secure (Exodus 17:12).

We're all like Moses. We all need people to hold up our hands. Therefore, we need to pray for and cultivate relationships that will enable us to hold up one another's hands in times of weakness.

JULY 3

Be of good courage, and let us behave ourselves valiantly for our people, and for the cities of our God: and let the LORD do that which is good in his sight.

1 Chronicles 19:13

These men were armed, trained, and ready to do battle - but they realized the results would have to be left to the Lord. They did what they could, but realized only the Lord could bring about ultimate victory.

I feel it's important we adopt a similar attitude - that we do the very best we can do in situations of spiritual warfare and ministry, and leave the rest with the Lord. I fear that we are sometimes reluctant to pray for the sick because we're worried they won't be healed. I fear we're hesitant to pray for those who are worried or depressed for fear that they will remain in their state. The Lord will do what's right in His sight. Our job is simply to prepare for the battle, to place ourselves in positions to do whatever we can do.

If you say to someone, "Dear brother, let me pray for you," and you pray the prayer of faith and seek the Lord, even if that situation does not seemingly or immediately improve or change, you will have done what you can do. Not only is that pleasing in the sight of the Lord, but it will inevitably be appreciated by the person for whom you pray. All too often, we don't pray or move in faith because we fear people will get disillusioned or disappointed if things don't work out the way we think they should.

I suggest that we should say, "We're going to do everything we can. We're going to pray fervently. We're going to work hard. We're going to see what we can do to the best of our ability. But then, Lord, we submit to Your sovereignty and Your wisdom to do what is right."

Pray for each other, dear saints. And don't let fear quench your desire or your aggressiveness in prayer.

JULY 4

And David said to Solomon his son, Be strong and of good courage, and do it: fear not, nor be dismayed: for the LORD God, even my God, will be with thee; he will not fail thee, nor forsake thee, until thou hast finished all the work for the service of the house of the LORD.

1 Chronicles 28:20

Paul was "confident of this very thing, that He Who began a good work in you will perform it until the day of Jesus Christ" (see Philippians 1:6). Therefore, as sure as a promise was made to Solomon, so the same promise is given to you. You can come to a point in your life where you realize that the dreams you had, the goals you set aren't going to happen. That can, if you're not careful, send you into an introspective crisis. But if you're a believer, there won't be a crisis because the promise of God is that what He wants to do in you will be completed. Period.

Zacharias was a priest. His wife, Elisabeth, was a priest's daughter. For years, they prayed that they might have a child. Suddenly, as Zacharias was serving in the Temple, an angel appeared and told him his prayer had been heard (Luke 1). Now, I bet Zacharias had stopped praying when Elisabeth passed the age of childbearing. I'm sure he had forgotten all about the prayer he had prayed. Maybe you can relate to that. At one time, you felt you were praying in harmony with God's heart - but nothing happened. Don't give up. The promise is that the work *will* be completed. It might take an entirely different course than what you thought, but God will complete His work for your life.

JULY 5

Then Solomon began to build the house of the LORD . . .

2 Chronicles 3:1 (a)

Like the Tabernacle, the Temple was divided into three main areas. The first part was the courtyard. And everyone was allowed to see the courtyard. Then, inside the Temple itself, there were two parts. The first was the Holy Place in which there was the Altar of Incense, the Candlestick, the Table of Showbread where the priests served. And behind the veil was the Holy of Holies containing the Ark of the Covenant and the Shekinah glory of God. On only one day could the high priest enter the Holy of Holies and experience the physical, tangible presence of God.

Even as the Temple has three parts, you are a triune being. You have an outer court: your body. Your soul is your holy place. Only a few people know your soul - your mind and your emotions. It's more exclusive. Lastly, there is your spirit, the holy of holies, reserved exclusively for God Himself and the high priest, Jesus Christ. It is where you commune with the Lord and give worship to the Lord. If you want to be a whole person, you need to give attention to all three areas - body, soul, and spirit - for they are intricately connected. If I am physically getting run down, it will affect the rest of my temple. If my mind is not being stimulated or developed, it will affect me spiritually and physically as well. If my spirit is not being tended, if I am not taking time to walk with the Lord and seek Him, it affects the rest of my being. This means if you're working out, worship the Lord while you do it. If you're in school, praise the Lord for the facts you're learning. Wherever you're at, take care of the whole person as much as possible.

The more important application, however, is that these three parts of the Temple show you where you're at in your service in the work of the Lord. Maybe you're in the outer court. It's where sacrifice was offered, the place of salvation. Maybe you're just enjoying the fact that your sins are forgiven. But there will come a time when you'll need to move out of the outer court into the Holy Place, the place where the priests went. You'll begin to lay out the bread, trim the lamps; you get involved in serving the Lord. After a season there, you'll be drawn to the Holy of Holies, which is worship and adoration. Like Mary, you'll choose the better part, sitting at the feet of Jesus.

Where are you at? Are you in the outer courtyard, have you moved into the place of service, or are you fellowshipping with the Lord in worship?

JULY 6

Now the rest of the acts of Solomon, first and last, are they not written in the book of Nathan the prophet, and in the prophecy of Ahijah the Shilonite, and in the visions of Iddo the seer against Jeroboam the son of Nebat? And Solomon reigned in Jerusalem over all Israel forty years. And Solomon slept with his fathers, and he was buried in the city of David his father: and Rehoboam his son reigned in his stead.

2 Chronicles 9:29-31

Solomon was wise, wealthy, and successful - but, nonetheless, miserable. In Ecclesiastes, we see from Solomon's own hand that, during this time of incredible prosperity, his life was full of misery. Solomon threw unbelievable parties, gained impressive education, had power, wealth, and influence that was unrivaled in the world. Yet he declared it all to be empty.

All of us think that happiness lies right around the corner - a little more money, and we'll be happy; a little more education or job security, and we'll be content. So too, poor Solomon. He was at the top of every conceivable arena. He had nowhere else to go, nothing else for which to strive or hope - and he was still wanting.

It is the wise person who learns from the wisest man who ever lived and sees the fallacy that can so easily penetrate our hearts in thinking that happiness lies right around the corner with the next job, raise, acquisition, spouse, or degree.

At the end of his days, Solomon turned to the Lord, realizing that He was what he was looking for all along . . .

> Let us hear the conclusion of the whole matter: fear God, and keep his commandments: for this is the whole duty of man.

Ecclesiastes 12:13

July 7

Thus saith the LORD, Ye shall not go up, nor fight against your brethren: return every man to his house: for this thing is done of me. And they obeyed the words of the LORD, and returned from going against Jeroboam.

2 Chronicles 11:4

Realizing his empire was divided, Rehoboam sought to reunite it by force. But the Lord sent a prophet, saying, "Don't fight your brethren in striving for unity."

The Lord never desired division, but He allowed it. Why? Under the reign of Solomon that lasted forty years, Israel experienced incredible prosperity. But at the same time, the nation was cracking and crumbling because of moral decay. So the Lord would actually allow the kingdom to split in order to save it.

From this, I understand that sometimes, although division is not the Lord's best, He sometimes allows it to accomplish His purpose. In Acts 2, we read that the Lord added to the church such as should be saved. In Acts 6, we read that the Lord multiplied the church. But in between Acts 2 and Acts 6 is Acts 5 - where we see not addition, not multiplication, but subtraction. Ananias and Sapphira were subtracted because they lied to the Holy Spirit. So, before there could be a further explosion of growth in the church, there first had to be a purging of the church.

In my own life, this same principle holds true. The Lord adds to my life and wants to multiply abundantly. But He sees He must do some subtracting first. So a season of purging follows. So too, if you're wondering why you're being purged, why you seem to be in a season of subtraction or division, it could very well be because the Lord is getting ready to do a great work of multiplication through you.

JULY 8

And it came to pass, when Rehoboam had established the kingdom, and had strengthened himself, he forsook the law of the LORD, and all Israel with him.

2 Chronicles 12:1

From 2 Chronicles 11:17, we know that Rehoboam, king of Judah, walked in the way of his grandfather, David, and honored the Lord - until he became strong. Then he forgot the Lord.

An elephant and a flea walked over a creaky wooden bridge. When they reached the other side, the flea said to the elephant, "Wow! We sure made that bridge shake, didn't we?" Rehoboam had that same mentality. And so can we. We walk with the Lord. God's blessing is poured out, and we begin to think, "We sure did something great, didn't we, Lord?" Are you in that place? Be careful. It's when we're doing well that we're most vulnerable.

When Paul had a vision of Heaven, the Lord sent a thorn in the flesh to buffet him. "Lord," he prayed, "take this thorn from me."

"Lord, remove this thorn from me," he prayed a second time.

After he prayed the same prayer a third time, the Lord said, "No, Paul. My grace is sufficient for you, for when you are weak, then you will be strong."

Paul went on to glory in his weakness, saying, "If God has to keep me weak that I might be dependent upon Him, so be it. I do not want to be strong if it means I'll be independent of Him" (see 2 Corinthians 12).

Why has God sent you a thorn in the flesh? Maybe it's a person. Maybe it's a physical problem or a situation that pokes and prods. It is very possible that its purpose is to keep you from making the mistake of Rehoboam, the mistake of relying upon yourself.

JULY 9

And he built fenced cities in Judah: for the land had rest, and he had no war in those years; because the LORD had given him rest. Therefore he said unto Judah, Let us build these cities, and make about them walls, and towers, gates, and bars, while the land is yet before us; because we have sought the LORD our God, we have sought him, and he hath given us rest on every side. So they built and prospered.

2 Chronicles 14:6-7

During the time of rest, Asa didn't kick back. He used the time of rest to prepare for future battles. And I believe his example is invaluable to us. If your life is going smoothly, praise the Lord and enjoy it - but prepare for the battles that are sure to come your way. If you're kicking back and watching TV in the time of peace, watch out because you don't know what tomorrow holds. And when the trial or difficulty confronts you, it will be too late to build your cities then. It will be too late to arm the soldiers then. When the attack comes, you'll kick yourself and say, "Why didn't I prepare when I had the opportunity? I didn't study and pray and meditate like I knew I should have, and now I'm sadly defeated." Asa is remembered as a godly man because he was wise enough to use the time of peace for a time of preparation.

They built and they prospered. So too, there are three ways the Bible tells us we can build, or edify. The first is through the Word of God. "As newborn babes, desire the sincere milk of the Word that you may grow thereby" (see 1 Peter 2:2). The word translated "grow" literally means "be edified." Peter doesn't address this exhortation to newborn babes or new believers. He doesn't say, "*If* you're a newborn babe, desire the sincere milk of the Word." No, he says, "*As* newborn babes, desire the milk of the Word." In other words, it as imperative for us as believers to take in the Word as it is for a newborn baby to take in a consistent and continual supply of nourishment.

The second way to build or edify is through our own words. Proverbs 18:21 tells us that life and death are in the power of the tongue. Every word you speak will either build up or tear down. You'll either build up your own or someone else's faith through words of encouragement and blessing, or you'll undermine your own or someone else's faith through cynicism and doubt.

Finally, we edify through love. Paul says in 1 Corinthians 13 that knowledge puffs up but love builds up. If you're striving with people, you're eroding the underpinnings of faith. But if you love people, you're building on a firm foundation.

Three practical ways you can build and prosper in the time of peace: Get in the Word; speak positive words; and love. In so doing, you will not only edify others, but your own faith will be built up and strengthened.

JULY 10

And he brought in the priests and the Levites, and gathered them together into the east street, and said unto them, Hear me, ye Levites, sanctify now yourselves, and sanctify the house of the LORD God of your fathers, and carry forth the filthiness out of the holy place.

2 Chronicles 29:4-5

Ahaz had allowed the Temple to be desecrated and defiled. Here, Hezekiah tells the Levites to clean it up.

So too, because we are the temple of the true and living God, there must be a continual cleansing of the filthiness that pollutes and penetrates our lives. It is interesting to me that virtually all of creation is concerned with cleanliness . . .

Mice and rats actually spend the majority of their waking hours grooming themselves. They carry disease, but are actually surprisingly clean. So are elephants. Elephants who become invaded with parasites cover themselves with dust. Then they rub themselves against trees. The dust suffocates the bugs. The tree acts like a towel to wipe the dead bugs from off their back. Finally, they give themselves showers by filling their trunks with water and squirting themselves. The gecko lizards in the desert in the southwest part of our country are interesting because they don't have any eyelids. Yet they live in a place where there is lots of dirt and sand. So what do they do? The gecko lizard has a long tongue which actually extends all the way to their eyes and thus is able to clean them.

There seems to be innately built into creation a desire to be clean. And yet when it comes to the heart of man, we allow corruption and pollution to affect us internally. Cleansing needs to be carried out daily. How? If we confess our sin, He is faithful and just to forgive us our sin and to cleanse us from all unrighteousness (1 John 1:9). This verse, one which you've maybe known since childhood, tells us that even if you feel defiled and desecrated, you can solve the problem right now simply by confessing. When you confess your sin, the blood of Jesus is immediately applied and it removes all the filth from the temple of your life.

JULY 11

In those days Hezekiah was sick to the death, and prayed unto the LORD: and he spake unto him, and he gave him a sign.

2 Chronicles 32:24

This story is recorded in 2 Kings 20 and Isaiah 38 as well. From these passages, we know that when God sent Isaiah to tell Hezekiah that it was time to go home, Hezekiah begged God to let him live. God granted Hezekiah's request and confirmed it by turning the sundial back ten degrees, or approximately forty-five minutes. But was it His will? I wonder. In the following fifteen years a couple of terrible things took place. First, Hezekiah fathered a son named Manasseh, who later would be the worst of Judah's kings and whose reign would lead to Judah's captivity.

Second, when Hezekiah miraculously recovered, the Babylonians sent a contingent of ambassadors with some get-well cards and congratulations. When Hezekiah took them on a personal tour of his storehouses, their report to their leader, Nebuchadnezzar, led to the attack by the Babylonians.

Hezekiah would have been far better off flowing with what the Lord was doing rather than demanding his own way. I don't want to demand my way because I don't know as much as God does. God knows what's right. My Father knows best. Yes, we are to bring our requests to Him. But ultimately we must say, "Not my will, but Thine be done, Father."

As they wandered in the wilderness, the children of Israel begged God for meat. When He answered their demand, Numbers 11:33 tells us they died even as they ate the quail. Of this the psalmist writes, "The Lord gave them their request, but sent leanness to their soul" (see Psalm 106:15).

Be careful, gang, that you don't demand from God without submitting it to His perfect will. He might give you your request. But you might find it wasn't what you were hoping.

JULY 12

And when he was in affliction, he besought the LORD his God, and humbled himself greatly before the God of his fathers, and prayed unto him: and he was intreated of him, and heard his supplication, and brought him again to Jerusalem into his kingdom. Then Manasseh knew that the LORD he was God.

2 Chronicles 33:12-13

In this time of his affliction, the Lord, in His amazing grace, heard Manasseh's prayer. Even though Manasseh had been living rebelliously for fifty-five years, the Lord heard his prayers. The psalmist said in Psalm 119:71, "It is good for me to be afflicted that I might learn thy statutes." It's when we're afflicted that, perhaps for the first time in a long time, we pick up the Bible. It's when we're afflicted that we finally cry out to the Lord in sincerity and desperation. If He heard Manasseh's prayers, don't you know He'll hear your prayer when you cry to Him?

I love to think about the grace of God because I need it. I love the way God my Father has been so very gracious to me. The problem is, when I hear about other guys - like Manasseh - who I think are awful and who have done evil, I don't want to hear about the grace of God extended to them. In other words, I have found that I compare their worst with my best. In reality, what the Lord would have for me is to compare my worst with their best - to find something that is good or right in them. If you're having difficulty wondering how God could be so gracious to others, it might be a time for you to compare your worst with their best.

JULY 13

And the men did the work faithfully: and the overseers of them were Jahath and Obadiah, the Levites, of the sons of Merari; and Zechariah and Meshullam, of the sons of the Kohathites, to set it forward; and other of the Levites, all that could skill of instruments of musick.

2 Chronicles 34:12

As the Temple was restored, musicians were playing. Music has a powerful impact and effect upon our spiritual lives . . .

As he waited on the Lord for a word from Him, Elisha called for a minstrel. And as the minstrel began to play, the Holy Spirit spoke to Elisha (2 Kings 3:15). How often have you begun to worship the Lord in song - when suddenly He begins to speak to you? How often have you found yourself encouraged as you've listened to praise music? Saul was haunted and hounded by a demonic spirit. He called for David to come and play his harp. As songs were played and worship ascended, Saul experienced relief (1 Samuel 16:23).

If you're discouraged, depressed, or defeated, if you want your temple restored, play music. It will build you up and cause your spirit to soar. In Job 38, God says that as the foundations of the earth were being laid, the angels were singing songs. In other words, He does His best work with background music. These guys created an atmosphere that was right spiritually. The Lord inhabits the praise of His people (Psalm 22:3). The demons are confused by praise. That is why Jehoshaphat sent a choir before he sent an army to do battle (2 Chronicles 20). Be a person of praise. Sing in your car. Sing in your shower. Sing when you're depressed. As Isaiah said, "Sing, O barren one" (see 54:1). If you'll develop this practice, you'll tap into a spiritual dynamic that will aid and assist you in the days of spiritual warfare.

JULY 14

And when they brought out the money that was brought into the house of the LORD, Hilkiah the priest found a book of the law of the LORD given by Moses. And Hilkiah answered and said to Shaphan the scribe, I have found the book of the law in the house of the LORD.

2 Chronicles 34:14-15 (a)

As the Temple was being remodeled, refurbished, and restored, someone found a copy of the Law. Manasseh and Amon evidently had destroyed all the copies of the Law. But one was found in the Temple in the midst of the rubble. Bookbinding wasn't developed until AD 900. Before that time, books were made from dried papyrus woven together and rolled into lengths of approximately one hundred feet. Because the process was not an easy one, books were not easily copied.

Throughout history, every lasting revival that has taken place has been linked to a rediscovery of the Word. The same thing will happen in our lives personally. That is, if we get into the Word, revival can't help but break out. A Bible that's falling apart usually belongs to a person who isn't. If you want your life to be revived and refurbished and renewed, read your Bible - but know that Bible study isn't always like the 4th of July. When I read the Word in the morning, I'm not always fired up. Sometimes it's just plain discipline. But it's a discipline that will bring about long-term maturity and real stability.

Think about the believers you know who have a real history in the Lord and are rich in the things of God. I guarantee their walks are not based upon "Holy Spirit goose bumps," or some new experience or hot tip. No, the men and women I've known who are deep and rich in their history and maturity with God are that way because of their knowledge of the Word. If you will center your life on Bible study, I guarantee you will have a rich, stable, mature Christian experience.

JULY 15

These are now the chief of their fathers, and this is the genealogy of them that went up with me from Babylon, in the reign of Artaxerxes the king.

Ezra 8:1

The number of men who responded to Ezra's invitation to return to Jerusalem following their captivity in Babylon - listed in verses 2 through 14 - was approximately fifteen hundred. Keep in mind that most of the Jews carried into Babylon had, over time, become comfortable there. In the first group, led by Zerubbabel, nearly fifty thousand went. In this second group, there are fifteen hundred who go. Most chose to stay.

The Holy Spirit is a perfect gentleman. He invites. He encourages. He inspires. He enlightens. But He doesn't force. That is why He is likened not to a vulture or an eagle, but to a dove, a bird of peace and gentleness (Matthew 3:16).

In Ezekiel 47, we see Ezekiel being led to a river - often a picture of the Spirit in Scripture (Joshua 3:13) - where he stepped in up to his ankles. Then he was led downstream, where he stepped in up to his knees. Further downstream, he stepped in up to his waist. Still further, he found himself over his head. What does this say to us? The Spirit of the Lord invites us to step in. Some step in up to their ankles. That is, they're standing in Christ, believing in Jesus. Others, however, choose to go deeper. They go to their knees, not only believing in the Lord themselves, but praying for others. Others go deeper still, sharing their faith and seeing others born again. And others ask the Lord to take total control of their lives, allowing the baptism of the Spirit to wash over them completely. At each stage, Ezekiel had a choice whether or not to step in. So do we. Will I do what the Lord invites me to do? Will I ask for the power of the Holy Spirit to come upon me? Will I believe that His Spirit will fill me? Will I witness for Him?

Gang, the Lord will take you as far and as deep in Him as you want to go - but not one step further. Why are some people seemingly so Spirit-filled? I suggest it is simply because they want to be, that they are those who say,

"Lord, take total control of me. Do whatever You want with my life. I want to be lost in You."

JULY 16

But it came to pass, that when Sanballat heard that we builded the wall, he was wroth, and took great indignation, and mocked the Jews.

Nehemiah 4:1

Sanballat's name literally means "thorn in secret." In other words, he was a pain - the Old Testament equivalent of Paul's own thorn in the flesh (2 Corinthians 12:7). A "Sanballat" was sent Paul's way to keep him from being puffed up in pride, to keep him in a place of humility and brokenness. I wonder what "Sanballat" the Lord has sent you. Maybe you look at him as a big pain or at her as a real problem. But could it be that the person who seems to be poking you or breaking your heart is actually allowed by the Lord to cause you to do what we'll see Nehemiah do - to pray? If so, Satan's tactics will backfire because they will draw you closer to the Lord than you otherwise would have been.

There were plenty of Sanballats in Jesus' day as well. When Jairus' daughter was nearly dead, he asked Jesus to heal her. As they made their way to his house, they found mourners weeping and wailing. Jesus looked at Jairus and said, "Don't believe them. This isn't the end of the story. She's just sleeping." When the people heard this, Matthew tells us they laughed Jesus to scorn (9:24).

Maybe at one time a promise was given to you - something you know the Lord has placed on your heart or a promise in the Word that practically jumped off the page. But now it seems dead. All you hear are voices inside that mock and laugh. You must do what Jesus did, for it wasn't until Jesus sent the mockers packing that resurrection took place. If you have a promise from the Lord that seems dead and hopeless, the Lord would say to you,

"Move out the mockers. Send the voices of cynicism and the whispers of doubt packing."

In the early days of Elisha's ministry, there was a group of young men who laughed at him, calling him a bald-headed man. What did Elisha do? He cursed them in the name of the Lord - and they were immediately devoured by bears (2 Kings 2). When doubts come our way in the temple of our spirit, saying, "It's not going to come about. It's too late. You're too old, bald-headed man," send the bears of the Word upon them. Tell them that all things are still working together for good (Romans 8:28). Tell them that God will indeed complete that which He began (Philippians 1:6). Move out the mockers by standing on the Word of God. And then watch resurrection life surge into the promise that He gave you.

JULY 17

And he spake before his brethren and the army of Samaria, and said, What do these feeble Jews? will they fortify themselves? will they sacrifice? will they make an end in a day? will they revive the stones out of the heaps of the rubbish which are burnt? Now Tobiah the Ammonite was by him, and he said, Even that which they build, if a fox go up, he shall even break down their stone wall.

Nehemiah 4:2-3

Just as Sanballat addressed an army, our adversary has an army of demons. This life is a battleground, gang. That's why we shouldn't be surprised if sometimes we wake up feeling as though tanks had rolled over us. There's a war going on and sometimes we feel the fallout from it.

"Will these feeble Jews fortify themselves?" Sanballat asks. "Will they launch a rebellion against the king from their walled city? Will they really sacrifice once the walls are up, or will they simply live lives of luxury?" Sanballat's questions are the same ones Satan asks us. All of these questions deal with the future - and the Lord doesn't always answer questions that relate to our future because He tells us to "take no thought for the morrow" (see Matthew 6:34).

In John 13, we read that it was because Jesus knew from whence He came and where He was going that He was able to wash the disciples' feet. He wasn't concerned about the past or the future. Consequently, He could minister in the present moment. That's always the way it is. Faith takes care of the past because our sins are washed away. Hope secures the future because we know we're going to Heaven. That allows us to love in the present.

We are to walk by faith. Faith means we don't know what's ahead or around the next bend. All we need to know is that God is with us right now. You might be having lots of questions and dealing with lots of issues about the future. But the Lord would have you know that He wants to give you peace not that comes from your understanding, but that passes it (Philippians 4:7) so that you can say, "I trust You, Lord."

JULY 18

And I sent messengers unto them, saying, I am doing a great work . . .

Nehemiah 6:3 (a)

Notice that Nehemiah didn't say he was doing a great job. Rather, he said, "I'm involved in a great work. You guys thought it was hapless or hopeless. But I see it as holy and glorious."

Nehemiah's name means "comforter from God." Thus, the "Nehemiah" within us - the Holy Spirit - is doing a great work in us both corporately and individually. Yet, because the enemy wants us to doubt this, we need to learn the lesson of Simeon. The promise had been given to him that he would not die until he saw the Messiah. After waiting all his life for this promise to be fulfilled, the Spirit led him to the Temple.

"This is it!" he must have thought. "I will see Messiah at last!"

I'm sure he listened for the sound of chariot wheels and soldiers marching. Surely Messiah would be a military leader who would rescue the Jews from Roman oppression.

But all Simeon heard was a Baby's cry.

At that moment, he had a choice to make. He could have thought, "This is what I've been waiting for all my life? A Baby? What a waste!"

Instead, he did what I'm challenging us to do. He took the Baby and said, "I bless You, Father. I believe what You are going to do is mighty and massive" (see Luke 2).

I wonder if the Spirit hasn't given you a vision in your mind or a desire in your heart that you know is of Him. When it comes, will you choose to embrace it regardless of how small or weak it initially might seem? Will you, like Simeon, choose to say, "I believe this is the beginning of the fulfillment of what You promised, Lord"?

"Too much rubbish!" some will proclaim.

"It will never last," others will protest.

"Even a fox will knock it down," others will predict.

Will you be the one to say, "No, it's a great work the Lord is doing"? It might not be exactly what you were expecting or what you envisioned. But if you choose to embrace it as from God, you, like Nehemiah, will exhibit the one quality necessary for His work: faith (Hebrews 11:6).

JULY 19

For if thou altogether holdest thy peace at this time, then shall there enlargement and deliverance arise to the Jews from another place; but thou and thy father's house shall be destroyed: and who knoweth whether thou art come to the kingdom for such a time as this?

Esther 4:14

"Even if you choose not to step out, deliverance *will* come," Mordecai said to Esther. "But you will miss a glorious opportunity. And you will be destroyed in the process."

So too, if you're not interested in God's work, if you'd rather complain about your difficult situation or cruise in your easy one, God will still get His work done, but you'll perish - not physically, but the vibrancy of your walk, the joy of service, the opportunity and blessing of being used will be absent.

"Maybe you've come into this place as queen of Persia for such a time as this," Mordecai said to Esther. And the same is true of you, dear saint. You are where you are because God is in the shadows, steering the ship of your life. God is in control and He's placed you in your location for such a time as this because there are people for you to minister to, lives for you to touch, work for you to do. Nothing is accidental to the child of God. Even if your situation seems difficult, the Lord has you right where He wants you to be. He has you right where you are "for such a time as this," for the sake of the Kingdom.

JULY 20

So they hanged Haman on the gallows that he had prepared for Mordecai.

Esther 7:10 (a)

Our God has an incredible way of taking what Satan means for evil in our lives and turning it around for good. Joseph's brothers sold him into slavery. Years later, Joseph found himself prime minister, second only to Pharaoh. His brothers came before him, begging for food. And Joseph revealed his identity. When his brothers reacted in fear, Joseph said, "Don't fear. You meant it for evil, but God has turned it for good to save many people alive this day" (see Genesis 50:20).

That's a promise for you as well. "No weapon that is formed against thee shall prosper; and every tongue that shall rise against thee in judgment thou shalt condemn. This is the heritage of the servants of the LORD, and their righteousness is of me, saith the LORD" (Isaiah 54:17). Any attempt of Haman to come against you and destroy you will not prosper. It might seem like it's going to. The gallows might be built. The noose might be readied. And you might think it's all over for you. But if you're a child of His, God will miraculously and faithfully turn it for good.

I think of Satan putting Jesus Christ on the gallows of the Cross thinking that he had won. But God turned the tables, for it was Satan who was defeated that day. Only God can do that.

JULY 21

Then Job arose, and rent his mantle, and shaved his head, and fell down upon the ground, and worshipped, and said, Naked came I out of my mother's womb, and naked shall I return thither: the LORD gave, and the LORD hath taken away; blessed be the name of the LORD. In all this Job sinned not, nor charged God foolishly.

Job 1:20-22

A man of remarkable insight and maturity, Job released his emotion not through ranting and raving, cursing and complaining, weeping and wailing but through worship.

When Paul and Silas were in the dank, dark dungeon, they began to sing praises to the Lord. They began to worship the One they loved and served. And as they did, the prison doors opened wide. The amazing thing is, not a single prisoner escaped. Why? I suggest it was because they were so amazed that Paul and Silas praised God in the dungeon that they wanted to stick around and see how the rest of the story would unfold (Acts 16).

The same can be true of us. When you feel as though it's dark and damp and dank and dungeony, when you feel as though everything you were hoping for, everything you trusted in has been taken away, it's your opportunity to do what Job did, to do what Paul and Silas did. That is, you can say, "I'm going to worship You, Lord, because You're in control and You know what's best."

Job didn't have chapter 1 to read. He didn't know what was going on. He wouldn't know anything about Satan's challenge throughout his whole ordeal - and perhaps not until he got to Heaven. But that didn't matter. He chose to worship nonetheless and untold millions of lives have been impacted by his example.

JULY 22

But he said unto her, Thou speakest as one of the foolish women speaketh. What? shall we receive good at the hand of God, and shall we not receive evil? In all this did not Job sin with his lips.

Job 2:10

"Are we simply going to love God in the good times and not trust Him in the dark days?" Job asked his wife.

This is the lesson of Job: God does not exist for you. You exist for Him. All things were made by Him and *for* Him (Colossians 1:16). God can use us any way He chooses. Therefore He can put us in situations that might seem uncomfortable or difficult for reasons we may not understand this side of eternity.

After setting them free from bondage in Egypt, God positioned His people with their backs to the Red Sea. In other words, they were boxed in - with Pharaoh closing in on them. It seemed they were about to be wiped out. But God said, "I'm doing this for a reason. I'm putting you in a tough situation in order that Pharaoh and the Egyptians might see My glory" (see Exodus 14:4). The Sea would part. Blessings would be bestowed. God's people would eventually reach the Land of Promise. But not immediately. Therefore, I have to remember as I go through life that the Lord may put me in situations from time to time that are uncomfortable or difficult - in part that I might ultimately see how He'll come through for me, but also that the Egyptians around me might see His glory and come to know Him personally.

If we don't remember this as we both go through the Book of Job and through each day of our life, we'll be confused. Job is fulfilling a huge purpose that deals with the honor and integrity of God in the eyes of all eternity. But he didn't know it at the time.

Job is in physical pain and misery. He's distraught and distressed emotionally. He's bankrupt and wiped out financially. Yet, he doesn't sin by charging God foolishly. And in his submission to God's sovereignty, he's silencing Satan.

Maybe you wonder what's going on in your own life. Maybe you feel like you're being beat up and run over and you don't know why. It might be that in your choosing to submit to the sovereignty of God by worshipping Him passionately and spending time in His Word consistently that you, too, are silencing Satan. I guarantee that when Job got to Heaven, when he finally saw what had taken place, he didn't say, "What a waste." No, I'm sure he said, "Thank You, Lord, for allowing me the privilege of silencing Satan by simply trusting in Your sovereignty, by worshipping You even though I didn't have a clue what was going on."

JULY 23

Remember, I beseech thee, that thou hast made me as the clay; and wilt thou bring me into dust again?

Job 10:9

In Psalm 103, we read that our Father remembers that we are made of dust. Oftentimes, I think we expect more out of ourselves than God expects of us. We mistakenly think we're more than dust. No wonder we're shocked by what we find ourselves thinking or doing. God, however, isn't shocked. He's not even surprised. He knows our frames. He knows what we're made of. But He also knows what we're going to be. He sees us as already glorified in Christ Jesus (Romans 8:30).

If the Anaheim Angels called me and said, "Jon, we heard you're in town and we really need a pitcher because we're headed for the World Series." And if I agreed to come and take a few practice pitches, the ball would have gone right over the catcher's head and into the stands. But if, for some reason, the coach and the owner liked me, I would be given a uniform. I would be on the team. Yes, I would sit on the bench - but I would be on the team. Then, when the Angels won the World Series and the bonus checks were cut and the rings were distributed, when the team photo was taken and the parade took place at Disneyland - there I would be. Why? I can't pitch my way out of a paper bag; but, simply because I was on the team, because I wore the uniform, I would get the ring, the photo, the check, the parade, the whole thing.

That's the Gospel. Our Heavenly Father is the Owner. Our Lord and Savior is our Coach. They happen to like us and chose us for reasons that are beyond me! We're on Their team. We get the photo, the ring, and Heaven simply because we're robed in the righteous uniform of Christ Jesus (Isaiah 61:10; 2 Corinthians 5:21). Oh, happy day!

JULY 24

Wherefore do I take my flesh in my teeth, and put my life in mine hand? Though he slay me, yet will I trust in him . . .

Job 13:14-15 (a)

And with these words, Satan lost his bet. Although Job didn't navigate his difficulty perfectly, he completely shuts Satan down right here. "Even if I don't understand what God is doing, even though it seems to be unfair, even if He should slay me in the process, yet I will trust Him," Job proclaims. Yes, Job's faith will falter - but here it's ignited.

It's one thing to have faith for healing. It's a greater thing to have faith for sickness. That is, it takes greater faith to say, "I come to You for healing. But, Lord, should You, as You did to Paul, say, 'My grace is sufficient,' I will still trust You. I have faith in You - not faith that I can get You to do what I want You to do - but faith that You will do what's best."

Even if the affliction doesn't go away, even if the problem continues, even if the solution doesn't come, faith says, "Though You slay me, I will still trust You because You were slain for me. You gave up everything because You love me. Therefore, I embrace whatever You decide to do. You see things I don't. You know things I can't."

Here, with his body broken out in boils, with his worldly possessions and his family taken from him, with his friends relentlessly accusing him, faith flares up in Job.

JULY 25

If a man die, shall he live again?

Job 14:14 (a)

This is the ultimate question: Can man live again? "All of the days of my life, I will wait for that, Lord," Job says. "When You call, I'll answer." Here, again, Job expresses hope.

If you're not going through a trial presently, you will at some point. And when you do, remember Job. When does his faith flare up? Whenever he talks about living again, whenever he remembers the reality of eternity. Although it's hazy to him, when he focuses on Heaven, suddenly there's hope in his heart.

That's why Jesus talked about Heaven immediately after telling His disciples one of them would betray Him and that He was about to die (John 13:33-14:3). For hopeless and heavy hearts, the solution is always Heaven. That's why the people of Israel were commanded by the Lord to put blue on the borders of their garments (Numbers 15:38). Blue is the color of

Heaven. Thus, they would be reminded that they were just passing through, that they were a Heavenly people, with every step they took.

"Let not your heart be troubled," Jesus said. "You believe in God, believe also in Me. In My Father's house are many mansions and I go to prepare a place for you, that where I am, you may be also" (see John 14:1-2). When we go through difficulties, trials, and heartaches, we can either let our hearts be troubled or keep them from being troubled. The choice is ours. It's not just a matter of positive thinking, but of thinking about what really matters. And what really matters is eternity. With every step you take, may your thoughts be of Heaven.

JULY 26

For I know that my Redeemer liveth, and that he shall stand at the latter day upon the earth: and though after my skin worms destroy this body, yet in my flesh shall I see God . . .

Job 19:25-26

The word "redeemer" or *goel*, speaks of one who can set free, purchase back, recoup what has been lost.

In chapter 9, Job said, "I wish I had a daysman" (see verse 33).

In chapter 16, he said, "I wish I had an advocate" (see verse 19).

Here in chapter 19, he says, "I know I have a Redeemer."

An increasingly clear and powerful revelation takes place as Job's tribulation continues. That's the way it works in spiritual life. Job is confused, but there are fantastic revelations that come his way in the midst of his personal tribulation - and that's what we will discover as well. In the time of tribulation, there is inevitably grand and glorious revelation of who our Lord is. From Genesis through Revelation, we see this theme over and over again. Whenever God's people go through tribulation and difficulty, testing and trial, they inevitably receive fresh understanding and revelation concerning the nature, the character, and the reality of our Lord.

We see not only revelation, but redirection. That is, when Job was at the bottom, he started thinking about eternity in a way he perhaps never would have had everything remained comfortable. I'm convinced that prosperity is a far greater problem for us than persecution is because when we're prosperous, we tend not to think about eternity or Heaven. We start living for this life. So, in His goodness, the Lord says to us, "In order to get you thinking about Heaven - where you're going to spend the next gazillion years - to get your focus off of the football game, your backyard, or your car, I will send challenges, trials, and difficulties your way. When you're at the bottom the only place you can look is up."

Tensions in relationships, setbacks in business, debilitating illnesses all make us long for Heaven. That's why the Lord allows them to come into our lives. Without them, we would be too rooted in a world that is passing away. And God loves us too much for that.

Job would have greater understanding of who God is and a greater hope for the future solely because of his losses and difficulties. "In my flesh, I will see God," he declares. "This is not the end of the road for me."

JULY 27

And unto man he said, Behold, the fear of the Lord, that is wisdom; and to depart from evil is understanding.

Job 28:28

After referring extensively to mining the earth for gems and jewels, Job ponders how to discover the gems and jewels of wisdom. He concludes that the way to do so is to listen to what the Lord declares and decrees. Solomon said it is the fear of the Lord that is the beginning of wisdom (Proverbs 9:10). Paul would go on to say that all the treasures of wisdom and knowledge are found in Jesus (Colossians 2:3). I rediscovered that this morning. Pondering some things, I grabbed my Bible and a cup of coffee and made my way to a small park. Enjoying the stars overhead as they broke through the clouds, I talked to the Lord about what was on my heart and my mind.

And I came away from that quiet place having the wisdom I needed for the morning. It's amazing! The Lord will *truly* meet us.

Everything you need to know about how to get through the rest of this day or tomorrow will be found in God - in talking to Him, in walking with Him, in being in awe of Him. The fear of the Lord is not an abstract concept. The fear of the Lord simply says, "Lord, You're awesome, gracious, and good. And I need You desperately. So I'm going to begin this day with You because in You are all the treasures of wisdom and knowledge."

If we don't fear the Lord, gang, we'll fear everything else. But if we fear Him, we'll have nothing else to fear.

JULY 28

I chose out their way, and sat chief, and dwelt as a king in the army, as one that comforteth the mourners.

Job 29:25

"I was both a commander and a comforter."

Remembering past blessings actually improves Job's present situation. This should not be surprising. In Deuteronomy 8, God declares, "Thou shalt remember all the ways the Lord thy God led thee." Fourteen more times in the Book of Deuteronomy alone, God commands His people to remember. In days of difficulty, in times of despair, in seasons of despondency, how important it is to simply remember God and the gracious blessings He showers upon us daily (Psalm 68:19).

> Will the Lord cast off for ever? And will he be favourable no more? Is his mercy clean gone for ever? Doth his promise fail for evermore? Hath God forgotten to be gracious? Hath he in anger shut up his tender mercies? Selah. And I said, This is my infirmity: but I will remember the years of the right hand of the most High. I will remember the works of the LORD: surely I will remember thy wonders of old. I will

meditate also of all thy work, and talk of thy doings. Thy way, O God, is in the sanctuary: who is so great a God as our God?

Psalm 77:7-13

Walking through his own dark days, the psalmist says, "Will I ever be blessed again?" Then he adds the word *selah* - an instruction to wait or stop. After that, he goes on to say, "I'm going to look back and remember what God has done for me - the grace He's shown me, the blessings He has sent my way."

In this day when so many are depressed, it's necessary to remember what God has already done and to realize that, because He saw us through in the past, He's sure to see us through in the future. C. H. Spurgeon said that too often too many of us write our blessings in sand and our infirmities in marble. We focus on our pain and problems - but that ought not be. We must be those who remember, recall, and reflect upon all God has done for us.

"How can this be?" the host of the wedding party said. "Most men serve the good wine at first and the cheaper wine at the end when no one would notice the difference. But you have kept the best for last" (see John 2). Why was the best wine saved for last? Because that's always the way of the Lord. He always takes us from glory to greater glory (2 Corinthians 3:18).

Job will lament in the next chapter - but here, he's saying, "Wait a minute. God has been good to me."

And so must we.

JULY 29

Hear, I beseech thee, and I will speak: I will demand of thee, and declare thou unto me. I have heard of thee by the hearing of the ear: but now mine eye seeth thee. Wherefore I abhor myself, and repent in dust and ashes.

Job 42:4-6

I believe this is the key to the entire Book of Job: "I heard about You, but now that I see You, I abhor myself." Remember, Job was the most righteous man on the face of the earth. And yet the most righteous man on the face of the earth realized he was nothing in the presence of God.

You might feel secure in your theology, but if you chatter endlessly, perhaps it's indicative that you've heard about God without seeing Him. Many Christians know a lot about God, but many have not had revelation of Him. Notice that Job doesn't say, "I abhor Eliphaz, Bildad, and Zophar." He says, "I abhor *myself.*"

If the most righteous man on the face of the earth needed to come to a place of repentance, how much more do I need to come before the Lord and say, "Lord, forgive me. Have mercy upon me. I need You to save me. I need Your blood to cleanse me."

Earlier, Job had maintained his righteousness and integrity. But now that he has seen the Lord, all he can say is, "I repent in dust and ashes." Does this mean he's getting right with God? I don't think this is the idea here. Rather, I think it proves that he has been right with God all along. Even though he had questions, even though he wrestled through problems, once the Lord comes on the scene and raises questions to him about creation, about spiritual issues and mysteries, Job responds accordingly.

Over many years, I have observed that at summer camp, the kids who respond at the campfire are not necessarily the ones who are just then getting right with God. More often than not, they're the ones who are already right with Him because their heart is sensitive enough to respond. It's the ones who don't respond who often have a problem.

James calls Job an example to us of what godly patience looks like (5:11). In Ezekiel 14, Job is in the category with Noah and Daniel as exceedingly righteous men. I believe these references give God's viewpoint of Job's character throughout his ordeal, not just at the conclusion of it.

JULY 30

So the LORD blessed the latter end of Job more than his beginning: for he had fourteen thousand sheep, and six thousand camels, and a thousand yoke of oxen, and a thousand she asses. He had also seven sons and three daughters.

Job 42:12-13

Some people find the end of this story a bit unsatisfying. They're happy that Job came out so well, but wonder why didn't God answer the questions Job raised. I suggest it is because, in the presence of the Lord, Job found every answer he needed.

Looking back over Job's incredible journey, I see six lessons for us . . .

First, trials and difficulties prepare us for eternity. God wants to develop our faith. That means we won't often see with our eyes what He's doing.

Second, Satan is silenced by submission to God's sovereignty. I'm convinced that when we get to Heaven, we're going to discover that a great deal of the difficulty we experienced on earth was simply God proving to the enemy that we're not mercenaries, that we're not hirelings, that He hasn't bought us off with blessings and ease.

When we go through difficulties and misunderstandings, hurts, pains and problems financially, mentally or emotionally; when we persevere, and like Job, do not curse God or rebel against Him - even though we might have questions for Him, if our attitude is one of worship - Satan is silenced. And when we see the Lord, He'll embrace us and say, "Well done, good and faithful servant. You silenced Satan - and you didn't even know it. Satan was accusing you day and night saying, 'If that marriage isn't healed, she'll curse You; if that job doesn't open, he'll deny You; if that answer doesn't come, he'll backslide from You.' But you didn't. I allowed Satan to touch you within certain parameters to prove that you are not a mercenary, that you really do love Me."

Third, suffering produces clearer vision of ourselves and of God. In suffering, Job finally saw he was a vile man. So too, when we go through trials and don't react properly, when we hear ourselves saying foolish things, we realize that we're less mature than we thought and say, "Lord, I need You. I'm vile. I need Your blood." If you've gone through deep waters, your understanding and vision of God will increase exponentially. You'll see the Lord in a new dimension. What does this do? It makes us no longer fear suffering the way we once did. Jesus becomes so real and precious that we begin to reach the point where we say, "Trials and testing are worth it because they allow me to see myself in my vileness and the Lord in His holiness."

Fourth, suffering produces compassion. It was when Job saw he was vile himself that he embraced his friends. When do we have compassion for others who are hurting and troubled? After we've been through our own difficulties and trials. That is why Paul would write, "Blessed be the Father who comforts us that we may be able to comfort others with the comfort we ourselves have received" (see 2 Corinthians 1:3-4).

Fifth, suffering teaches us humility. It was when Job was humble that he saw the Lord. Humiliation always brings revelation, for it's when we're going through hard times that we get fresh insight into the Lord and receive revelation of the Lord.

Finally, suffering has a happy ending. Even if you are never healed, you will be in Heaven. Even if you're poor on this earth, you'll live in a mansion in eternity. Peter talks about the trial of faith and about the angels who desire to look into these things (1 Peter 1:12). This means that what we go through is not just about us. It's about eternity. It was for the joy that awaited Him that Jesus endured the Cross (Hebrews 12:2). Even on earth, at the end of the story, Job was given twice as much as he had before. That's always the way of the Lord, as He takes us from glory to greater glory (2 Corinthians 3:18), from sorrow to unspeakable joy (John 16:20).

JULY 31

How long wilt thou forget me, O LORD? for ever? How long wilt thou hide thy face from me? How long shall I take counsel in my soul, having sorrow in my heart daily? How long shall mine enemy be exalted over me? Consider and hear me, O LORD my God: lighten mine eyes, lest I sleep the sleep of death; lest mine enemy say, I have prevailed against him; and those that trouble me rejoice when I am moved. But I have trusted in thy mercy; my heart shall rejoice in thy salvation. I will sing unto the LORD, because he hath dealt bountifully with me.

Psalm 13:1-6

In six verses, David goes from a sigh to a song, from the blues to being blessed. Why? Simply because he prayed. Feeling forsaken and forgotten, he prays. And by the time he's done, the Lord has met him.

I think sometimes we believe the lie from the enemy that says, "It can't be that simple. It will take many months of prayer to break through and get victory over my depression, over my addiction, over my situation." But I suggest this psalm tells us differently. In no more time than it takes to pen these six verses, David finds release, relief, and victory. In other words, it doesn't take as much as we think.

"Don't think you'll be heard because of your much speaking," Jesus said (see Matthew 6:7). And, as if to underscore this, the model prayer He gave His disciples was only sixty-five words long (Matthew 6:9-13).

About a year and a half later, the disciples came to Jesus and said, "Lord, teach us to pray." No doubt they were thinking the first model prayer He gave was fine for beginners. But now that they had walked with Him, they could handle something more complex. What did Jesus do? He gave them the same prayer He had given them earlier - but shortened it to fifty-eight words (Luke 11:2-4). The disciples were no doubt expecting volumes. I suggest it was with a twinkle in His eye that the Lord said, "It's simpler than you think."

Like David, I have discovered that, no matter how overwhelming the situation, if I'll just pull away and pray, the Lord meets me. He really, truly does. Talk to the Lord. Question Him. Be honest with Him. And you'll find that the Lord will meet you. The old adage that prayer changes things is true. But the real thing prayer changes is us.

AUGUST 1

Keep me as the apple of the eye, hide me under the shadow of thy wings.

Psalm 17:8

Scripture records that, even in the "waste howling wilderness," God kept Jacob as the apple of His eye (Deuteronomy 32:10). Here, David asks that Jacob's protection be extended to him.

The apple of the eye is the pupil. We are told that the reflex which covers the eye is the quickest reflex in the body. When there's danger coming toward your face, your eye will close in 1/10,000[th] of a second. And the speed with which your eyelid closes to protect your eye is the speed with which the Lord protects His children.

An eagle makes a massive nest; eggs are laid; and Ernie eaglet is born. Hatching out of his egg, Ernie enjoys the grand view. Day by day, he grows bigger until one day, Mama Eagle jars the nest and Ernie is knocked out. Squawking and frantically flapping his little wings, Ernie thinks he's dying as he falls, falls, falls hundreds of feet, headed for certain destruction on the rocks below. But right then, Mama swoops down, catches Ernie on her wings, and puts him back in the nest. No sooner does Ernie calm down than Mama jostles the nest again. Angry and upset, Ernie falls again. And again, right before certain death, Mama is there, bearing him on her wings. The process is repeated until something happens - until instead of being sore, Ernie begins to soar.

"I'm not going to let you hit bottom," the Lord says to us. "But I will tip your nest from time to time because I want to teach you to fly."

August 2

The king shall joy in thy strength, O LORD; and in thy salvation how greatly shall he rejoice! Thou hast given him his heart's desire, and hast not withholden the request of his lips. Selah.

Psalm 21:1-2

This refers, of course, to the Kings of kings, Jesus Christ. What is Jesus' heart's desire? In John 17, He prayed,

Father, the hour is come; glorify thy Son, that thy Son also may glorify thee: as thou hast given him power over all flesh, that he should give eternal life to as many as thou hast given him. And this is life eternal, that they might know thee the only true God, and Jesus Christ, whom thou hast sent.

John 17:1-3

In other words, the desire of the King of kings is that you might know Him. In Psalm 20, we read, "May the Lord grant the king according to his heart" (see verse 4). Here, the Lord has given Him His heart's desire.

Psalm 37:4 says, "Delight yourself in the LORD: and he shall give thee the desires of thine heart." This is the great thing about being a believer. This is how the Lord works in guiding and directing us. He writes His will upon the table of our hearts. Jeremiah calls it the New Covenant (31:31). Paul says it's God working in us both to will and to do of His good pleasure (Philippians 2:13).

If you're delighting in the Lord and staying connected to Him, He will give you the desires of your heart because those desires will be from Him. That's the way He directs and guides.

God puts desires in my heart, but I still have the responsibility to pray, to ask for those things stirring within me. "You have not because you ask not," James plainly says (see 4:2).

"Ask and it shall be given. Seek and you shall find. Knock and it shall be opened to you," Jesus said (see Matthew 7:7). The verb tense is literally

"*Keep* asking, *keep* seeking, *keep* knocking." Why? Because in the very act of prayer, our desires are adjusted.

"Father, if it be possible, let this cup pass from Me," Jesus prayed. "Nevertheless, not My will, but Thine, be done," He added, committing Himself to obey His Father no matter the cost (see Luke 22:42).

AUGUST 3

I will bless the LORD at all times: his praise shall continually be in my mouth. My soul shall make her boast in the LORD: the humble shall hear thereof, and be glad.

Psalm 34:1-2

Fleeing from Saul, David found himself in Goliath's hometown, the city of Gath. Achish, the king - also known as Abimelech - welcomed David. But when the people recognized him as the one who killed their hero, Goliath, David knew he had to leave. So he pretended to be insane. Spittle ran down his beard as he clawed at the gate.

"I don't need another madman in this city," Achish said.

So David was released (1 Samuel 21).

At this time of difficulty - a time when he was being hunted by the enemy, shunned by his countrymen, threatened by the Philistines - David penned this psalm of praise. Notice his determination. He says, "I will bless the LORD." The word "bless" means "to confer happiness or prosperity upon another." It's amazing to think that we actually have the ability to bring happiness and prosperity to the God of the universe. Yet He genuinely enjoys hearing our praise. We are those who have been blessed by the Lord. But we also have the ability to bless Him back.

"I will bless the LORD," David declared - not just in good times, not just in easy times, but in *all* times.

"That's easy for David," you say. "He was a king in a palace with servants and all of the money he wanted."

Wait a minute. This psalm was not written under those conditions. In fact, with the king of Israel hunting him and the entire city of Gath suspicious of him, I suggest that not one of us is in a more perilous place than was David when he penned this psalm.

I'm convinced that one of our Father's favorite attitudes is that of gratitude because we see story after story where His people ended up in big trouble - bitten by snakes, swallowed by the earth - when they murmured and complained (Numbers 16; 21).

C. H. Spurgeon wisely said, "He who praises God for blessings will always have blessings for which to praise God." One of the reasons I believe David was so blessed was because he purposed in his heart to be one who praised God.

AUGUST 4

O continue thy lovingkindness unto them that know thee;
and thy righteousness to the upright in heart.

Psalm 36:10

"O continue thy lovingkindness," or literally, "Draw out at length, stretch out Your lovingkindness to those who know You." Jeremiah 31:3 tells us that God has loved us with an everlasting love. It just goes on and on and on.

The famed opera house in the city of Paris was scheduled to host a well-known operatic singer. The day of the performance, the singer came down with the flu and had to cancel his engagement. But it was too late to alert the ticket holders. So when the guests arrived in the great opera hall, the host came before the people and said, "We regret to inform you that our singer could not be here tonight. He is ill. A local singer will be singing tonight instead." The local singer took the stage. The audience greeted him with silence. The man sang with all his heart. People listened patiently, but were not very impressed. So when he finished, there was no applause whatsoever. But then, from the top balcony, a little voice was heard to say, "Daddy, I think you were wonderful."

Upon hearing that, the entire opera house began to clap and eventually gave the singer a standing ovation.

Others might not be very impressed by you. But there is One in your balcony who says, "I think you're wonderful." And He's the only One who matters because it's God Himself.

AUGUST 5

The steps of a good man are ordered by the LORD: and he delighteth in his way. Though he fall, he shall not be utterly cast down: for the LORD upholdeth him with his hand.

Psalm 37:23-24

If you love the Lord, your steps are being ordered by Him. The events in your life - the circumstances where you work or study, the situations at home - are all ordered by the Lord. And if you stumble along the way, He won't cast you off. He won't kick you out. He'll just pick you back up and keep you going with His own hand . . .

"Lord, save me!" Peter cried as he sank beneath the waves. And Matthew says Jesus stretched forth His hand, lifted a drenched Peter out of the water, and plopped him back in the boat (Matthew 14:30-31). That's a strong hand!

Riding on an unbroken donkey, the hand of Jesus was able to control the animal (Matthew 21:7). That's a strong hand!

Jesus was able to overturn tables and throw out the moneychangers (John 2:15). That's a strong hand!

The hand of Jesus is strong yet scarred, for there is a hole in it from the nail driven through it to pay the penalty for my sin. It is this very hand that picks you up and sees you through.

AUGUST 6

For I said, Hear me, lest otherwise they should rejoice over me: when my foot slippeth, they magnify themselves against me. For I am ready to halt, and my sorrow is continually before me.

Psalm 38:16-17

In this psalm of remembrance that David has the entire nation sing, he says, "I am ready to halt," or literally, "I'm about to fall."

I think of two stories . . .

One day, Jesus went to the pool of Bethesda where a man was lying. "Rise, take up your bed, and walk," Jesus said to him. And immediately that man stood, took up his bed, and walked. But when the religious leaders asked him who it was that healed him, the man couldn't tell them. He was evidently so thrilled to be healed that he didn't have time to wonder who had done it (John 5:13).

The second man was a can-do kind of guy. So clever was Jacob that he was able to talk his own brother out of his birthright and blessing. Following that, everything Jacob touched seemed to turn to gold. Everything seemed to be going well until he heard that his brother was coming to see him - accompanied by four hundred fighting men. Jacob was worried. As he camped by the brook Jabbok on the evening before he would meet his brother, the Angel of the Lord came to him and wrestled with him. "I'm not going to let you go until You bless me," Jacob vowed. As morning dawned, the Angel of the Lord dislocated Jacob's hip as if to say, "You're not going to be Jacob - or "heel-snatcher" - any longer. You're going to be *Israel*, or "governed by God." Jacob arose - but would walk as a broken man who would need to lean on the Rock of his salvation, who would need to be governed by God each step of the way. Thus, in his weakness, he was indeed made stronger (Genesis 32).

Sometimes the Lord allows us to limp permanently because it forces us to lean on Him. "Why am I still struggling with that?" we wonder. "Why is that temptation or problem back again?"

I suggest it is the Lord saying, "I want you to lean on Me. You'll draw close to Me in ways you never would have otherwise." Maybe you've been set free - but perhaps the Lord is taking you into deeper water. He wants to do more than give you victory, He wants to be your Victor. I suggest that is why David declares that he is ready to halt if that's what it takes for him to lean on the Lord every step of the way.

AUGUST 7

As the hart panteth after the water brooks, so panteth my soul after thee, O God. My soul thirsteth for God, for the living God . . .

Psalm 42:1-2 (a)

Maybe in a dry region, the psalmist saw a deer drinking water from a stream. Maybe it was this sight that prompted him to say, "That's exactly how I feel. My heart is thirsty. My soul is longing for God."

Augustine put it this way: Our hearts are restless until they find their rest in Thee.

Although people might not be aware of it or be able to articulate it, the fact is, God is what every soul craves. That is why Jesus said that it was only he who drank of the water He gave who would never thirst again (John 4:14).

Sometimes, late at night, I'll think I'm craving something. So I'll pour a bowl - or two - or three - of Mini-Wheats. When that doesn't satisfy me,

I'll watch the news or read *Time* magazine. But then, when I finally come to my senses, I turn off the TV, throw away the empty box of cereal, and say, "Lord, what I really need is just to spend time with You." And, without fail, as I do, I am truly, deeply satisfied and fulfilled.

If you're thirsting, perhaps it's because you've been drinking at the old watering holes, trying to find satisfaction in the world. Come to the Lord. Drink of Him. Draw nigh to Him and He'll draw nigh to you. That's not my word. It's His (James 4:8).

AUGUST 8

Why art thou cast down, O my soul? and why art thou disquieted within me? Hope thou in God: for I shall yet praise him, who is the health of my countenance, and my God.

Psalm 42:11

"I shall yet praise Him" doesn't mean "someday I'm going to praise Him," or "someday I'll be able to look back and honor Him." No, the Hebrew language is clear that the psalmist would praise God presently.

This is so powerful and so practical. Even as he's working through his own emotional difficulty, the psalmist says, "Here's what I'm going to do: I'm going to hope in God - absolutely expecting things are going to work out for my good and His glory. I'm going to talk to God. I'm going to be honest with the Lord. He knows what I'm thinking, anyway. So I'm just going to tell Him when I feel forgotten."

The psalmist hopes in God. He talks to God. And he praises God. It is so important that we learn to be people who praise God. It was one thing when Miriam and the congregation of Israel praised the Lord after they were delivered from the oncoming Egyptians (Exodus 15). But how much better it would have been had they praised God *before* the Red Sea parted. The key is to say, "Lord, even though I don't see how this is going to work out, I know You'll never leave me nor forsake me. And I know that all things work together for good for me. Therefore, I'm going to praise You in advance."

When Silas and Paul were in the Philippian prison at midnight praising the Lord, an earthquake jolted the doors open. Assuming all the prisoners had fled, the jailer was about to take his life when Paul said, "Wait a minute. We're all here" (Acts 16). Why had no one left? I suggest it was because the other prisoners saw something in Paul and Silas that so intrigued them that they wanted to stick around and see how it all played out. They wanted to be free like Paul and Silas were - not only externally but, more important, internally.

That's what happens in our lives as well. When we say, "I'm going to hope in You, Lord," the imprisoned world around us takes note and is drawn to Him.

Before the Red Sea parts and before the prison doors open is your moment for greatness. Don't miss it.

AUGUST 9

Be merciful unto me, O God, be merciful unto me: for my soul trusteth in thee: yea, in the shadow of thy wings will I make my refuge, until these calamities be overpast.

Psalm 57:1

Psalm 57 deals with the mercy of God. Hiding from Saul, David was camped out in a cave at En-Gedi, near the Dead Sea. When Saul made his way into the same cave, not knowing David was already there, David's men were jubilant. "This is your opportunity to wipe Saul out!" they said. But David wouldn't do that. Instead, he merely cut a piece of cloth from Saul's skirt - more than likely from the hem of the garment, which would have spoken of Saul's pedigree and position. You see, in Bible days, knots were tied to the hems of garments in such a way that they signified a man's family, tribe, and position. Thus, by cutting the garment of Saul, David, in a sense, was cutting off Saul's position. Later, we are told, David's heart smote him, for he knew he must not touch the Lord's anointed (1 Samuel 24:5).

Maybe there's someone chasing you down, hurling spears in your direction, trying to wipe you out, treating you unfairly or cruelly. Here's what you need to remember: that person is anointed by the Lord to work His purposes in your life, to make you into the man or woman He desires you to be in order that you might rule with Him more effectively. If I retaliate and throw spears back, I'm missing the point, missing what God is doing in my life. The Lord knows. He'll remove Saul in due season. But in the meantime, any given person or situation in your life could be the very instrument God is using to make you into a better person than you otherwise would be. And David understood this.

In clipping Saul's garment, David knew that he had missed God's best. So he asks the Lord to be merciful to him. "Blessed are the merciful," Jesus said, "for they shall obtain mercy" (Matthew 5:7). David had shown mercy in not lopping off Saul's head. Thus he could ask for mercy to be shown to him.

In Luke 6, Jesus talks about the importance of mercy . . .

> But love ye your enemies, and do good, and lend, hoping for nothing again; and your reward shall be great, and ye shall be the children of the Highest: for he is kind unto the unthankful and to the evil. Be ye therefore merciful, as your Father also is merciful. Judge not, and ye shall not be judged: condemn not, and ye shall not be condemned: forgive, and ye shall be forgiven: give, and it shall be given unto you; good measure, pressed down, and shaken together, and running over, shall men give into your bosom. For with the same measure that ye mete withal it shall be measured to you again.
>
> Luke 6:35-38

"Give, and it shall be given unto you." Jesus isn't talking about money. He's talking about mercy. Every one of us is in need of mercy. We all drop the ball. We all fall short. God has been merciful to us - but we need mercy from each other as well. Therefore, if you want to receive mercy in your hour of difficulty, be merciful to others.

When people were spitting on Him, hurling curses at Him, Jesus didn't pray, "Father, forgive them when they realize what they've done and repent of it." No, He prayed, "Father, forgive them even now because they don't understand what they're doing" (see Luke 23:34).

That's always the way it is. When people are mean-spirited and throwing spears, it's because they don't see the big picture, the Biblical perspective. That is why we need to do what Jesus did. We don't need to be vengeful, we need to be merciful. We don't need to throw spears back at them. We need to pray for them.

AUGUST 10

For thy mercy is great unto the heavens, and thy truth unto the clouds. Be thou exalted, O God, above the heavens: let thy glory be above all the earth.

Psalm 57:10-11

Sometimes people say, "I know I'm not supposed to be bitter at her or upset with him, but I can't help it. What can I do?" I suggest two simple keys: First, pray for your enemies. Who is the person who bugs you? I dare you to pray, "Lord, bless him. Guide his steps. Draw him to You. Work wonders in his life." You see, when we pray that way for our enemies, something happens. Yes, they may change - but whether or not they change, my feelings and perspective about them changes because I pour treasure into them through prayer. And Jesus said that wherever our treasure is, there will our heart be also (Luke 12:34). I've found time and again that when I pray for people who irritate me, I become interested in them, wondering what the Lord is doing in answer to my prayer.

Second, come to the Lord's Table. Eat of His body and drink of His blood. And as you do, remember that His blood was shed and His body was broken not only for you, but for the very person who bugs you. Jesus is passionately in love with the very person who irritates you. He paid completely and fully for their sin - just as He did for yours.

How did David ultimately feel about Saul? What did he do when Saul died? The man after God's own heart wept (2 Samuel 1:11).

AUGUST 11

God be merciful unto us, and bless us; and cause his face to shine upon us; Selah. That thy way may be known upon earth, thy saving health among all nations.

Psalm 67:1-2

Psalm 67 swings on the hinge of the first word of verse 2: That. "Bless us God," the psalmist writes, "*That* Thy way may be known upon the earth." In other words, "Bless us, God, so that we, in turn, might be a blessing."

So many teachings center on how we can be healthy, wealthy, or happy - as if health, wealth, and happiness were ends in themselves. God does want to bless us, but the purpose is that all the earth may be brought to Him. This was God's intention all along for the people of Israel. They were chosen to be a blessing, a light to all the nations . . .

> I will also give thee for a light to the Gentiles, that thou mayest be my salvation unto the end of the earth.
>
> Isaiah 49:6

"I'm choosing you, Israel, that you might be a light unto the nations, that they might see in you My beauty, My reality, and be drawn to Me," God said. The Jews were to be looking out, reaching out to a world that was lost in darkness. They were to be a light, a witness of who God is. But they lost sight of this calling. In fact, they eventually began to view Gentiles as simply fuel to keep hell hot. They had no compassion for the Gentiles and, as a result, turned inward. As they did, things began to sour.

The same thing can happen to us. Like Israel, we can begin to turn inward. We can lose our desire to share our faith. And, I know from experience, that when I stop sharing my faith, I tend to turn inward and become dry.

In the north of Israel lies the Sea of Galilee. It teems with life. But in the south, there is another body of water: the Dead Sea. There's no life there. Why? In the Sea of Galilee, there is inflow and outflow. The Jordan River comes in and flows through. In the Dead Sea, however, although there is an inflow, there is no outflow. Consequently, the saline content of the water has built up to the point where nothing can grow. The same thing can be true of us spiritually. If you feel like the Dead Sea, it could very well be because there is not an outflow in your life.

If I'm not looking for people to reach out to, I miss my calling, my purpose, and suddenly, my walk is dry. Bible study will be boring. Prayer will be meaningless. Devotion will be nonexistent. Praise will be an effort. But when I say, "Lord, bless me so I can go to work and share the Gospel, so that I can tell someone he's loved by You," suddenly my prayer life will have purpose, the Word will come alive, and praise will overflow once again.

AUGUST 12

Blessed is the man whose strength is in thee; in whose heart are the ways of them. Who passing through the valley of Baca make it a well; the rain also filleth the pools. They go from strength to strength, every one of them in Zion appeareth before God.

Psalm 84:5-7

The psalmist is thinking about those who would make their way to the Tabernacle, and later, to the Temple. Leaving their villages, as all of the men were commanded to do three times yearly, families would travel together to Jerusalem to worship the Lord. No doubt, they would anticipate coming into the city and being in the presence of the Lord. But on the way, they would pass through the valley of Baca. The root of the word *baca* means "weeping." We're not sure where this valley is geographically. It could even be a poetic picture the psalmist is painting. However, whatever the case historically, we can find ourselves going through tearful valleys presently.

The tears we shed on our way to the house of the Lord - toward Heaven, ultimately - actually form pools that provide refreshment for others on their own pilgrimage. That is why Paul would write, "Blessed be the Father of mercy, the God of all comfort who comforts us in our trouble in order that we may be able to comfort others with the comfort we ourselves have received (see 2 Corinthians 1:3-4).

You can't be a comforter unless you've been comforted. And you can't be comforted unless you've been uncomfortable. So God allows us the privilege of being made uncomfortable from time to time, to walk through the valley of Baca, so that the One who wipes away every tear can minister deeply to us in order that we can help others (Revelation 21:4). The Lord is so good to allow us to experience what Paul calls the fellowship of suffering (Philippians 3:10) that we might help others and let them know the Lord will see them through, even as He has done for us.

AUGUST 13

For the LORD God is a sun and shield: the LORD will give grace and glory: no good thing will he withhold from them that walk uprightly.

Psalm 84:11

The Lord is a sun to warm us and a shield - or, literally, shade - to protect us. Grace is unmerited, unearned, undeserved favor. Glory, or *chabod* in Hebrew, means "substance" or "weightiness." What a dynamic combination: the substance of glory and the gift of grace.

If I'm walking with the Lord - not perfectly, but simply if my heart is right - I can be absolutely assured that there is not one good thing He'll hold back from me. We make our requests to Him. We talk things over with Him. We cast our cares upon Him. And we can know with absolute certainty that whatever we desire will come our way - if it's a good thing. If it doesn't come our way, it simply means it's not truly good.

Even as she worshipped Him, Jesus realized Salome had another agenda. I picture Him with a smile on His face and a gleam in His eye as He said to her, "Tell Me what you want. "

"Can my two boys, James and John, be on Your right hand and left hand when You come into Your kingdom?" Salome asked.

Jesus looked at her and said, "Can they drink of the cup that I drink of and be baptized with My baptism?"

James and John answered, "Yes" (Matthew 20:20-22).

A few days later, at the foot of the Cross, Salome must have heard the thief say to Jesus, "Lord, remember me as You come into your kingdom" (see Luke 23:42).

And when Jesus said, "Today you will be with Me in paradise," His answer must have hit her like a ton of bricks. No wonder He didn't grant her request. She was unknowingly asking that her boys be crucified on His right and left.

If you're praying and things aren't happening, know that the Lord sees what you don't see and knows what you can't know. Remember Salome - and trust Him to do what's best for you.

AUGUST 14

Blessed is the people that know the joyful sound: they shall walk, O LORD, in the light of thy countenance. In thy name shall they rejoice all the day . . .

Psalm 89:15-16 (a)

How can you rejoice all the day? If you really want to be happy, consider the names of the Lord . . .

He identified Himself to Moses as I AM THAT I AM (Exodus 3:14). I'm sure Moses thought, *"You are . . . what?"* But the implication is that God would be whatever Moses had need of.

"I am Jehovah-Ropheka," God declared (Exodus 15:26), the God Who heals. Is your heart hurting? Is your spirit wounded? Call upon Jehovah-Ropheka.

He is Jehovah-Jireh (Genesis 22:14), the Lord who provides.

He is Jehovah-Nissi (Exodus 17:15), the Lord our banner, or covering. If you feel exposed or insecure, call upon Jehovah-Nissi.

He is Jehovah-Tsidkenu (Jeremiah 23:6), the Lord our righteousness. Do you feel flawed? God is your righteousness.

He is El Shaddai (Genesis 17:1). *El* speaks of strength. *Shad* speaks of the breast. Thus, this is the picture of a God Who is strong, yet as tender as a mother with her newborn baby.

He is Abba (Mark 14:36), our Father. When I feel I just need to talk things over with someone and receive wisdom and direction, I turn to Him, my Abba.

The names of the Lord cause our hearts to rejoice indeed.

AUGUST 15

My mercy will I keep for him for evermore, and my covenant shall stand fast with him. His seed also will I make to endure for ever, and his throne as the days of heaven.

Psalm 89:28-29

When David wanted to build a Temple for the Lord, the Lord said to Nathan, "Tell him that, although he can't build Me a house, I will build him a house" (see 1 Chronicles 17:4-10). The Davidic Covenant is the promise God made to David that his house - his family - would endure forever. Scripture says that when David heard this, he sat down before the Lord speechless (1 Chronicles 17:16-18).

September 8, 1998. Those in attendance at Camden Yard that day didn't know they would be watching history made - not by what they saw but by what they didn't see. It was on that day that Cal Ripken, Jr. went to his manager and said, "Scratch me from the starting lineup." After playing in 2,643 consecutive games, it was the first time in 16 years that Cal Ripken, Jr. wouldn't be playing.

Sixteen years is quite a streak - but it pales in comparison to the streak of the One who will sit on the throne forever. During Cal Ripken's sixteen years, there were weeks where he never connected with the ball. So too, there were times when David dropped the ball and was far from perfect. But God made a promise to him and He would keep His promise because His steadiness and His faithfulness were on the line.

God's steadiness and faithfulness are what keep us going as well. It's not how good we're doing. It's that He is faithful. "I'll never leave you nor forsake you," He said. "Nothing can separate you from the love I have for you." God is truly with us, gang. He is for us. He's not going to give up on us. He made a covenant with us - the New Covenant (Hebrews 12:24). The blood of His Son washed away our sin. And that streak isn't going to end after sixteen years, no matter how many times we strike out.

AUGUST 16

O come, let us worship and bow down: let us kneel before the LORD our Maker. For he is our God; and we are the people of his pasture, and the sheep of his hand.

Psalm 95:6-7 (a)

Here, the psalmist says, "Let us bow down. Let us kneel." Clapping hands, standing in awe, lifting the head are all spoken of in the Scriptures as ways we can demonstrate worship. Although worship is stimulated in the heart and can be demonstrated through the body, I have found that sometimes demonstration through my body works stimulation in my spirit. That is, when I'm dry and I don't sense the Lord's presence as I once did, I find that when I bow my knees before Him or lift my hands to Him, something happens deep within me and my heart is stirred.

In the morning - when my mind might be foggy and my body might be tired - if I'll kneel down before the Lord, if I'll lift up my hands and praise His name, if I'll sing loudly in my study, if I'll worship enthusiastically, even though my spirit may not initially be on board, it doesn't take long for it to respond accordingly. That's why the psalmist doesn't say, "Do these things if you feel like it." He says, "Do these things, period." Worship is not based on feeling. Worship is based on who God is. And He is merciful, generous, wonderful, and loving.

When the wise men made their way to Bethlehem, bearing gold, frankincense, and myrrh, Jesus was not yet two years old. Thus, they obviously weren't hoping to get anything from Him. Instead, they brought their gifts to Him simply because they realized that He was the Promised One, the King. Whether they felt anything or not was irrelevant.

All things were made by Him and for His pleasure. Therefore, when I am pleasing the Lord by worshipping Him, I am actually fulfilling the very purpose for my existence (Revelation 4:11).

AUGUST 17

To day if ye will hear his voice, Harden not your heart, as in the provocation, and as in the day of temptation in the wilderness: when your fathers tempted me, proved me, and saw my work.

Psalm 95:7 (b)-9

The reference here is to Meribah (Exodus 17). After the Lord had set His people free from their bondage in Egypt, after He had parted the Red Sea for them, they found themselves hot and thirsty. They could have trusted God. Instead, they murmured and complained. The result was hardened hearts.

So too, at any given moment, I'm either going to be worshipping or murmuring. Thanksgiving leads to grace and glory. Murmuring, on the other hand, leads to discouragement and depression. Murmuring will take us down faster than anything else. When do we murmur? More often than not, as with the children of Israel, it's when we're going through a dry spell. And when we're dry, we're vulnerable to complaining. "Don't let that happen," the psalmist says.

The Israelites had seen God's work. So have we. We have seen Him save us from hell, take up residence in our hearts, adopt us as sons, and plant us in His Kingdom. Therefore, regardless of how dry the day might be, we have more than enough reason to rejoice and worship Him enthusiastically.

AUGUST 18

O sing unto the LORD a new song; for he hath done marvellous things: his right hand, and his holy arm, hath gotten him the victory. The LORD hath made known his salvation: his righteousness hath he openly shewed in the sight of the heathen.

Psalm 98:1-2

In Luke 2, we find the story of a man named Simeon, an old man who waited day after day for the coming of Messiah, the One who would set His people free. One day, Simeon was told by the Spirit, "Today is the day. Today is the day you have been waiting for." As Simeon made his way to the Temple that day, he was no doubt listening for the rumble of chariot wheels. No doubt there would be an awesome army that would march into Jerusalem, led by Messiah, to liberate Israel from the oppression of Rome. Simeon listened. He watched. He waited. But there were no chariots. There was no army. Instead, there was just a peasant couple who had come to dedicate a little, tiny Baby. And Simeon had a choice to make right then. He could have said, "You're kidding me. I've been waiting decades for a teenage girl, a poor carpenter, and a tiny Baby?" But he didn't. We are told he took the Child in his hands and blessed the Father for making known His salvation.

Oftentimes, we pray for and focus on a specific person or event to come our way, to solve our problem, to set us free. But more often than not, what God sends our way isn't at all what we expect. We look for an army, and God sends a baby. We think it's going to be a powerful presentation. Instead, it's a peasant couple. At that moment, like Simeon, we have a choice to make. We can either say, "What's the use of praying? God surely doesn't answer prayer" - or we can say, "I don't understand this, Lord. But I bless You and trust that somehow what You've brought to me today is going to be what's best."

AUGUST 19

I will lift up mine eyes unto the hills, from whence cometh my help.

Psalm 121:1

The psalmist was not drawing inspiration from the mountains, but rather from the location of Jerusalem in the midst of the mountains. Making his way to Jerusalem, the psalmist says, "I can see the hills. I'm getting close."

Beginning with *The Little Engine That Could* from our earliest days we have been taught that if we try hard enough, that if we think we can, we can. But the problem is, sometimes the battles before us are just too great. Sometimes the obstacles that loom over us are just too large . . .

Facing our cross-town rival, Leigh High School, my football coach moved me from my usual position on the line to outside linebacker. Leigh had the best runner in the state that year. Mike Franz was tough, indeed. So the coach put me and another guy as outside linebacker to try and stop the sweep, Mike's favorite play. All week long, I psyched myself up. I watched the films. I worked out. I told myself that I was unbeatable and unstoppable. Then came the day of the game. The first play Leigh called was a sweep to my side, with Mike Franz carrying the ball. I saw him coming my way. Our linemen had fought off Mike's interference so it was just me and him, one on one. I had a clear shot at him. I stuck my helmet right into his gut. I speared him just like I was taught.

"All right!" I thought. "I got him!" - until I found myself flat on my back with his cleats running over me as he went on for twenty-five yards.

After I got off the ground, the next play Leigh called was exactly the same sweep. Again, I made contact with Mike. Again, he ran right over my body. The third play Leigh called was a sweep to my side once again. I wrapped my arms around Mike's legs - and he busted on through for twenty-five yards. In three plays, Mike gained about seventy yards - all over me. Following the third play, I can still hear the cheerleaders yelling, "You can do it. You can do it. You can, you can."

I clearly remember getting up, looking at them, and thinking, "*You* can do it."

Try as I might, I just couldn't tackle the problem I was facing. So too, sometimes no matter how much we psyche ourselves up, we encounter problems that are just too great for us. So then what do we do? All too often, we look to someone else to give us help. But, although people are sometimes willing to help, they're not capable . . .

I remember doing a set of squats as a junior at Biola College. Squats are done by doing deep knee bends with a barbell on our shoulders. Because I was attempting to set a personal record, two of my friends were there as spotters, available to help if I couldn't make the lift. I went down and knew I was in trouble when I heard a "pop" in my lower back. I called out, but these friends of mine were fooling around and didn't see what was happening until it was too late. I went crashing to the floor, writhing in pain. Although my friends were available, they were very incapable!

The psalmist had a better idea. He knew the key wasn't to look in to himself or out to his friends, but to look up to the Lord.

AUGUST 20

My help cometh from the LORD, which made heaven and earth.

Psalm 121:2

Jerusalem was located in the hills on a rocky plateau twenty-five hundred feet above sea level. Thus, what the psalmist and the pilgrims were saying was, "We're lifting our eyes as we head to Jerusalem because our help is found in coming to the Temple, into the presence of God. Our help is found in meeting with the Lord, in pouring out our hearts before Him."

Before Jesus fed a hungry multitude with a little boy's lunch, Matthew says He lifted His eyes toward Heaven and gave thanks (14:19). The night before He was crucified John tells us that Jesus lifted His eyes to the Father and prayed (17:1). Jesus looked up to His Father and received the very help He needed.

Sometimes my problems seem really big. But that's because my perspective is all wrong. I'm so close to the problem that it blocks my perspective - just as I can block out the sun with my thumb. Remembering that the God to whom I pray is the One who made Heaven and earth makes my problems shrink to a workable size in light of His power.

How great is God's power? Look at the heavens. The most powerful telescopes we have are said to spot sextillion stars. How big is sextillion? It is a one with twenty-one zeros after it. That's a lot of stars, gang. And yet Psalm 147:4 tells us that not only did the Lord put each of those stars in place but that He calls each of them by name. Einstein's theory of an expanding universe has recently been verified by experiments conducted in outer space. This means that our understanding of God's power increases as well.

How great is God's power? Look at the earth, specifically at the bumblebee. Scientists tell us that it is theoretically impossible for a bumblebee to fly because his wings are too short and his body is too heavy. How he flies is a mystery to scientists, yet Deuteronomy 29:29 tells us the secret things belong to the Lord. To create and keep in operation the intricacies of our own planet speaks of a power of ingenuity and creativity beyond anything we can even begin to fathom.

Few of us doubt the ability of God to solve our problems. But many of us struggle with His willingness to do so. But listen to what He says: "Fear thou not; for I am with thee: be not dismayed, for I am thy God: I will strengthen thee; yea I will help thee; yea, I will uphold thee with the right hand of My righteousness" (see Isaiah 41:10). That's a promise not for those who are good enough, but for all of us.

AUGUST 21

The LORD is thy keeper: the LORD is thy shade upon thy right hand.

Psalm 121:5

"Now unto Him Who is able to keep you from falling and to present you blameless and faultless on that day," Jude writes (see verse 24). I'm so glad I don't have to keep myself. I'm so thankful I don't have to struggle and strive to make it in my Christian experience. I'm so relieved that the Lord is the One who promises to keep me.

The story is told of a man who wanted to cross a frozen lake. He got on his knees by the edge and tapped on the ice to make sure it was solid. Then he carefully scooted out on his hands and knees and tapped some more. When he found it was still solid, he scooted still farther. Every few feet, he would tap the ice to make sure it was strong enough to hold him. The hours went by. His face turned blue. His knuckles turned red. He was almost to the other side when he heard a rumble behind him. As he looked back, he saw twelve Clydesdale horses pulling a heavy wagon. They made it across the lake in a few minutes, leaving the man to think how foolish he had been.

We're like that man. We wonder if we're going to make it in our Christian experience. "Tap, tap, tap, I wonder if the Lord's going to keep me," we say. "Tap, tap, tap, I wonder if He's going to continue to work in my life." Doubt fills our minds. Discouragement fills our hearts because we don't realize that we're on *solid* ground. The Lord has promised that He will never leave us, that He will never forsake us, that we are in His hand, and that no man can pluck us out. What a difference it makes when the truth sinks into our hearts that we can rest in God's keeping power.

Newer translations render the word "shade" as "shield." In battle, soldiers would be exposed on their right side because they wielded the sword with their right hand. Here, the psalmist is saying that the Lord is the shield in the area which is vulnerable to attack.

You know the areas of strength and weakness in your own life. Here, the Lord says He will shield, protect, and cover me in the areas where I am most vulnerable.

AUGUST 22

They that trust in the LORD shall be as mount Zion, which cannot be removed, but abideth for ever.

Psalm 125:1

Those who trust in the Lord will be as strong and as stable as a mountain. That's why I need to have devotions tomorrow morning - not to impress my Lord or to earn righteousness, for that's already secured by the work of the Cross - but to become stable, because if I don't spend time with the Lord, I can get shaken up real easy.

I'm convinced we become slack in our devotional life because, usually, we don't have feelings when we have devotions. That is, we don't feel God's presence. We don't feel a "tingle." But, gang, how we feel is not the issue.

When a horse is shod, nails are driven through a horseshoe into his hoof. The horse doesn't feel a thing. But when he goes out on the trail, if he encounters broken glass or sharp rocks, he won't feel their effect because the shoe has been placed on his hoof. That's what the devotional life does. I might not feel one thing when I'm reading the Word. I might not feel one thing when I'm praying and worshipping. But once I get on the road of life that day, inevitably I encounter broken glass, rocks, and nails - and I feel the difference then if the "hooves" of my heart aren't shod. I get uptight. I get tense. I say the wrong thing. Inevitably, I pay the price if I don't take the time with the Lord in the morning. So, next time you have devotions and don't feel anything, remember the horse - and let the Lord prepare you for what only He knows lies ahead.

AUGUST 23

Yea, if thou criest after knowledge, and liftest up thy voice for understanding; if thou seekest her as silver, and searchest for her as for hid treasures; then shalt thou understand the fear of the LORD, and find the knowledge of God.

Proverbs 2:3-5

To know God and to understand Him requires a certain amount of effort and work. Solomon likens the process to a miner searching for gold, silver, and precious stones. If you dig in and get serious about your pursuit of wisdom, wisdom will be yours. But it doesn't come easily. There's a price to pay for wisdom: digging in the Word day after day.

In 1 Timothy 5:17, we read that we are to labor in the Word. The Greek word Paul used for "labor" means "to work to the point of perspiration." Why do we have to labor? Why do we have to mine for wisdom like gold? Because what I mine is mine. That is, what I learn through the grace of God as I dig in and wrestle with a text becomes His Word spoken to me personally. And what is mined stays in the mind. I never forget it.

The story is told of a young man who came to Socrates and said, "Give me understanding, wisdom, and knowledge."

Socrates said one sentence: "Follow me."

As the young man followed the great philosopher, Socrates walked through the city until he came to the edge of the ocean. He walked out waist-deep in the ocean, grabbed the young man by the neck, and thrust him beneath the water.

Finally, the young man fought his way up for some air and gasped, "Master, what are you doing?"

Socrates said, "When you want knowledge and wisdom and understanding as badly as you wanted that breath of air, that's when you begin the journey."

Solomon is saying the same thing. When you really want to dig in and commit yourself to that process, it will be yours. Labor in the Word, gang. Moisten this Book with the sweat of your brow. And God will meet you in that place and reward you greatly with hidden treasures, with real gems.

AUGUST 24

Trust in the LORD with all thine heart; and lean not unto thine own understanding. In all thy ways acknowledge him, and he shall direct thy paths.

Proverbs 3:5-6

Trust in the Lord. Even if it doesn't seem to make sense, follow the leading of the Lord according to His Word.

When I went skydiving, a man on the ground held a big arrow that he turned to show which way the wind was blowing and which way we were to go to catch it. I remember that when I regained consciousness after jumping out of the plane, I saw the guy turning the arrow. But I thought his direction was wrong, that he was leading me into a power line. His direction didn't make sense to me. Do I follow the arrow? I wondered. Or do I follow my own judgment? For a moment, I ignored the arrow. And then I thought I better follow it. So follow it I did - flying right over the power lines and landing in the right spot.

It's tempting to think we know more than the arrow. It's tempting to think, "Well, Lord, I know I'm not to lean on my own understanding. I know I'm to trust You. But what You're doing doesn't seem to make sense." At that point, we have a decision to make - whether to follow the arrow or to do our own thing.

How I encourage you to follow the arrow, gang. Even if you can't figure it out, follow the leading of the Lord according to His Word. You'll dodge the deadly power lines of the wicked and land right in the center of the field every time.

AUGUST 25

Strive not with a man without cause, if he have done thee no harm.

Proverbs 3:30

"Don't strive with a man for no reason," Solomon says. But, as always, it is Jesus Who gives us the final word when He said . . .

> Ye have heard that it hath been said, An eye for an eye, and a tooth for a tooth: but I say unto you, That ye resist not evil: but whosoever shall smite thee on thy right cheek, turn to him the other also. And if any man will sue thee at the law, and take away thy coat, let him have thy cloke also. And whosoever shall compel thee to go a mile, go with him twain.

Matthew 5:38-41

It's not practical to turn the cheek, to give the coat, to walk the extra mile. But the genius of what Jesus is saying is that the person who refuses to fight back is actually the person in control of the situation. The teachings of Jesus are radical. Entire societies change when people embrace them.

The subcontinent of India was changed simply because Mahatma Gandhi understood this principle. Although he was not a Christian, he embraced the reality of what Jesus taught. Had the Indians fought back, the British would have wiped them out. But the British themselves were defeated by a force more powerful than they: the force of love.

When your friends, parents, children, coworkers, or neighbors strike out at you, you have a choice to make: to strike back or turn the other cheek. Don't worry about getting walked on. You'll actually see the release of a greater power. Love will prevail.

AUGUST 26

A false balance is abomination to the LORD: but a just weight is his delight.

Proverbs 11:1

Measuring was done with weights and balances. The problem is, people would use one set of weights when they were buying and another set when they were selling.

Every day, the farmer delivered a pound of butter to the baker. But the baker began to notice that the pound of butter was becoming smaller and smaller and smaller. "My goodness," he thought, "I'm being systematically cheated." So he reported it to the town constable.

The baker and the constable went to the farmer's farm, where the farmer was accused of shortchanging the baker.

"But the butter I give him weighs one pound," the farmer insisted.

"What are you using for a weight?" the constable asked.

"The baker's one-pound loaf of bread," the farmer stated.

Thus, the baker was caught in his own trap.

It's interesting how we try to connive to get the best possible deal. That's the tendency of the human heart. But the Lord doesn't reward such a tendency.

To Him, manipulation is an abomination. This doesn't only apply to our own businesses or lifestyle, but to spiritual things as well.

You see, there's something that far outweighs our sin and failure: a little tiny piece of bread and cup of juice. If you'll come to the Lord's Table and receive what He did for you on the Cross, you will find that whatever sins you've been involved in, whatever stuff you're struggling with, whatever things you're bogged down by will be far outweighed by His righteousness.

A just weight is the Lord's delight. And we are just that because of what Jesus did on the Cross (Romans 3:26).

AUGUST 27

He that keepeth his mouth keepeth his life: but he that openeth wide his lips shall have destruction.

Proverbs 13:3

President Calvin "Silent Cal" Coolidge was asked why he spoke so little. "I never have regretted anything I didn't say," he answered. How true. We often regret what we do say, but rarely what we don't say. That is why James said it is better to be a listener than a talker (verse 1:19).

It would do us well first to *think* about what we're about to say . . .

T is it truthful?
H is it helpful?
I is it inspiring?
N is it needful?
K is it kind?

If what you're speaking is all of those things, go ahead and speak. Otherwise, keep quiet.

AUGUST 28

Every prudent man dealeth with knowledge: but a fool layeth open his folly. A wicked messenger falleth into mischief: but a faithful ambassador is health.

Proverbs 13:16-17

We are messengers, for Jesus has entrusted us with the message of the Gospel, the good news of salvation (Mark 16:15).

In 2 Kings 5, we read of a Syrian man of power and importance named Naaman who was plagued with leprosy. He heard about a man of God named Elisha and came to meet him. Elisha, however, sent his servant, Gehazi, saying, "Go tell Naaman to dip seven times in the Jordan and he'll be healed."

Upon hearing this, Naaman was angry. "Elisha didn't even come to meet me," he fumed. "And now he's telling me to dip in this muddy river? I'm not interested."

"Wait a minute," his servants said. "What do you have to lose?"

Naaman took their advice, and when he came out of the river, his leprosy was gone. He immediately went to meet with Elisha, saying, "Let me give you silver and fine clothes. Let me reward you for what you've done for me."

Elisha, however, refused Naaman's offer, and Naaman headed back to Syria. But Gehazi caught up with him and told him that Elisha had a change of mind, that he would accept some silver and fine clothes to give to his students. He took Naaman's silver and clothes, intending to keep them for himself. Upon his return, however, not only was Gehazi confronted by Elisha, who knew what he had done, but he was struck with leprosy as well.

"Freely ye have received, freely give," Jesus said (Matthew 10:8). It's the wicked messenger who, like Gehazi, manipulates the message for his own selfish gain. This applies to every one of us. When we share and witness is it simply because of our love for Jesus? Or is it because we want something out of it - a testimony to share Sunday night, a notch to place in our Bible, a proof of our own spirituality? All kinds of subtle things can creep into our hearts oh, so easily. And we can become wicked messengers ourselves.

As you share the Gospel, make sure you're doing it as a faithful messenger, a faithful ambassador, because of the work God has done in your own life. "It's the love of Christ that constrains me," Paul said (see 2 Corinthians 5:14). In other words, "Jesus loves me so much, has shown such grace and kindness to me, has done so much for me that I can do nothing but tell others about Him." We have a message, gang: "Jesus loves you. Your sins are forgiven." And we must share it faithfully.

AUGUST 29

A fool hath no delight in understanding, but that his heart may discover itself.

Proverbs 18:2

A fool places more stock in his feelings than in the facts. This is a very real hazard for all of us. "I feel God doesn't want us together any more," a wife said concerning her decision to leave her husband.

"Are there reasons for leaving him and your children?" I asked.

"No. I just don't feel God wants me with him any more."

But it is the foolish person who bases his decision simply on how he feels.

It has been said that faith, fact, and feeling are like three men walking along the top of a fence. Fact is in front; faith is in the middle; and feeling is at the end. As long as faith looks straight ahead at fact, he'll be all right. But once faith turns around to check out feeling, he'll lose his balance and fall.

Whenever I have taken my eyes off the facts and instead analyzed how I'm feeling, I've stumbled. My faith must be based upon the facts of what God's Word says - not upon how I feel on any given day. For example, God's Word says He will never leave me nor forsake me (Hebrews 13:5). If I keep my focus on that fact, I'll do fine. But if I start to say, "I don't think God is with me today because I don't feel His presence," I'll stumble and fall.

AUGUST 30

The king's heart is in the hand of the LORD, as the rivers of water: he turneth it whithersoever he will.

Proverbs 21:1

Whether we are speaking of the pharaohs of Egypt or the kings of Babylon, the chairman in China or the president of America, any ruler is there only as God allows him to be (John 19:10-11). In reality, although they seem powerful in our perspective, they're really only puppets for God's sovereign purpose.

Caesar Augustus was one of the greatest leaders of all time - at least in the eyes of man. When he decided to tax the whole world, he no doubt felt potent as he ordered the entire world to go to the cities of their birth. In reality, however, who was pulling the strings of Caesar Augustus' heart? God. You see, when Jesus was about to be born, Mary was in the Galilee area in the city of Nazareth. Yet Micah had declared that Messiah would be born in Bethlehem, the city of David (5:2). So what would compel Mary and Joseph to make the journey to Bethlehem? God the Father simply pulled the strings of His puppet, Caesar Augustus, to order everyone to their home towns to be taxed. And in so doing, Joseph and Mary traveled to Bethlehem, perfectly fulfilling Micah's prophecy.

Because God is on the throne, we don't have to panic about government policies. Yes, we are to pray for our leaders. Yes, we are to be engaged as citizens of this country. But we're not to perspire, pout, panic, or plot. Instead, we're to pray, knowing that God is in complete control. And as we do, we'll be at peace.

AUGUST 31

A poor man that oppresseth the poor is like a sweeping rain which leaveth no food.

Proverbs 28:3

If someone who is poor oppresses someone else who is poor, like a hard rain, he's a big drip, he's all wet. Certainly the poor should have compassion upon the poor.

We are poor in spirit. We realize the poverty, the inadequacy of our own lives. Therefore, we should be compassionate and forgiving of the problems, mistakes, and weaknesses of others.

In Matthew 18, we read of a king who forgave the debt of a man who owed him the equivalent of ten million dollars. Once exonerated, however, the man found a person who owed him the equivalent of two thousand dollars and demanded full payment. When the king heard about this, he said to the man he had forgiven, "You will be cast into prison until you pay the full ten million dollars because, although I forgave you much, you wouldn't forgive another man little."

We have no right to hold anything against anyone else because we've been forgiven so much. So if I oppress others, come down on others, heap condemnation on others, I'm like the poor oppressing the poor - and I'm all wet.

SEPTEMBER 1

Then shall the dust return to the earth as it was: and the spirit shall return unto God who gave it.

Ecclesiastes 12:7

Aging is inevitable, essential - but, praise God, not eternal because we're only here for a short time. We'll discard these bodies and move on to our glorious, new resurrected state where there shall be no aging or disease. Aging is not an eternal process. It's short - then on to Heaven, where we'll have new bodies designed for eternity.

That is why Solomon says, "*Today* is the day to remember your Creator (see Ecclesiastes 12:1). You're not dead yet. You still have your mind. Your heart is still pumping." *Now* is the time because most people think, "As soon as I get out of high school, then I'll really live for God," or "As soon as I get through college and finish my studies, then I'll be serious about seeking the Lord," or "As soon as my kids grow up, then I'll have time to wait on God," or "As soon as my kids get out of the house . . ."

The truth, however, is that it will never be easier than now for you to serve God. Never. It will never be easier for you than now to develop devotions. It will never be easier for you than now to begin to minister. It will never be easier than now to worship. It does not get easier as you get older. That's what Solomon is saying. Physically, you start to fall apart. Mentally, you're vulnerable to depression. So now is the day, in the day of your youth, to act decisively on behalf of God.

You see, the greatest misunderstanding is that when we get older, we automatically become wiser. Not so. If you are not spending time in the Word now, worshipping God now, serving God now, when you get older, you'll just be an old, cranky fool. And society is loaded with people like that.

But if you decide now to walk with God and commit your life to Him, you will age gracefully, become wise increasingly, and be a blessing to so many.

SEPTEMBER 2

For God shall bring every work into judgment, with every secret thing, whether it be good, or whether it be evil.

Ecclesiastes 12:14

The author of the Book of Job was a dramatist, a quintessential playwright. The authors of Psalms were poets par excellence. The author of Genesis and Exodus, a wonderful novelist. The author of Jonah was a storyteller. But here, I see Solomon not so much a storyteller or dramatist but rather a photographer. He takes pictures of life and lets us look at them in order to see they're all bogus. Then, on the last page of his photo album, he says, "This is the key: Fear God and keep His commandments" (see Ecclesiastes 12:13).

But you know what? I close this photo album and still feel discouraged because the problem is, I've broken the commandments, and therefore, fear judgment.

In the Sermon on the Mount, Jesus said, "Be ye therefore perfect" (Matthew 5:48). But I'm not. So, although Solomon's conclusion is correct, I haven't followed it. I haven't obeyed God perfectly.

But our Greater-than-Solomon - Jesus Christ - appears and says, "Come unto Me and I will give you rest, for except your righteousness exceed that of the scribes and Pharisees, unless it's better than the most religious individuals, you will not inherit eternal life" (see Matthew 5:20; 11:28).

So it is then I say, "Lord, I failed. But You didn't. You took my sin upon Yourself and died in my place. Oh, what grace. And now, Lord, by Your grace, I can walk in Your ways and keep Your commandments. By Your grace, Lord, I not only fear You, but I love You."

And life has meaning - not under the sun, but in the Son.

SEPTEMBER 3

Awake, O north wind; and come, thou south . . .

Song of Solomon 4:16 (a)

The north wind is a cold wind. Perhaps you feel cold presently - you don't feel the intense love for Jesus that you would like to or once did. You feel distant and alone. That is the blowing of the north wind. Let the wind blow - because the times that are devoid of tingly feelings or "Holy Ghost goose bumps" provide unique opportunity for you to demonstrate your love for the Lord through diligence in worship, prayer, and study of His Word - even though you don't feel His presence.

Gang, an absence of feelings doesn't mean the Lord has forsaken you. On the contrary, He is allowing you to go through a cold season in order to grant you the privilege of learning to walk by faith and not by feeling. Feelings are so fickle. They're affected by what you ate last night, by what your family said to you this morning, by the news, the weather, the economic outlook. Not so faith. It is a constant because it is totally independent of outside circumstances. Therefore, the Lord, wanting the best for His people, desires us to walk in the surety and stability of faith.

Can you, like the maiden, say, "Lord, I'm willing to go through a week, a month, or even a year of the blowing north wind in order to give to You without expecting the sense of Your presence in return"? Can you say, "Lord, if I can best demonstrate what You have done in my life through periods of coldness, so be it"?

Most of the time, whenever I give to God, I get so much back that I can't really call it giving at all! I start to worship and say, "Lord, this is a sacrifice of praise to You," when suddenly, finding myself flooded with feelings of joy, I think, "This is no sacrifice at all. Am I doing this to give - or am I doing this to receive?" But when I feel somewhat distant from the Lord, it's an opportunity for me to give without necessarily receiving anything in return.

If you're going through a cold spell today, if the north wind is howling, rejoice. You have a unique opportunity to minister to Jesus, to give to Him worship and adoration, praise and thanksgiving regardless of your feelings.

The south wind, on the other hand, is a hot, arid wind. Perhaps you are presently walking through days of difficulty and times of fiery trials. That is the blowing of the south wind. If this is your situation, remember that it's not when you're prospering and cruising through life that others can see Jesus in you. It's when they see you walking through difficult days by the grace of God that they know He is real to you.

SEPTEMBER 4

. . . blow upon my garden, that the spices thereof may flow out.

Song of Solomon 4:16 (b)

At Applegate Lake, I was sitting on the grass when, all of a sudden, I smelled something. My mouth began to water and my stomach started to growl as the fragrance of barbecued steak worked its way down the hillside into my nostrils.

So too, when the winds of adversity and difficulty blow through our lives, a fragrance is released. It is either a foul odor of bitterness and hostility, jealousy and anger, or it is the sweet-smelling savor of praise and thanksgiving, worship and adoration. You see, the wind itself doesn't determine what the fragrance will be. It merely releases the fragrance already present. Therefore, when I find bitterness, anger, jealousy, or hostility coming forth from my life, I must say, "Father, the problem isn't him, her, them, or it. It's *me*. Father, forgive me. I thought I was farther along than that. Oh, Lord, have mercy!"

Gang, if instead of saying, "It's his fault," or "They don't understand," or "Why is she doing that?" you say, "Oh, Lord, the fragrance in my life is not what it should be. I repent, Father. Change my heart," you will find a pleasing fragrance emanating from your life.

SEPTEMBER 5

Let my beloved come into his garden, and eat his pleasant fruits.

Song of Solomon 4:16 (c)

Take special note of this verse, saints. The key to life is saying, "I'm Your garden, Lord. Eat of me. I exist for Your pleasure and Your glory. That is why I am alive today. That is why I will awake tomorrow. I exist for one reason: not to heap pleasure upon myself, not even to please others - but to please You."

Why do you exist?

To bring pleasure to the Lord (Revelation 4:11).

Tomorrow will be a fabulous, wonderful, exciting, fulfilling day if you'll say, "Lord, I'm here to please You all day long. I'm taking You out for lunch. We'll grab a burger and then I'll meditate on Your Word, talk to You, and worship You. Lord, on my coffee break, my thoughts and prayers will be ascending to Your throne. I'm going to carry a verse in my pocket so that my thoughts might be upon You as I meditate upon it at various intervals throughout the day."

You exist to bring the Lord pleasure, gang. You are His garden.

SEPTEMBER 6

This is my beloved, and this is my friend, O daughters of Jerusalem.

Song of Solomon 5:16 (b)

Some married couples are passionately in love but fight like cats and dogs and tell me they're not even friends. Romantically and physically, they're in love - but they don't like each other very much.

Such is not the case with Jesus, for He's not only our Lover, He's also our Friend (John 15:15). And He desires to cultivate a deep and meaningful relationship with us.

If you spent as much time with your best friend as you spend with the Lord on a daily basis, how deep would your friendship be? If you spent four minutes a day, five minutes every other day, or twenty minutes every third week together, what kind of friendship would you have? So often, when we say, "I just don't feel the presence of the Lord. I don't enjoy His company," it's because we haven't invested time in cultivating His friendship.

"Be not deceived," warned Paul. "Whatever a man sows, that shall he also reap" (see Galatians 6:7).

Jesus enjoys me. Even though many times I don't even like myself, He continues to call me friend. What a great and marvelous mystery!

SEPTEMBER 7

How beautiful are thy feet with shoes, O prince's daughter!

Song of Solomon 7:1 (a)

The king compliments his bride upon the beauty of her feet, which is somewhat unusual since feet are not necessarily the prettiest part of a person. But therein lies an interesting thought. You see, according to Ephesians 6:15, we are shod with the preparation of the Gospel of peace. That is, we stand on the Gospel of peace - not upon our own efforts, works, or righteousness, but on the good news of God's peace with us.

When Moses stood on holy ground, what did God instruct him to do? Remove the sandals *from* his feet (Exodus 3:5). When the prodigal son returned home, what did his father do? He put sandals *on* his feet (Luke 15:22). Why? Because Moses speaks of the Law, while the prodigal speaks of grace.

If you think you can stand on the Law, take off your shoes because you'll never make it. You cannot earn or deserve God's blessings. But if you're at a place where you say, "I need God's forgiveness, grace, and mercy in my life," then, like the prodigal, you will experience the Gospel of peace being placed upon your feet.

Dear Church, dear Bride, hear this: We do not stand on what we do or how we behave. We stand on the finished work of the Cross. We stand on what Jesus Christ has done for us. We stand on the Gospel of peace.

SEPTEMBER 8

Many waters cannot quench love, neither can the floods drown it: if a man would give all the substance of his house for love, it would utterly be contemned.

Song of Solomon 8:7

"Love will persevere," says the bride. "But if a person tries to buy love, it will be condemned."

Church, rejoice in the fact that the Lord has you on His heart and upon His shoulders. Challenges will come in your relationship, but love will overcome. And yet if you try to buy His love, that love will be condemned.

Don't try to buy the Lord's love. Don't say, "The Lord must really love me today because I had devotions for an hour. What a day this is going to be!

I really earned God's love today." That kind of love is useless because it is based upon your works instead of His grace.

"Then why have devotions?" you ask.

Because we love our Lord and want to spend time with Him. We gain strength in His presence and receive understanding. But we're not trying to prove or earn a greater love. Did you know that if you had devotions every day this week for seven hours the Lord wouldn't love you any more than if you didn't have devotions at all?

Now, if you have devotions for seven hours, there will inevitably be a glow on your face and strength in your heart. You would be changed - but God's love for you would not be affected because His love for you is not based upon your actions. It is based solely upon His own nature. That is why Paul wrote that nothing shall separate us from His love (Romans 8:38-39).

Don't work for God's love, gang. Don't try to deserve it. Just enjoy it!

SEPTEMBER 9

The ox knoweth his owner, and the ass his master's crib: but Israel doth not know, my people doth not consider.

Isaiah 1:3

"The ox and the donkey are smarter than My people," God says. The ox is not known for his brilliance. In fact, to this day we say, "He's as dumb as an ox." The donkey is known only for his stubbornness. And yet God says they're smarter and wiser than His people for at least they know their master. "My people don't consider Me at all. Here, I have blessed them, but they have forgotten Me," He says.

At this point, Judah was experiencing a time of unparalleled prosperity. And yet, as is so often the case, because times were good, apathy had crept in. In Deuteronomy 6, God warned of this. "I will bless you," He said. "I will bring you into a Land of Promise where you will dwell in houses you didn't build, drink from pools you didn't dig, eat from vineyards you didn't plant. But when you come into the Land, beware lest you become full and forget the Lord your God."

What an important word this is for us. Beware when things go well because the tendency can be to be dumb as an ox, as stubborn as a mule, and to forget the blessings of God.

SEPTEMBER 10

The word that Isaiah the son of Amoz saw concerning Judah and Jerusalem. And it shall come to pass in the last days, that the mountain of the LORD's house shall be established in the top of the mountains . . .

Isaiah 2:1-2 (a)

This prophecy concerns the rebuilding of the Temple in Jerusalem. Must it be rebuilt before we're raptured? No. But it must be rebuilt before Jesus comes back to rule and reign in Jerusalem. At that time, there will be peace at last. Swords will be beaten into plows. Spears will be shaped into pruning hooks. Annapolis, West Point, and the Pentagon will be shut down. How we look forward to that!

In verse 2, we see the location of the Temple. It is in the mountains. As the temple of God, we, too, must be in the mountains. We must be built on Mount Sinai, where the Word of God was given. We must commit ourselves to the proclamation and meditation of the Scriptures. We must also be built on Mount Pisgah, where Moses stood before he died and saw the Promised Land, for we, too, must see things not from a worldview, but from a Heavenly perspective. We must also be built on Mount Carmel, where Elijah called down fire from Heaven, for the Church is the place where the fire of the Holy Spirit can burn brightest. We must also be built on Mount Hermon, the Mount of Transfiguration, for we must be those who are transformed and those who see each other in that way. Finally, we must be built on the Mount of Olives, where Jesus prayed, for the House of God is to be a house of prayer (Matthew 21:13).

Why would we want to pray with intensity, seek the Holy Spirit with fervency, hear the Word of God as Moses did, become visionaries like Isaiah? Because of another mount - Mount Calvary. I want to be a man of the mountain - a man of prayer, a man who can look at people supernaturally, a man of vision, a man of the Spirit - because of the incredible price Jesus paid for me.

SEPTEMBER 11

Therefore as the fire devoureth the stubble, and the flame consumeth the chaff, so their root shall be as rottenness, and their blossom shall go up as dust: because they have cast away the law of the LORD of hosts, and despised the word of the Holy One of Israel. Therefore is the anger of the LORD kindled against his people, and he hath stretched forth his hand against them, and hath smitten them: and the hills did tremble, and their carcases were torn in the midst of the streets. For all this his anger is not turned away, but his hand is stretched out still.

Isaiah 5:24-25

"You brought judgment and destruction upon yourself," God says, "but My hand is outstretched still." Look at that hand. It's not stretched out to strike you down. As I look at that hand, I see the scars where a nail pierced and penetrated the palm and I realize that His hand is stretched out not to come down on me but to reach out and save me.

God's hand is stretched out to our country, gang. The mistakes we've made personally, as a church family, as a community, and as a country have been forgiven and covered by the blood of Jesus Christ if we'll simply respond and say, "Thank You, Lord, for reaching out, for stretching out Your hand on the Cross, for absorbing My sins. I repent. I change direction. I'm turning away from my old paths to walk in Your way."

God comes to the vineyard of our nation and looks for the fruit of thanksgiving, rightness, holiness, love, mercy, and compassion, but all He finds is sour grapes and wild fruit. What is the solution? Repentance. Nations don't repent. People repent. Therefore, it's time for us to accept our part in the corrupt state of our society. It's time for us to change our activity and pray on behalf of our country.

SEPTEMBER 12

Also I heard the voice of the Lord, saying, Whom shall I send, and who will go for us? Then said I, Here am I; send me. And he said, Go, and tell this people, Hear ye indeed, but understand not; and see ye indeed, but perceive not. Make the heart of this people fat, and make their ears heavy, and shut their eyes; lest they see with their eyes, and hear with their ears, and understand with their heart, and convert, and be healed.

Isaiah 6:8-10

Isaiah didn't passively say, "Lord, if You want, You can use me." Rather, the original text indicates he said, "Behold me." Look at me, Lord. Thus, with the enthusiasm of an eager first-grader who knows the answer, Isaiah raised his hand to get the Teacher's attention and said, "Send me, Lord."

It has been said that Isaiah's calling can be summarized as Woe, Lo, and Go.

"Woe is me," Isaiah said in verse 5.

"Lo, this iniquity is taken away," the seraphim said in verse 7.

"Go," the Lord said in verse 9.

"Who will go?" the Lord asked.

"Count me in," Isaiah answered. "How can I not go? I've seen You. I've been touched by You. I'll go."

Will *you* go? Whether that means across the seas or across the street, around the block or around the office, will you tell people about the One who saved your soul? Daniel 12 says those who win souls are wise and that they shall shine as the stars forever. But if that concept is too hard to grasp, ask anyone who's been witnessing or on the mission field and they'll tell you they find it to be wonderfully fulfilling and addicting in the best sense of the word. You see, the Holy Spirit is like electricity. He'll only go into an object if there is a way out of that object. People wonder why the Holy Ghost isn't moving in their lives, but it's because there's no outflow. Plug into ministry, sharing, missions - and you will feel the current of the Holy Ghost flowing through you.

Isaiah sees the Lord. He's humbled before the Lord. He's touched by the Lord. He offers himself to the Lord. But what does the Lord say? "Go and preach - but no one will be converted. No one will listen or respond. You'll open your home for Bible study and no one will come. You'll witness and people will walk away."

Why would the Lord say this? In Matthew 13, Jesus referred to this very passage when He said He spoke in parables lest the people understand what He was saying and be converted. Why wouldn't Jesus want everyone converted? Because God allows man to make his own choice. God won't force His will on anyone. If a person says, "I do not want to know the Lord. I want to be my own God," the Lord will allow his ears to be stopped and his eyes to be made blind lest they be converted against their own will.

God wanted Isaiah to speak His Word and to be His witness in order that people might see how they were either rejecting or responding to Him. So too, our calling is not to be successful in ministry. Our calling is simply to be obedient to the Master. Those who are elected will respond. Others won't. Our message just shows people where they're at.

SEPTEMBER 13

In the year that Tartan came unto Ashdod, (when Sargon the king of Assyria sent him,) and fought against Ashdod, and took it; at the same time spake the LORD by Isaiah the son of Amoz, saying, Go and loose the sackcloth from off thy loins, and put off thy shoe from thy foot. And he did so, walking naked and barefoot. And the LORD said, Like as my servant Isaiah hath walked naked and barefoot three years for a sign and wonder upon Egypt and upon Ethiopia; so shall the king of Assyria lead away the Egyptians prisoners, and the Ethiopians captives, young and old, naked and barefoot, even with their buttocks uncovered, to the shame of Egypt.

Isaiah 20:1-4

Tartan was the general of the invading Assyrian army. Ashdod was one of the five cities of the Philistines. It was when Assyria invaded Ashdod that the Lord told Isaiah to take off his clothes and shoes and to walk naked and barefoot as a sign to the people of Egypt and Ethiopia. Why would the Lord have His prophet walk around naked? Because He loves people deeply (2 Peter 3:9).

You see, God was not concerned only about the nation of Israel. I think of Jonah. God cared about the Assyrians so much that he sent Jonah to Nineveh, their capital city, to tell them to repent. In Exodus 19:6, God told the people of Israel that they were to be a kingdom of priests. A priest is one who stands before the people on behalf of God and stands before God on behalf of the people. Therefore, Israel was to be a spokesman for God to all of the other nations of the world. Israel was to be a missionary nation. Entrusted with the Word of God, they were to reflect and radiate God's reality to the entire world.

But Israel made the mistake that we are sometimes vulnerable to making. That is, Israel kept the word to herself and saw the surrounding nations as nothing more than fuel for the fires of hell. We must not fall into Israel's error, having no compassion or concern for those around us who are headed for hell.

We want to be powerful men of God or women of faith - as long as people marvel at our spirituality. But what about when we're told to walk naked? Oh, God won't call any of us to be physically naked. He does, however, call us to share the naked truth, the honest truth with candor. And yet I see us shirking away from the truth. Consequently, we live next to people year after year without ever saying, "I must be honest with you. God loves you but the wages of sin is death. And, according to John 3:36, he that has the Son has life but the wrath of God abides on the one who doesn't have the Son. You might be angry with me for saying that, but I must be honest with you. You need Jesus. You must be born again or you'll be destroyed."

How long has it been since you bared your heart to an unbeliever? God not only told Isaiah to bare his soul, but later He Himself would do the same thing. As the Son of Man, He would bare His soul in His teaching, bare His life by speaking honestly, and bare His body on the Cross of Calvary - all to bear the sins of humanity. He could have said, "I will not be humiliated. I will not be disgraced by these savages." Instead, He said, "Father, forgive them. They know not what they do." Jesus died naked and exposed because He cared about me personally. He cared about you passionately.

Is it any wonder Isaiah would obey the command - no matter how embarrassing - of a God like that?

SEPTEMBER 14

And the vision of all is become unto you as the words of a book that is sealed, which men deliver to one that is learned, saying, Read this, I pray thee: and he saith, I cannot; for it is sealed.

Isaiah 29:11

Here, the Lord says to these people at this time that, because they chose to be apathetic, they would remain unenlightened. That is, neither the educated nor the uneducated individual would have understanding of the Word.

In this is an important truth. That is, if you don't want to understand Scripture, you won't. If you're not interested in doing the will of God or knowing the heart of God, the Bible will become meaningless to you. Regardless of how educated or uneducated you are, you will find the Word to be dry, boring, and an unsolvable mystery. We receive illumination when we approach the Word with a submitted spirit, saying, "Lord, this Book is talking to me and talking about me. Therefore, change me, Lord. Deal with my heart and life."

Are your devotions dry and tedious? Are they difficult? Perhaps it's because you're approaching the Word without intending to be submitted to what it says. What a difference it makes when we approach it, saying, "Lord, today, use these Scriptures to change my life, to convict me of sin, to change my attitudes and heart within."

SEPTEMBER 15

Strengthen ye the weak hands, and confirm the feeble knees.
Say to them that are of a fearful heart, Be strong, fear not:
behold, your God will come with vengence, even God with
a recompence; he will come and save you.

Isaiah 35:3-4

How are we to strengthen people who feel weak or fearful? We are to tell them the Lord is coming. That's not "pie in the sky" theology. It's God's Word given to us practically. The way to strengthen people - whether yourself or others - is to say, "Fear not. Be strong. Your God will come and save you."

We're pilgrims, gang, on our way to a city with foundations (Hebrews 11:10) - a place that is solid and secure, a place that won't shift with the changing winds of commerce or culture - Heaven. If we lose sight of this, if we begin to think this is all there is, we become vulnerable to discouragement and depression. "Lord," we'll cry, "will I ever get the job I want? Will I ever lose the weight I want? Will it ever be right between sisters and brothers?" I can get so discouraged if I think this is all there is. But if I realize God's coming back and will set all things right, I can go on.

SEPTEMBER 16

Speak ye comfortably to Jerusalem, and cry unto her, that her warfare is accomplished, that her iniquity is pardoned: for she hath received of the LORD's hand double for all her sins. The voice of him that crieth in the wilderness, Prepare ye the way of the LORD, make straight in the desert a highway for our God.

Isaiah 40:2-3

How was Isaiah to comfort God's people? First, he was to tell the nation that her warfare would come to an end and that her iniquity was pardoned. So too, how are we to comfort others? By telling people that warfare is coming to an end, that life is short, that life goes fast, that Jesus is coming back.

In Isaiah's day, if you couldn't pay your creditors, a violation of your contracts would be posted on your house with a warning that in a short time, the house would be repossessed and you would be evicted - unless there was a redeemer who could pay your debt. In that case, the paper would be folded up, tacked to the wall, and marked "Paid."

That's the message of the New Testament. Our sins are forgiven. Therefore, tell the person who feels guilty, depressed, discouraged, or defeated that Jesus is coming back and that their sins are forgiven - for those are comforting words, indeed!

"Comfort My people," Isaiah was instructed. "And prepare them for the coming of Christ."

John the Baptist used this passage when he was asked by the Pharisees who he was.

"Are you the Christ?" they asked. "Are you Elijah? Are you that prophet?"

"No," he said. "I am a voice crying in the wilderness, preparing a way for the coming of the Lord" (see John 1:19-21).

That's the essence of ministry for you and me as well. We are not to draw attention to ourselves, but rather we are to prepare the way for Jesus. I can't be like Elijah - raising the dead and calling down fire from Heaven. But I can be like John. I can talk about Jesus, preparing a way for Him.

SEPTEMBER 17

Every valley shall be exalted, and every mountain and hill shall be made low: and the crooked shall be made straight, and the rough places plain: and the glory of the LORD shall be revealed, and all flesh shall see it together: for the mouth of the LORD hath spoken it.

Isaiah 40:4-5

The valley of depression, discouragement, and defeat needs to be filled in. The mountain of pride and prayerlessness and haughtiness needs to be taken down. The crooked place of errors needs to be straightened out. And the rough places of irritation need to be made smooth. I don't have time to be in the valley of depression or to feel sorry for myself. I've got work to do. I don't have a right to be proud or irritated because I have a job to do. We need to forget about our own problems and pain, hurts and heartaches. We need to realize that we have the same call John the Baptist did: to prepare a way in the wilderness of this world for Jesus.

SEPTEMBER 18

Have ye not known? have ye not heard? Hath it not been told you from the beginning? Have ye not understood from the foundations of the earth? It is he that sitteth upon the circle of the earth, and the inhabitants thereof are as grasshoppers; that stretcheth out the heavens as a curtain, and spreadeth them out as a tent to dwell in.

Isaiah 40:21-22

We read in Numbers 13 that the people of Israel didn't initially enter the Promised Land because they felt like grasshoppers in the eyes of the people who lived there. Here, God is saying, "You might be grasshoppers in their sight, but they're grasshoppers in My sight."

The same is still true. Whoever or whatever stands against you is as a grasshopper in God's sight. Therefore, rather than worrying, believe that your Father loves you and will see you through.

"I have a hard time believing that," you say. "Maybe it's because I'm not praying right."

I think of the little girl who came to her father and said, "Daddy, would you please put gasoline on my lips?"

"Sure, honey," the father said as he went into the bathroom, opened the medicine cabinet, and pulled the Vaseline off her shelf. Yes, the little girl got her words mixed up, but did her father say, "You want gasoline on your lips? Then gasoline is what you're getting"? Of course not! He's her father. He knew what she meant.

"If you, being evil, know how to give good gifts to your children, don't you know that the Heavenly Father will give good gifts to His?" Jesus asked (see Matthew 7:11). Listen, dear folks, your vocabulary might be all mixed up. You might not pray with eloquence, but your Father knows what's in your heart. And even if you get it all jumbled up, He's not going to say, "Gasoline, huh? Gasoline it is!"

SEPTEMBER 19

A bruised reed shall he not break, and the smoking flax shall he not quench: he shall bring forth judgment unto truth. He shall not fail nor be discouraged, till he have set judgment in the earth: and the isles shall wait for his law.

Isaiah 42:3-4

Jesus doesn't smash the reed that bends under the heat of the sun. Nor does He douse the smoking flax that doesn't ignite easily. In fact, as evidenced by the parable of the lost sheep (Luke 15), Jesus seems to be most interested in the person who is hurting or struggling. Over and over again, Satan will tell you that if your reed is bruised or your flax is nothing more than smoke that Jesus is really tired of you and about to give up on you. But that's a lie. Jesus doesn't break the bruised reed. He doesn't extinguish the smoking flax. You might look at yourself as hopeless. But He doesn't. He sees you as you're going to be. He's not discouraged because, although you might fail time and again, He won't.

SEPTEMBER 20

Thus saith the LORD that made thee, and formed thee from the womb, which will help thee; Fear not, O Jacob, my servant; and thou, Jeshurun, whom I have chosen. For I will pour water upon him that is thirsty, and floods upon the dry ground: I will pour my spirit upon thy seed, and my blessing upon thine offspring.

Isaiah 44:2-3

Here, the Lord is encouraging Israel - here called Jacob and *Jeshurun*, or "righteous nation," to not be afraid, that He would pour out the water of His Spirit upon a dry land. We know from Joel 2 that, as the tribulation period comes to a close, the Spirit will be poured out in such a way that perhaps multiplied millions of people will turn to the true and living God in that great and terrible day.

This outpouring was previewed on the Day of Pentecost, but it was not completely fulfilled, for Joel 2 speaks of signs in the sky, of the moon turning to blood, and various symbols associated with the tribulation period. But it also speaks to us personally, for the Lord promises that He will pour water upon him who is thirsty and blessing upon his offspring. I like that because I need the Spirit to be poured upon me and upon my family.

To whom does the Lord pour out His Spirit? Simply to those who are thirsty. And, in that, is a real key. We over-complicate and over-mystify the work of the Spirit in many cases when, in reality, the prerequisite for an outpouring of the Spirit upon your life is simply to say, "Lord, I'm thirsting for more of You." That's why Jesus said the woman who acknowledges her thirst is blessed, why the man who admits his hunger will be filled (Matthew 5:6).

If you're not thirsty, if you don't have a desire to experience a fuller measure of the Spirit flowing through your life, how do you become thirsty? Ask a jogger or a basketball player. If you start expending energy and start sweating a bit, you'll find yourself feeling thirsty real fast. The key is to get out and start ministering. Start sharing, loving, and caring - for it is when you're in the place of loving your neighbor, of sharing with your friends and family, of witnessing to your co-worker, of expending energy, that you begin to thirst for more of the Lord.

SEPTEMBER 21

Look unto me, and be ye saved, all the ends of the earth: for I am God, and there is none else.

Isaiah 45:22

When the children of Israel were bitten by poisonous snakes, the Lord instructed Moses and Aaron to make a brass pole and to place a brass snake upon it. Then they were to tell the congregation that whoever looked at the snake on the pole would be saved (Numbers 21). Brass is the metal of judgment. A serpent is a symbol of sin. Therefore, it was a picture of Jesus Christ, Who bore the judgment for our sins on the Cross. If we simply look to Him and believe in Him, we'll be saved from Satan's poisonous sting of eternal damnation.

What do you have to lose by looking to the Lord?

Nothing.

What do you have to gain?

Eternity.

SEPTEMBER 22

Hear ye this, O house of Jacob, which are called by the name of Israel . . .

Isaiah 48:1 (a)

Abraham was the father of Israel, the first Jew. Called from Ur of the Chaldees, God made a new nation from him. Abraham had a son named Isaac, who had a son named Jacob. Jacob had twelve sons who became the fathers of the twelve tribes of Israel. Jacob's name, which means "heel snatcher," or "supplanter," was appropriate because he was one who lived by his wits - conning and tricking people. But one night, seeing no way out of his circumstances, he wrestled all night with the Angel of the Lord, saying, "I will not let You go until You bless me."

In the morning, the Lord said, "You're no longer Jacob, but you're going to be called Israel, which means 'governed by God.' You'll no longer rely on your schemes and tricks but will cling to Me" (Genesis 32).

How I want to be more Israel-like and less Jacob-like. Oh, how much Jacob is still in us. We rely upon our own abilities and personalities, our own plans and principles. But, like Jacob, we need to come to the end of ourselves and say, "Lord, You govern me."

SEPTEMBER 23

For my name's sake will I defer mine anger, and for my praise will I refrain for thee, that I cut thee not off. Behold, I have refined thee, but not with silver; I have chosen thee in the furnace of affliction. For mine own sake, even for mine own sake, will I do it: for how should my name be polluted? And I will not give my glory unto another.

Isaiah 48:9-11

"I deferred My anger toward My people for My name's sake," the Lord declares. "I wanted to refine you in the furnace of affliction, but found no silver." What a tragic indictment for God to level at His people: "You wouldn't let the fiery furnace, the hard trials, purify you. Therefore, no silver was found."

Sometimes we wonder why we face one affliction after another. Could it be it's because we're not learning our lesson? Could it be that we're so stubborn that the Lord has to continually take us through the fire of affliction? Has the Lord been speaking to you about some issue? Is there something the Lord has told you needs to be changed but about which you persistently say, "Maybe later, Lord"? We all go through fiery trials and many are absolutely mandated. But, as we watch the people of Israel, we see that other trials are the result of our own stubbornness concerning lessons God wants to teach.

SEPTEMBER 24

Hearken to me, ye that follow after righteousness, ye that seek the LORD: look unto the rock whence ye are hewn, and to the hole of the pit whence ye are digged.

Isaiah 51:1

Here, the Lord is saying, " Look back and remember where you came from, the pit from which you were rescued." If you think it's hard to be a believer, pause and remember what it was like before you invited Christ into your heart - the meaninglessness, the emptiness, the frustration, and the insecurity you felt before Jesus took up residence.

The eyes of one of the most powerful preachers in the early days of colonial America - a Puritan preacher - filled with tears whenever he talked about the Lord. Week by week, year by year, he showed tremendous tenderness toward Jesus and the people who were lost. When he was asked what made him so tender, he said, "Every Saturday night, I spend at least an hour reflecting on the days before I was saved. I remember what it was like not knowing the Lord. I remember the futility and vanity and it makes my heart break. It makes me appreciate Jesus and feel compassion for sinners all the more."

SEPTEMBER 25

Art thou not it that hath cut Rahab, and wounded the dragon? Art thou not it which hath dried the sea, the waters of the great deep; that hath made the depths of the sea a way for the ransomed to pass over? Therefore the redeemed of the LORD shall return, and come with singing unto Zion; and everlasting joy shall be upon their head: they shall obtain gladness and joy; and sorrow and mourning shall flee away.

Isaiah 51:9 (b)-11

"Lord, aren't You the One who dealt with Rahab - or Egypt - in days of old? Aren't You the One who opened the Red Sea for Your people to pass through?" Here, the prophet is saying what we sometimes feel. We read the stories of God's power and deliverance, but wonder where He is in our own trouble and difficulty.

In verse 10, Isaiah wondered why the Lord wasn't working. Here, in verse 11, he is sure that the Lord will work. What caused him to change his mind? I suggest it was in the very act of pouring out his heart to the Lord in prayer that the answer to his question, the solution to his frustration was found. "You parted the Red Sea," he said in verse 10. And, as he did, he must have realized that, with Pharaoh's army barreling down on them, the Israelites must have felt even more forsaken than he did. But he also realized that God had made a way, that God had come through - and that He would do the same for him.

I believe one of the greatest advantages of prayer is that, as we talk to the Lord, we begin to get insights and understanding that will see us through another day - maybe just one more day, but that is all we need. It is a very good thing to pour out your heart to the Lord because, as was the case with Isaiah, so often the answer is found in the very questions and frustrations we share.

SEPTEMBER 26

Seek ye the LORD while he may be found, call ye upon him while he is near.

Isaiah 55:6

Seek the Lord while He may be found. Why? Because in Genesis 6:3, God said His Spirit would not always strive with man. If you're not saved, there will be a time when you may seek the Lord, but you won't be able to find Him. There comes a time when all hope of salvation is lost and all that's left is despair.

Hearing the crowds gather, Bartimaeus asked what was happening. "Jesus of Nazareth is coming," he was told.

When he heard Jesus and His disciples walking down the road, he cried, "Son of David, have mercy upon me."

"Be quiet!" the crowd scolded. But Luke tells us Bartimaeus cried all the more, causing Jesus to stop and ask him what he wanted.

"That my eyes might be opened," Bartimaeus answered.

And at that point, Bartimaeus was healed (Luke 18).

What if Bartimaeus had said, "Jesus is coming, huh? I've heard He can do some amazing things. Next time He comes by, I'm going to cry out to Him. Next time He's in the area, I'll call out to Him." If Bartimaeus had not cried out at that time, he would never have been healed.

So too, the Holy Spirit comes by us and whispers, "Go pray. Take a half hour and read the Word. Go for a walk through your neighborhood with Me." Rather than an audible voice, these are impressions that tug on our hearts. If you put them off, you may find you missed a unique opportunity to receive a healing, a blessing, a work of God in your life.

SEPTEMBER 27

. . . ye that make mention of the LORD, keep not silence, and give him no rest, till he establish, and till he make Jerusalem a praise in the earth.

Isaiah 62:6 (b)-7

Through Isaiah, God says, "Give Me no rest until the things that are upon My heart are accomplished."

Jesus said the same thing. In Luke 11, teaching about prayer, He said, "At midnight, there was a knock on the door of a man's house. 'Go away!' the man said. 'It's late.'

"But the cry came from the other side of the door, 'I'm your friend. Open up!'

"'No,' the homeowner said. 'My kids are all in bed. I don't want to wake them up.'

"But the man kept knocking. Finally the homeowner arose and let him in - not because of their friendship but because of his importunity. The guy just wouldn't stop knocking!"

Jesus was saying, "If a man who doesn't want to get out of bed responds to constant knocking, how much more readily will your Father respond to you?"

Jesus used this story as an illustration of what prayer is to be. "Ask and it shall be given," He would say. "Seek and you shall find. Knock and the door shall be opened unto you" - or literally, "*Keep* asking. *Keep* seeking. *Keep* knocking" (see Matthew 7:7).

"Give Me no rest until these things be established," God says. I wonder how much is not established in our lives simply because we stopped praying. I wonder how many miracles, how many blessings we missed because we stopped knocking. It's not that God is teasing us. Rather, He wants to cultivate a relationship of faith, of perseverance, of affection, of communication with Him.

SEPTEMBER 28

For since the beginning of the world men have not heard, nor perceived by the ear, neither hath the eye seen, O God, beside thee, what he hath prepared for him that waiteth for him.

Isaiah 64:4

As Isaiah is praying, he says, "Lord, we don't even know the amazing things You have ahead for us."

Paul would echo this same thought . . .

> But as it is written, Eye hath not seen, nor ear heard, neither have entered into the heart of man, the things which God hath prepared for them that love him.

1 Corinthians 2:9

If you're living for your job, your bank account, your possessions, or even your family, you'll miss out on the life God has for you both now and eternally. But if, like Isaiah and Paul, you set your heart on Heaven, you'll have abundant life on earth thrown in!

If, like Isaiah, we would just say, "Lord, we are looking and waiting for that which You have in store for us in Heaven," you'll not only end up there, but you'll enjoy life as well. If you're living for your job or your bank account or your possessions, you'll miss both. Why doesn't God speak more to us about Heaven? Because we couldn't comprehend it.

SEPTEMBER 29

And they shall go forth, and look upon the carcases of the men that have transgressed against me: for their worm shall not die, neither shall their fire be quenched; and they shall be an abhorring unto all flesh.

Isaiah 66:24

Sadly, while the Kingdom is celebrating, there will be incredible suffering as those who reject the King will be left to the consequences of their own will.

Many a person has been brought into Heaven by being scared out of hell. That's why I was saved. I became a Christian when I heard a sermon on hell. At 3 ½ years old, I usually slept in the pew in the Assembly of God church my parents attended. But one particular Sunday night, the preacher preached on hell and I listened intently. "Satan has a stopwatch in his hand," he said, "and he sees his time coming to an end. Therefore, he's chasing you harder and faster and more energetically than ever because he sees his time is running out and he wants you."

Me? I thought. So when the invitation was given, I slid off the pew, went forward, and got saved that night. My parents prayed with me later on in the evening and I gave my life to Jesus right then.

I knew God's love, but what I needed to know was the reality of hell. Maybe you know people who aren't responding to the goodness of God and committing their life to Jesus. Very respectfully, I say, "Give them hell." Let them know that if they're not going to respond to the love of God, they will have to deal with eternity apart from God.

September 30

Then the LORD put forth his hand, and touched my mouth. And the LORD said unto me, Behold, I have put my words in thy mouth. See, I have this day set thee over the nations and over the kingdoms, to root out, and to pull down, and to destroy, and to throw down, to build, and to plant.

Jeremiah 1:9-10

Here, we see the power given to Jeremiah as the Lord put His words in Jeremiah's mouth. The Word of God is quick and powerful, sharper than any two-edged sword (Hebrews 4:12). Therefore, just as He provided Jeremiah His words, He has provided us with His Word. True power comes not from sharing with people what we think, but what God's Word says; not from our ideas or philosophies, but what Scripture states with certainty and authority.

The ministry of a prophet is always profitable but not always pleasant. It's not simply planting and building, but the ministry of a prophet is also pulling down, throwing down, tearing up, rooting out. There had to be a breaking before there could be a building. There had to be a tearing up of the land before there could be a planting of the seed. Jeremiah knew this. He saw it in his father and in the priestly community that ministry wouldn't always be easy.

"To every thing there is a season," Solomon declared, "and a time to every purpose under the Heaven: a time to be born, and a time to die; a time to plant, and a time to pluck up that which is planted; a time to kill, and a time to heal; a time to break down, and a time to build up . . ." (see Ecclesiastes 3:1-3). Building up is always more fulfilling than pulling down, planting always more exciting than destroying, yet, like Solomon, Jeremiah was told he would have to root out, pull down, destroy, and throw down before he could build and plant. And so must we. Paul tells us we are to pull down strongholds and cast down imaginations that seek to have preeminence over Christ in our thoughts and minds (2 Corinthians 10:4-5).

True ministry is not about getting people to like us but rather speaking as the Lord directs in humility and integrity - even if that means rooting out and throwing down in order that God may build up and plant deep.

OCTOBER 1

Moreover the word of the LORD came to me, saying, Go and cry in the ears of Jerusalem, saying, Thus saith the LORD; I remember thee, the kindness of thy youth, the love of thine espousals, when thou wentest after me in the wilderness, in a land that was not sown.

Jeremiah 2:1-2

The first part of Jeremiah's message is simply summarized in the word, "remember."

"Remember how it was when you first loved Me," the Lord says to His people through Jeremiah - "even when the land was yet wilderness, before it was prosperous."

I think of the words of Jesus to the church at Ephesus when He says, "I know all your good works, all your activities, all the ministry you're doing. But I have something against you. You've left your first love. Your love for Me has diminished. Remember from whence thou art fallen" (see Revelation 2:2-5).

Can you remember a time when you loved the Lord more than you do now? Was there a time when your love for Him was real and fresh and vital? Have things changed? Are devotions a drag? Is church a drudgery? Are the things of God a burden? "Remember," God would say, "how it was when you really sought Me. They may have been wilderness times, difficult times, but you loved Me and were wholly committed to Me."

OCTOBER 2

And it shall come to pass, when ye shall say, Wherefore doeth the LORD our God all these things unto us? then shalt thou answer them, Like as ye have forsaken me, and served strange gods in your land, so shall ye serve strangers in a land that is not yours.

Jeremiah 5:19

Although He had given them His Word and had sent them His prophets, knowing His people would claim to be mystified by His action, God gives a crystal-clear explanation. That is, "Because you have served foreign gods in your own land, you will now serve them in a foreign land." The irony is that, although they served foreign gods in their own land, they would eventually return to their own God in a foreign land - but the lesson would be a painful one.

If you're pursuing the gods of materialism, lust, pleasure, intellectualism, or any other god, take heed. Whom the Lord loves, He chastens (Hebrews 12:6). Therefore, like the people of Judah, you will have no reason to be surprised if He allows you to in some way be removed from the blessings of your own land and plunged into an unfamiliar, brutal, foreign land in order to ultimately draw you back to Him.

OCTOBER 3

To whom shall I speak, and give warning, that they may hear? behold, their ear is uncircumcised, and they cannot hearken: behold, the word of the LORD is unto them a reproach; they have no delight in it.

Jeremiah 6:10

In Jeremiah 4:4, the Lord said the hearts of His people were uncircumcised. Here, He says their ear is uncircumcised as well.

Before the people of Israel entered the Land of Promise after being released from Egypt and wandering in the wilderness for forty years, an entire generation grew up that had not been circumcised. The Lord told Joshua to stop at Gilgal before they went into the Land and circumcise the people again, for before they could experience the blessings of the Promised Land, they had to deal with their flesh (Joshua 5).

Maybe you and I are not experiencing the land of blessing or the fruitfulness God has for us because we have failed to stop at Gilgal and allow the Lord to deal with our flesh - those parts of our lives that prevent a real relationship with Him. If the Word of God no longer interests us because flesh has begun to cover our heart, how we need to be circumcised again.

OCTOBER 4

Is this house, which is called by my name, become a den of robbers in your eyes? Behold, even I have seen it, saith the LORD.

Jeremiah 7:11

Through Jeremiah, God refers to the Temple as a den of robbers. Centuries later, Jesus would come on the scene and say the same thing . . .

> And Jesus went into the temple of God, and cast out all them that sold and bought in the temple, and overthrew the tables of the moneychangers, and the seats of them that sold doves, and said unto them, It is written, My house shall be called the house of prayer; but ye have made it a den of thieves.

Matthew 21:12-13

Religious leaders were using the people of God and the things of God for their own gain. But before we indict them too severely, we must ask ourselves if we do the same thing. Do we use the things of God to find a girlfriend or a boyfriend? Do we use the things of God to make business connections or even to establish a name in ministry? Do we subconsciously ask ourselves how we can use the Lord rather than how we can honor Him?

> And the blind and the lame came to him in the temple; and he healed them.
>
> Matthew 21:14

Jesus kicked out those who were using Him, but reached out to those who were choosing Him, those who knew they didn't see the way they could or walk the way they should. So too, when we realize how blind and lame we are, Jesus will reach out to us as well. In Philippians 2:13 we read that it is God Who works in us both to will and to do of His good pleasure. In other words, He changes our desires and then gives us the ability to carry out the desire He's placed within us. That's the beauty of the living Lord. He's not saying, "Get it together." He's saying, "Let Me have your life."

"I am crucified with Christ," Paul declared. "Nevertheless, I live. Yet not I, but it's Christ Who lives in me" (see Galatians 2:20). It's not a matter of trying to be like Jesus. It's not keeping outward rituals or spiritual customs, as the people were doing in Jeremiah's day. Growth in the Christian life comes from saying, "I'm a sinner, Lord, and the only way I can be changed is by You forgiving Me through Your blood and living in me through Your Spirit. So I come to You with brokenness and honesty, asking You to live Your life through me."

OCTOBER 5

O that my head were waters, and mine eyes a fountain of tears, that I might weep day and night for the slain of the daughter of my people!

Jeremiah 9:1

Jeremiah didn't deliver his prophecies condemningly, with fingers pointing. He delivered them from a broken heart and with tear-filled eyes. That's why God chose him.

Some people come into our lives and say, "Woe is you," as they condemn and point their fingers. Not Jeremiah. He shared the message of God accurately, but not without weeping compassionately. I believe we have no right to judge any other person or situation if we're not brokenhearted about it. If I don't feel compassion and tenderness, brokenness and love, I need to keep my mouth shut. I don't have any right to point out the dirt on another's feet unless I'm willing to do what Jesus did - to get down and start washing. If I'm not willing to get involved in restoring, loving, weeping, and caring, I'm missing the mark entirely.

OCTOBER 6

Thy words were found, and I did eat them; and thy word was unto me the joy and rejoicing of mine heart: for I am called by thy name, O LORD God of hosts.

Jeremiah 15:16

In contrast to the rejection he felt from the people around him, Jeremiah speaks of the joy that God's Word produced within him. For years, the Law was lost. There was no copy of God's Word in all of Judah. When a copy was discovered - perhaps even by his own father (2 Kings 22:8) - Jeremiah had an insatiable appetite to take it in.

Job felt the same way. Even though he, too, went through some incredibly heavy times, he prioritized the Word even above physical food (Job 23:12). "Man shall not live by bread alone," Jesus said, "but by every word that proceeds out of the mouth of God" (see Matthew 4:4).

If it comes down to a choice, do we have morning devotions with the Lord or do we have breakfast instead? Somehow, we always find time to eat, but my prayer is that we would be like Jeremiah and Job and reach for the Word before we reach for the Wheaties.

OCTOBER 7

The heart is deceitful above all things, and desperately wicked: who can know it?

Jeremiah 17:9

We have a tendency to think we don't have to abide in the Lord, that we can do some pretty good things on our own, that we're not that bad. The average person thinks he's just a couple of steps away from perfection. But that's due to the deception of the heart. When I used to play basketball with Peter John, I was awesome. With my hook shots, rebounds, and lay-ups, I was unstoppable. When he turned twelve, however, things got a little more difficult!

We can always find people to compare ourselves to and feel okay about. But when you compare yourself to the true standard - not your friend, not your neighbor, but Christ Jesus, Who lived life the way it was meant to be lived - you realize you're not as hot as you thought. The more you get to know the Lord, the more you realize how far you are from where you should be. When you're first saved you think, "Once I get off cocaine, I'll be perfect." But as you walk with the Lord, you realize there are so many subtleties in your heart - motives, attitudes, and perspectives that are amiss. The closer you get to Him and the more you realize you need His grace, the more you enjoy His forgiveness and marvel at His patience.

OCTOBER 8

And the burden of the LORD shall ye mention no more: for every man's word shall be his burden; for ye have perverted the words of the living God, of the LORD of hosts our God.

Jeremiah 23:36

This group of prophets spoke continually about the burden of the Lord. But the Lord said He didn't want to hear that phrase any more.

"Come unto Me all you who are weary and heavy laden," Jesus said, "and I will give you rest, for My yoke is easy and My burden is light" (see Matthew 11:28-30). As a carpenter, it is possible Jesus made yokes. If so, He would have designed them to fit each animal perfectly. He does the same for us. The yoke He asks us to bear is custom-made for us. It takes into account our personalities, interests, and temperaments. That's what makes it easy.

When two animals are yoked together, there is a lead animal and one who follows. The lead animal carries most of the weight. If you wonder why your walk with the Lord is so hard and burdensome, it's likely because you're not flowing with what the Lord is doing. Consequently, you're pulling against His lead and getting bruised by the yoke in the process. In Ezekiel 44, the Lord said very clearly that the priests were to wear no garments made of wool because wool causes sweat. In other words, He doesn't want the work we do for Him to be troublesome. You'll know you're in the right ministry when it's a joy rather than a burden to you.

OCTOBER 9

Thus saith the LORD of hosts, the God of Israel, unto all that are carried away captives, whom I have caused to be carried away from Jerusalem unto Babylon; Build ye houses, and dwell in them; and plant gardens, and eat the fruit of them; take ye wives, and beget sons and daughters; and take wives for your sons, and give your daughters to husbands, that they may bear sons and daughters; that ye may be increased there, and not diminished.

Jeremiah 29:4-6

Jeremiah's letter didn't tell the Babylonian captives to gather weapons, start assassinating every leader they saw, ruin the economy, or overthrow the government. Instead, he told them they might as well dig in because they would be there for a long time. They were to plant gardens, get married, and build houses. It was God's plan for those people to be in captivity and difficulty for seventy full years until His purposes were accomplished.

This has implication for me. I must realize that if the Lord allows friends of mine to be in hard places, I am not necessarily to try to run in and get them out. There are some times when it is the Lord's plan to keep a person or even a nation in the place of difficulty for a season to accomplish what He wants to do in them. For example, historically, the Church has been the strongest in places where persecution has been the hardest. Therefore, we must, like Jeremiah, react according to spiritual discernment rather than according to political persuasion.

OCTOBER 10

For I know the thoughts that I think toward you, saith the LORD, thoughts of peace, and not of evil, to give you an expected end.

Jeremiah 29:11

Here, God says to His people, "You'll be in Babylon for seventy years, but know that the thoughts I think of you are of peace, to bring you to a glorious end. I'm doing something special in you." And indeed He was. When the Jews went into Babylon, they were idolatrous people. When they came out, never again did they worship idols. They were purged. They were healed. They were matured in those difficult days of the Babylonian captivity.

This verse is one of my favorites in all the Bible, for it speaks to me and you that even in the times things look bad, when the Babylonians are carrying you away, the Lord is using it for something glorious.

OCTOBER 11

*And ye shall seek me, and find me, when ye shall search for
me with all your heart.*

Jeremiah 29:13

Kirk was an all-state basketball player for the high school I attended. Kirk
wore contact lenses and, not infrequently, one of them would pop out during a game. When that happened, Kirk, his teammates, the coach, the ref-
erees, and even the opposing team searched with all their hearts to find the
missing lens so that the game could continue. That's the kind of diligence,
the kind of single-heartedness the Lord wants from us in seeking Him.

Why does God want us to search for Him with that kind of intensity? It's
not that He's playing hard to get, but that He wants to strengthen us. You
see, the only way we'll be prepared for the ages to come is if we learn how
to pray, worship, and walk by faith this side of eternity. This earth is boot
camp, gang. It's spring training. The Lord is training us because He knows
what lies beyond this life and He wants to get us in shape for it. That's why
He doesn't respond to those who seek Him halfheartedly or lethargically.

OCTOBER 12

*Behold, I will bring them from the north country, and gather
them from the coasts of the earth, and with them the blind
and the lame, the woman with child and her that travaileth
with child together: a great company shall return thither.
They shall come with weeping, and with supplications will
I lead them: I will cause them to walk by the rivers of waters
in a straight way, wherein they shall not stumble: for I am a
father to Israel, and Ephraim is my firstborn.*

Jeremiah 31:8-9

Both at the beginning of their long history with idolatry and at the end, neither the Lord's love nor His plan for His people wavered. Thus, He would make a way for them back to Him. The only thing that could prevent this would be their own hesitancy.

"Follow Me," Jesus said.

"Let me first bury my father," came the reply.

"Follow Me," Jesus said.

"Let me first say good-bye," answered another (Luke 9:59-61).

God's promise to His people in Jeremiah's day was that, as He had done for them seven hundred years earlier when He led them from Egypt, He would lead the way, make straight the path, provide water and nourishment for them. The only thing they had to do was follow. Jesus called His own to do this as well, but their ties to this world rendered the majority too blind and lame to do so.

He calls you to follow Him today. Don't allow any seeming infirmity or inability to stand in your way. Make the first step and you'll find yourself walking by "rivers of water in a straight way" - and you'll stumble no more.

OCTOBER 13

Therefore the word of the LORD came to Jeremiah from the LORD, saying, Thus saith the LORD, the God of Israel; I made a covenant with your fathers in the day that I brought them forth out of the land of Egypt, out of the house of bondmen, saying, At the end of seven years let ye go every man his brother a Hebrew, which hath been sold unto thee; and when he hath served thee six years, thou shalt let him go free from thee: but your fathers hearkened not unto me, neither inclined their ear. And ye were now turned, and had done right in my sight, in proclaiming liberty every man to his neighbour; and ye had made a covenant before me in the house which is called by my name. But ye turned and polluted my name, and caused every man his servant, and every man his handmaid, whom ye had set at liberty at their pleasure, to return, and brought them into subjection, to be unto you for servants and for handmaids. Therefore thus saith the LORD; Ye have not hearkened unto me, in proclaiming liberty, every one to his brother, and every man to his neighbour: behold, I proclaim a liberty for you, saith the LORD, to the sword, to the pestilence, and to the famine; and I will make you to be removed into all the kingdoms of the earth.

Jeremiah 34:12-17

Because Zedekiah and the people broke the covenant they had made concerning freeing the Hebrew slaves, sword, pestilence, and hardship would be free to do their work upon them.

The Lord set us free. He released us from the penalty of every sin in our lives. Therefore, we are to forgive others. And sometimes we do that for a while. But then we remember what he said about us or what she did to us and, like Zedekiah, we change our minds and back into our debt we go.

Jesus told a parable of a man who was released from a two-million-dollar debt. But when he found someone who owed him a few dollars, he demanded to be paid on the spot. When the king heard about this, he brought the man before him and said, "I released you of a two-million-dollar debt. Yet you demand payment of a man who only owes you a few dollars? You're going to prison and you won't get out until you have paid every penny (Matthew 18). How could the man earn money in prison to pay his debt? He couldn't. There was only one way out of prison: he had to die.

How will you get out of the prison of bitterness and judgment, depression and criticism? There's only one way out: die. Die to yourself and your disappointments, your disillusionment and discouragement and say, "Lord, I've been forgiven so much. Help me to die to what others have said about me or done to me."

This is so important because bunches of us are in prison right now mentally and spiritually because we've brought back into bondage people we once forgave. Whether it's a girlfriend, a husband, a boss, or a neighbor, truly forgive them and resist the temptation to bind them again.

OCTOBER 14

Then Jeremiah called Baruch the son of Neriah: and Baruch wrote from the mouth of Jeremiah all the words of the LORD, which he had spoken unto him, upon a roll of a book.

Jeremiah 36:4

The Word was given to Jeremiah, who then dictated it to a man named Baruch. In this, we see an interesting illustration of inspiration - how the Bible came into being. The Lord's Word was revealed to Jeremiah. Jeremiah, in turn, related it to Baruch, who actually wrote the words down on parchment. This is a picture of the way inspiration works. Whether it be Jeremiah or John, Peter or Paul, the Word of the Lord was revealed to these men. It was revealed, then recorded, and finally regarded as God's Word.

Some people have a problem with this process. "What if Jeremiah made a mistake in sensing God's heart or hearing His voice?" they ask. "What if

Baruch wasn't listening carefully and wrote something down wrong? Can it truly be regarded as the Word of God?"

We could talk about the scientific accuracy of the Bible. Although it is not a book of science, when it does speak of science, it is absolutely accurate. Or we could talk about the archaeological confirmations of the Word. The Bible talks about cities and civilizations whose existence scholars denied for years that were eventually verified by the archaeologist's spade. We could talk about the Bible's miraculous unity - the fact that there are sixty-six individual books united in theme, message, and philosophy yet written over a period of fifteen hundred years.

We could talk about science and archaeology, unity and history - but it all gets down to one simple question. Is God Who He says He is? If God is omnipotent, a Father who cares about His children, a King who is concerned about His Kingdom, do you think that if mistakes were made when the Bible was either being penned or compiled that He was powerless to do anything about it? If God is a Father who loves us and wants to communicate with us, and if He chose to do it through a book, don't you think He would have safeguarded the writing and compilation processes?

October 15

Then the king commanded Ebed-melech the Ethiopian, saying, Take from hence thirty men with thee, and take up Jeremiah the prophet out of the dungeon, before he die. So Ebed-melech took the men with him, and went into the house of the king under the treasury, and took thence old cast clouts and old rotten rags, and let them down by cords into the dungeon to Jeremiah. And Ebed-melech the Ethiopian said unto Jeremiah, Put now these old cast clouts and rotten rags under thine armholes under the cords. And Jeremiah did so. So they drew up Jeremiah with cords, and took him up out of the dungeon: and Jeremiah remained in the court of the prison.

Jeremiah 38:10-13

Ebed-melech went to the king and interceded on Jeremiah's behalf. Then he gathered ropes and put rags around them so Jeremiah wouldn't be bruised.

You might not be able to perform miracles. You might not have musical talent. You might not be an evangelist. You might feel like an Ethiopian, without anything to offer. But you can find a person in the pit - in your community, your school, your office. You can intercede on his behalf. Then you can do something to help him practically. You can pull him out of the pit . . .

> Brethren, if a man be overtaken in a fault, ye which are spiritual, restore such a one in the spirit of meekness; considering thyself, lest thou also be tempted.

Galatians 6:1

Has there been someone who, seeing you were in a pit of some kind, found a way to do something, to say something, to share something that lifted you up? I've had those Ebed-melechs in my life and I thank God for them. Ask the Lord to show you someone in the pit, and God will honor your prayer.

OCTOBER 16

Thus saith the LORD of hosts; Behold, I will break the bow of Elam, the chief of their might.

Jeremiah 49:35

Elam is present-day Iran. The Elamites were known as superior archers. Here, the Lord said He would break their bow. That's often the way of the Lord, even with us. That in which we're most secure, that about which we're most confident is often that which the Lord takes away. It's not because He's capricious or spiteful, but because He realizes that if we're depending on our own strength or ability, we'll be limited in what we can accomplish because no matter how strong we are at any given point, our strength is limited.

God's principle is always brokenness. It's when we're weak that He can show Himself strong (2 Corinthians 12:10). His strength is infinitely greater than our strength. Therefore, if we're trusting in our bow - be it occupationally, financially, relationally - it's our bow He'll take away. When your bow gets taken away, gang, it's not by an angry God Who says, "I want to destroy you," but a loving Father who says, "I see that your bow is giving you a limited, false security, and I love you too much for that."

OCTOBER 17

In those days, and in that time, saith the LORD, the iniquity of Israel shall be sought for, and there shall be none; and the sins of Judah, and they shall not be found: for I will pardon them whom I reserve.

Jeremiah 50:20

Even after they ignored His warnings, imprisoned His prophets, and missed His illustrations; even after they sinned willfully, knowingly, and arrogantly,

God said that, because they had been chastened and had turned back to Him, no sign of the sin of His people would remain.

We have been given the same incredible promise because, if we confess our sin, the blood of Jesus cleanses the sins we have already committed, are committing, and will commit (1 John 1:9). The forgiveness of God is truly overwhelming. If you read Jeremiah and only see judgment, you're missing the most astounding part of his message - God's incredible, unspeakable mercy.

OCTOBER 18

But thou hast utterly rejected us; thou art very wroth against us.

Lamentation 5:22

This would better be translated as a question. "Have You utterly rejected us? Are You still angry with us?" Thus, Jeremiah ends his book with a question - one that will be answered as the history of God's people and His faithfulness to them unfolds.

Lamentations is a heavy book, but it's necessary for our growth. It reminds us not only that sin always brings sorrow but that blues can be battled, that depression can be defeated. Second, it causes us to ask ourselves if we weep for the lost. Our theology says that people who don't know the Lord will be damned. But what would happen if we really knew that our mothers and fathers and friends and brother were truly going to hell? I believe if we really understood that, we, like Jeremiah, would not be whining about ourselves any more but weeping for the lost and living to share the Gospel.

Finally, Lamentations reminds us that God entrusts tough messages to tender men. Jeremiah was perhaps the most tender man in all of the Bible, yet he had the toughest message of all. When G. Campbell Morgan watched D. L. Moody preach, he concluded that Moody had the right to preach on hell for he always talked about it with tears in his voice.

Lord, make us like Jeremiah - not preaching condemningly, but sharing compassionately.

OCTOBER 19

Now it came to pass in the thirtieth year, in the fourth month, in the fifth day of the month, as I was among the captives by the river of Chebar, that the heavens were opened, and I saw visions of God. In the fifth day of the month, which was the fifth year of king Jehoiachin's captivity.

Ezekiel 1:1-2

It was as he sat by the river Chebar, a captive away from home, no doubt feeling lonely and isolated, that the heavens opened to Ezekiel. Therefore, if you feel isolated, cut off from family or separated from friends, as though something is going on that is uncomfortable or uncertain, take hope. Ezekiel had this glorious vision of the reality of God when he was in a place of isolation.

The Bible speaks of the opening of the heavens on a number of occasions. In Matthew 3:16, it was when Jesus was baptized - a picture of death, burial, and resurrection - that the heavens were opened. So too, when we get to the place where we say, "Lord, I'm dying to self and living for You," the heavens will be opened. We'll have visions, new insights, new understanding.

The heavens were opened again in Acts 6. There we see Stephen being stoned to death, martyred for his belief in Jesus. As the rocks were flying, he looked up and saw Jesus standing, ready to receive Him. So too, when you go through persecution, Heaven becomes more real.

In Acts 10, Peter was on the rooftop praying when suddenly the heavens were opened and he had a vision of a sheet descending from Heaven bearing food forbidden to Jews. It was then that the Lord began to deal with him, saying, "You're not under the Law any longer. I'm doing something new." So too, when we seek the Lord and pray with intensity, we'll hear the Lord's voice to a greater degree.

Finally, in Malachi 3, we are told that when we give our tithes to the Lord, He opens the heavens and pours out blessing upon us. When you give to the Lord, when you seek the Lord, when you take a stand for the Lord, when you die to self and live for the Lord, the heavens will be opened to you. The problem is, we don't sit by a river, we float down it. We don't go up to the mountain, we ski down it. When we're going through hard times, we think we've got to get away for recreation. But how much better it would be to get away for meditation and contemplation.

OCTOBER 20

And I saw as the colour of amber, as the appearance of fire round about within it, from the appearance of his loins even upward, and from the appearance of his loins even downward, I saw as it were the appearance of fire, and it had brightness round about. As the appearance of the bow that is in the cloud in the day of rain, so was the appearance of the brightness round about. This was the appearance of the likeness of the glory of the LORD. And when I saw it, I fell upon my face, and I heard a voice of one that spake.

Ezekiel 1:27-28

It's not surprising that He Who is the Light of the world appears as bright as fire (John 8:12). Ezekiel saw not only the fiery glow of God's glory but also the bow of His grace (Genesis 9:16). Here, the Lord on the throne is as bright as fire but with a gracious bow emanating from Him. The glory of God and the grace of God walk hand in hand.

Seeing these things, Ezekiel fell on his face. So did the Apostle John (Revelation 1:17). When you see the greatness of God, it's inevitable that you fall on your face in brokenness and humility.

This chapter is important for two reasons. First, it guards against a loss of transcendence. That is, it serves as a reminder that God is great and awesome, beyond description and understanding, that He is "other." He's not our buddy or "the Man upstairs." There is a mystery and majesty concerning the God we serve that should cause us to fall on our face. Failure to acknowledge the transcendence of God results in a lack of worship of God. People who have God all figured out theologically, all boxed in doctrinally will not worship because there's no mystery. That's why visions like this are invaluable to us, even though we don't fully understand them.

Second, this chapter guards against a loss of imminence. Yes, God is "other" - but He's also here, among us. Here is this awesome mysterious Being revealing something of Himself to Ezekiel, dwelling in the midst of these living creatures, making Himself known by coming as a Man, Jesus from Galilee. Loss of imminence results in cold formality. People might worship, but it will be dead ritualism.

Transcendence and imminence are always necessary in the Church corporately and in our lives personally. The first time I went to Candlestick Park, I was in third grade. I saw Willie Mays hit the first pitch of the first inning out of the park. From that day on, he was my hero. Then I had the opportunity to meet him at a dinner through a friend's dad. I sat two rows away from him. He was there, present, but he was totally "other." He was very gracious, but I was aware of his transcendence. That's the way it is with our Lord. He rejoices over us with song. He loves to be in our midst. He calls us friends. And yet He is bigger and more "other" than we can ever imagine.

OCTOBER 21

And he said unto me, Son of man, stand upon thy feet, and I will speak unto thee. And the spirit entered into me when he spake unto me, and set me upon my feet, that I heard him that spake unto me.

Ezekiel 2:1-2

After Ezekiel fell upon his face in chapter 1, the Lord tells him to stand on his feet here in chapter 2. Then the Spirit Himself stood him on his feet. Isn't that always the way of the Lord? He's not only the commander, but also the enabler. What He says, He does. If He tells you to love your enemies, it is He Who will give you the power to do it. If He tells you to forgive your sister, it is He who will give you the ability to do just that.

When you read the Bible and the Lord tells you something specific to do, know that by virtue of the fact that He tells you to do it, He will enable you to do it. He never says, "Here's the goal. Good luck." He says, "Here's My Word and here's My Spirit."

OCTOBER 22

And say, Ye mountains of Israel, hear the word of the Lord GOD; Thus saith the Lord GOD to the mountains, and to the hills, to the rivers, and to the valleys; Behold, I, even I, will bring a sword upon you, and I will destroy your high places.

Ezekiel 6:3

The term "high places" appears throughout the Old Testament. The high places were groves or little gardens built by the Canaanites in which they would worship their gods in garden-like settings. When Joshua was told to conquer the land, he did a fairly good job, but let the high places remain. Why? Perhaps because they were pleasant to look at. But as the years progressed, the people of Israel were drawn to these little gardens and, there, learned of the worship rituals of the Canaanites.

The warning to us is that sometimes there are sins about which we say, "That's not a big issue in my life. I don't have to deal with that particular thing. It's under control. Besides, it's kind of pretty. I'll deal with everything else and I'll let that high place be."

God, however, says the groves have got to go not because He doesn't want us to have fun, but because He knows they'll eventually destroy us.

"Oh, but it's just a small part of my life," we protest.

"It will destroy you," a loving Father answers. "These groves have got to go - now."

Satan's biggest lie - one that he's told ever since the garden of Eden - is to whisper in our ears that God is holding back something really good from us (Genesis 3:5). But that's not true. God says to us that the groves must go because our bodies will be left on the floor of pagan altars. In other words, we'll be destroyed.

OCTOBER 23

I will recompense thee according to thy ways and thine abominations that are in the midst of thee; and ye shall know that I am the LORD that smiteth.

Ezekiel 7:9 (b)

Throughout Scripture, various names of God are revealed. In Genesis 22:14, we see *Jehovah-Jireh*, the Lord our provider. In Exodus 17:15, we see *Jehovah-Nissi*, the Lord our banner, or covering. In Judges 6:24, we see *Jehovah-Shalom*, the Lord our peace. In Jeremiah 23:6, we see *Jehovah-Tsidkenu*, the Lord our righteousness. We like those names. But here we see He's also *Jehovah-Makkeh*, the Lord who smites because God is not only our provider, He is also a smiter. And when we come to the Lord, we get the whole package. We can't say, "I'll take *Jehovah-Jireh* and *Jehovah-Shalom*, but I'm not interested in *Jehovah-Makkeh*." That's not the way it works. When we say, "You are my God," we get His person in totality.

God is indeed the God Who smites. But, instead of smiting you and me the way we deserve to be, He smote His own Son on a hill called Calvary.

Yet it pleased the LORD to bruise him; he hath put him to grief: when thou shalt make his soul an offering for sin, he shall see his seed, he shall prolong his days, and the pleasure of the LORD shall prosper in his hand.

Isaiah 53:10

Our glorious, awesome, powerful Father will not wink at sin. He is *Jehovah-Makkeh*. But He is also the One who loves you and me so intensely that He provided a way whereby we wouldn't be smitten eternally. Jesus took our place. Therefore, if we walk away from the One who gave everything to die in our place, we deserve to be smitten eternally.

OCTOBER 24

. . . and according to their deserts will I judge them; and they shall know that I am the LORD.

Ezekiel 7:27 (b)

"My people insisted on having their own way," the Lord declares. "But when I judge them accordingly, they will know that I am the Lord."

Three things strike me as I come to the close of this dramatic presentation. The first is the absolute integrity of God's message. We have a tendency to want to be liked. God, on the other hand, is committed to declaring the truth. And He knows that sin must be judged or it will bring judgment. One of the key components of conversion is for a man to realize he's a sinner. If he doesn't realize this, he will walk away from the One who was made sin for him (2 Corinthians 5:21). That's why the Old Testament is so important. It's a schoolmaster to show us that what we call personality quirks or idiosyncrasies are actually sin (Galatians 3:24).

Second, I see the remarkable flexibility of God's method. In Ezekiel, He communicates through drama, poetry, art, foot stomping, and hand clapping. Whatever it takes to communicate, God will use. Therefore, next time you think some ministry is bizarre, think of Ezekiel, for God will sometimes use methods that seem shocking to church people to reach a world that is no longer listening to traditional means.

Finally, I see the potential expendability of God's men. Our God has work to do. And He'll use those who are willing to say, "Use me." But it's not always going to be easy. He might say to you, "The way I will use you is to be a model to this community of how a man dies from cancer while keeping his faith intact." God might call some of you to the ministry where you will have churches that grow to the number of seven people after thirty years of preaching. God's ministry for you might be to show the world how to be faithful when you're not seeing results outwardly. He might give you songs to sing but no one comes with recording contracts.

Surely, Ezekiel didn't enjoy all of his assignments. But do you think he's in Heaven saying, "What a rip-off. I can't believe God made me do those things"? I don't. I think when he heard, "Well done, good and faithful servant" - it was all worth it.

In Heaven, there are rewards, blessings, and fulfillment that we can't possibly imagine now. And, like Ezekiel, we'll say "Thank You, Lord, for letting me suffer, for not allowing me to see my name in lights, for going through hard times because now it all makes sense. I feel honored." If it takes us going through hard times to allow God to do His work, so be it. God does not exist to make us comfortable. He has a job to do through us.

OCTOBER 25

For, behold, I am for you, and I will turn unto you . . .

Ezekiel 36:9 (a)

"I am *for* you," God declares. Could there have been any music sweeter to the ears of His people than these words? Maybe, like them, you feel you are held captive, far from where you should be because of sin and rebellion. Take heart, dear people, God is for you, just as He was for His people - and if God be for you, none can stand against you (Romans 8:31).

Eighteen times in this chapter God says, "I will." That's always the way it is. God does the work. All that's left for His people to do is to respond.

I remember when my daughter, Mary Elizabeth, was about 1 ½ years old. She came to me with a pink balloon not yet inflated. I blew it up for her until it was about as tall as she was. As I handed it to her, I cautioned her to be careful. With a smile on her face, she grabbed the balloon and toddled off. But she wasn't gone two minutes before she came back, blowing into a pink piece of plastic hanging from her mouth. The balloon had popped. The warning was not heeded. I see the same thing happen to a lot of us. Something blows up. Something pops. The bubble bursts. And what do we attempt to do? We blow and blow in our own strength. We try to put the marriage back together, raise the child, meet the need ourselves. But we get nowhere. Here, the Lord is saying something wonderful to Israel - and to any of us who are aware of a burst bubble, a popped balloon - "I am for you."

OCTOBER 26

Thus saith the Lord GOD; I will yet for this be inquired of by the house of Israel, to do it for them; I will increase them with men like a flock. As the holy flock, as the flock of Jerusalem in her solemn feasts; so shall the waste cities be filled with flocks of men: and they shall know that I am the LORD.

Ezekiel 36:37-38

The Lord promises to restore and revive, and yet there is a price - but it's a joyous one. "I want you to inquire of Me, to ask that I will do it," He says. "You don't need to impress Me with your spirituality or motivate Me with your intensity. All I ask is that you come to Me and ask." Why does God say this? Because He wants us to partner with Him in what He's doing.

Prayer is the one part we play in this restoration process. Jesus told us to ask, seek, and knock (Matthew 7:7). James declared that we have not simply because we ask not (4:2).

I think of Elisabeth. Week after week, year by year, no doubt she and her husband, Zacharias, prayed for a child. They believed the Lord and claimed the Word in prayer - yet nothing happened. But when Zacharias was an old man, serving in the Temple, an angel came to him and told him that his prayer had been heard. And indeed a baby was born to them - one who would grow up to be John the Baptist (Luke 1). But it took time.

"I will rebuild," the Lord says to us today. "I will revive. I will freely give you all things (Romans 8:32). And all I ask of you is, 'Will you be like Elisabeth and Zacharias? Will you pray?'"

OCTOBER 27

Then brought he me out of the way of the gate northward, and led me about the way without unto the utter gate by the way that looketh eastward; and, behold, there ran out waters on the right side. And when the man that had the line in his hand went forth eastward, he measured a thousand cubits, and he brought me through the waters; the waters were to the ankles. Again he measured a thousand, and brought me through the waters; the waters were to the knees. Again he measured a thousand, and brought me through; the waters were to the loins. Afterward he measured a thousand; and it was a river that I could not pass over: for the waters were risen, waters to swim in, a river that could not be passed over. And he said unto me, Son of man, hast thou seen this?

Ezekiel 47:2-6 (a)

"Have you seen this?" The Lord asks us the same question because that's the order of what happens in our walk. We're walking with Jesus and we get our feet wet up to our ankles.

"This is great," we say. "I'm on solid ground. I'm standing in the Lord. I'm born again. My sins are forgiven. I'm on my way to Heaven!"

Then the Lord says, "Let's go a little deeper." So he ⸺ one thousand cubits and says, "Go in again." This time, we ⸺

"I want you to learn what it means to pray - not only to stand, pray because you're aware of the challenges and problems and strug⸺ life."

Then the Lord says, "We're going deeper still." So we walk in up to our loins - the place of reproduction. As we grow in the knowledge of God, as we stay in His Word, as we learn how to pray, we're going to reproduce spiritually. If a congregation is healthy, it will naturally grow because healthy sheep naturally reproduce. It's inevitable.

Then the Lord says, "There's one more stop. This time you're going over your head in water so deep you can swim in it. You can be refreshed by it, but you can no longer control it. You're over your head." Praying in the Spirit, dying to self, worshipping with consistency, walking in power - have you seen this?

Where are you? Are you up to your ankles? Have you just begun your walk with Jesus? If you have, that's great - but move on. Get on your knees. Learn how to intercede, to pray, and to be faithful in your devotional life. Are you a prayer warrior? Great, then start reproducing. Start witnessing and sharing. But if you're still desiring more, take the plunge today. Step in deeper still to the place where you want to be used by the Lord no matter the price.

Where are you now? Where do you desire to be? The Lord will take you as far down the river as you want to go.

OCTOBER 28

It was round about eighteen thousand measures: and the name of the city from that day shall be, The LORD is there.

Ezekiel 48:35

The people to whom Ezekiel prophesied were captives in a foreign land. They had heard reports that their country had been obliterated, that the Temple had been destroyed. But suddenly they hear a message from God, telling them not only that the Temple would be rebuilt, that the Levites would be in place, that the priests would be in attendance, that all twelve tribes would be reunited and given a portion of the land - but, above all, that the city would be named *Jehovah-Shammah*, or "the Lord is there."

Maybe, like the Jews in Ezekiel's day, you feel displaced or forgotten, out of touch and out of hope. If you don't know the Lord, leave the captivity of sin behind and turn to Him, for He is as near as your confession of faith in Him (Romans 10:8-10).

And if you do know Him, take heart, for all Scripture is given by inspiration of God and is profitable for instruction in righteousness - including Ezekiel 48 (2 Timothy 3:16). Through this otherwise-obscure passage, the Lord would say to you, "Fear not. I haven't left you nor forsaken you. In fact, I have something planned and all measured out for you. The Kingdom is right around the corner - and the best part about it is that I will be there."

OCTOBER 29

And the king communed with them; and among them all was found none like Daniel, Hananiah, Mishael, and Azariah: therefore stood they before the king.

Daniel 1:19

You just can't out-give God. Daniel, Shadrach, Meshach, and Abed-nego gave themselves wholeheartedly to the Lord and what happened? They found favor with both God and man. When you give God your energy, talent, money, or ability, He will not "owe you one." He'll give back to you exceedingly abundantly above all you can ask or think (Ephesians 3:20).

The disciples certainly didn't lose out by loaning their boat to use as a floating pulpit, for in return He blessed them with so many fish their boat almost sank (Luke 5). When the little boy gave his lunch to the Lord, he was one of the five thousand in attendance who were filled to overflowing (Mark 6). When the widow gave her last bit of meal and oil to Elijah, she never lacked again (1 Kings 17).

One of the great lies of Satan is to try and get kids to think that if they serve Him, they will be unpopular and ostracized. That's just not true. Parents, show your kids the example of Daniel, Shadrach, Meshach, and Abed-nego. Say, "Here are some young men who refused to give in to the pressures and pleasures of the world - and they found favor with God and with men as well." Yes, you will experience persecution if you give your life to the Lord, but there will be a sterling quality about your life and an attractiveness that comes only from walking with God. Violate that and you'll miss out on so much that God wants to do in your life.

OCTOBER 30

Daniel answered and said, Blessed be the name of God for ever and ever: for wisdom and might are his: and he changeth the times and the seasons: he removeth kings, and setteth up kings: he giveth wisdom unto the wise, and knowledge to them that know understanding: he revealeth the deep and secret things: he knoweth what is in the darkness, and the light dwelleth with him. I thank thee, and praise thee, O thou God of my fathers, who hast given me wisdom and might, and hast made known unto me now what we desired of thee: for thou hast now made known unto us the king's matter.

Daniel 2:20-23

Daniel stopped and offered praise before he went out to save lives. I think that's an invaluable lesson. So often the Lord shows us something or gives us something and we can't wait to get going. In reality, before we run out, we should slow down and look up. We should worship and give thanks.

I think of the ten lepers in Luke 17. Jesus told them to go their way and show themselves to the priest. And as they went, they were healed. All ten rejoiced, but only one came back and thanked the Lord. "You are made whole," Jesus said to him. All ten were healed, but only the one who came back and worshipped was made whole, which speaks not only of his body but of his soul and spirit as well. Are we like the nine or are we like the one?

I like Daniel because he wasn't just a prayer warrior, but a praiser and a worshipper.

"But that's not efficient. Time is running out. You don't have time to pray." That's the voice of Judas. As Mary offered the alabaster box of oil to Jesus, Judas said, "That money could have been used for something much better, for feeding the poor."

But Jesus said, "What she is doing shall be spoken of throughout the world wherever the Gospel is preached" (see Mark 14:9).

Like Daniel, Mary was a praiser, a worshipper. And the Lord commended her.

OCTOBER 31

Shadrach, Meshach, and Abed-nego, answered and said to the king, O Nebuchadnezzar, we are not careful to answer thee in this matter. If it be so, our God whom we serve is able to deliver us from the burning fiery furnace, and he will deliver us out of thine hand, O king. But if not, be it known unto thee, O king, that we will not serve thy gods, nor worship the golden image which thou hast set up.

Daniel 3:16-18

In the answer of these three godly men, we see a very important lesson. "God is able to deliver us," they said. But then they added, "Even if He decides not to, we're still not going to bow down." They didn't doubt God's power to save them. But they submitted to His will concerning whether He intended to save them. They weren't doubting God's ability. They were submitting to His sovereignty.

> . . . Who through faith subdued kingdoms, wrought righteousness, obtained promises, stopped the mouths of lions, quenched the violence of fire, escaped the edge of the sword, out of weakness were made strong, waxed valiant in fight, turned to flight the armies of the aliens.

Hebrews 11:33-34

By faith, Shadrach, Meshach, and Abed-nego "quenched the violence of fire." In other words, because they had faith, they weren't burned. But faith in what? They didn't have faith in faith. They had faith in their Father.

When we pour out our requests to God and say, "If You decide not to heal me, bring me that financial windfall, or save my business, it doesn't matter. All I want is your will" - that is true faith. How I pray we can learn this.

NOVEMBER 1

Then this Daniel was preferred above the presidents and princes, because an excellent spirit was in him; and the king thought to set him over the whole realm.

Daniel 6:3

Darius realized there was an "excellent spirit" within Daniel. What was this excellent spirit? The Holy Spirit.

Daniel interpreted dreams. He prayed with effectiveness. He understood visions. He moved in prophecy. He experienced the miraculous. In other words, he was a man who was filled with the Spirit. That's what made him so successful all the days of his life.

In 2 Chronicles 16:9, we read that the eyes of the Lord go to and fro throughout the whole earth, looking for a man in whom He might show Himself strong, whose heart is perfect toward Him. Our Father is still looking for men and women in whom He can show Himself strong - as He did with Daniel.

November 2

Then king Darius wrote unto all people, nations, and languages, that dwell in all the earth; Peace be multiplied unto you. I make a decree, that in every dominion of my kingdom men tremble and fear before the God of Daniel: for he is the living God, and stedfast for ever, and his kingdom that which shall not be destroyed, and his dominion shall be even unto the end. He delivereth and rescueth, and he worketh signs and wonders in heaven and in earth, who hath delivered Daniel from the power of the lions. So this Daniel prospered in the reign of Darius, and in the reign of Cyrus the Persian.

Daniel 6:25-28

No less real than the lions that surrounded Daniel, Peter tells us that Satan is a roaring lion seeking whom he may devour (1 Peter 5:8). He has two basic ways to destroy and devour us. That is, he gets us involved in sin and then accuses us concerning our sin.

> . . . for the accuser of our brethren is cast down, which accused them before our God day and night.

Revelation 12:10 (b)

Satan whispers in our ear constantly. It's not a loud roar, but a soft purr: "You're a sinner," he whispers. "You have no right to pray to God. You'll never be used by Him." If Satan and his demons can't devour you through sin, they'll make constant accusations against you until you're ready to give up and walk away from the Lord. But, because you and I found ourselves damned because of sin and doomed to spend eternity in the lion's den of hell, God sent His Son - the ultimate Messenger - to come down to this earth, to stand with us, to die for us, and to go to hell in our place. Every sin we've ever done, are doing, or will do has been paid for by Jesus. Therefore, to overcome Satan's roaring accusations, we plead His blood (Revelation 12:11).

Satan is a roaring lion to be sure - but he got tangled up in a cat fight with the Lion of the tribe of Judah and he lost.

NOVEMBER 3

In the first year of Darius the son of Ahasuerus, of the seed of the Medes, which was made king over the realm of the Chaldeans; in the first year of his reign I Daniel understood by books the number of the years, whereof the word of the LORD came to Jeremiah the prophet, that he would accomplish seventy years in the desolations of Jerusalem.

Daniel 9:1-2

Although Daniel was a seer, he was still a student. Although he was a prophet, he was still a pupil. That is, he was one who read the Word regularly and studied it carefully. Now, if Daniel was one given to reading and researching the Scriptures, how much more do I need to do the same.

Here, Daniel comes to the 25th chapter of Jeremiah and sees that Jeremiah foretold that Nebuchadnezzar and the Babylonians would carry the Jews into captivity. God allowed this because not only had they embraced idolatry but they had ignored God's Word continually - specifically as it related to the Sabbath year.

You see, according to Leviticus 25, every seventh year, God's people were to do no plowing or tilling of the ground. The land was to rest. We now know agriculturally and scientifically why this would be important. But they were simply to take it on faith. On the sixth year, the Lord would give them twice as much in order to see them through the seventh year. But for four hundred ninety years, they ignored that commandment. In other words, the land missed out on seventy years of rest. Therefore, the Lord told Jeremiah that His people would be carried away captive for seventy years. And while they were gone, the land would indeed rest.

Now the seventy years was up. So what did Daniel do? Jeremiah's writings didn't simply stimulate his curiosity but they moved him to activity - and that's always the purpose of prophecy. After reading Jeremiah's prophecy, Daniel was prompted to pray.

Many times, people don't pray because they're not studying or meditating on the Word. When they try to pray, they don't know what to talk about. I have news for you: God is a great conversationalist and He initiates the conversation through His Word. That's why reading the Bible is important and studying it is essential. As I read the Scriptures, I discover the things I should talk about in prayer.

NOVEMBER 4

And I set my face unto the Lord God, to seek by prayer and
supplications, with fasting, and sackcloth, and ashes.

Daniel 9:3

After the prompting to prayer, we see the preparation for prayer. Daniel set his face, which speaks of determination. Sackcloth is a hairy garment, camel's hair usually, turned inside out so the bristles of the camel continually rub against one's skin. What was Daniel doing? He was showing he was serious in seeking the Lord.

Fasting is a way we can seek the Lord in seriousness. Fasting is an important tool in the Christian arsenal both in doing battle with the enemy and in seeking our Father and His blessings. All day long, we're bombarded by advertising and noise. Not only are our senses bombarded, but our stomachs are constantly craving certain kinds of food. We're stuffing ourselves with this, that, and the other. Fasting is a practical way of saying, "I'm not going to continue showering myself with physical sensations and stimuli. I'm going to slow it down."

Physiologically, you actually become a clearer thinker when you're fasting. Many tests confirm this. Fasting is good for us physically and helpful to us mentally. Fasting is not a way to score points with the Lord but an avenue to deny our flesh physically in order to concentrate on the spiritual realm with greater intensity. Fasting is not meant to prove something to God but to simply place ourselves in a position where we can hear Him more clearly.

As a teenager, Daniel understood the importance of the fast. Here he is now, at eighty-six years of age, still fasting.

NOVEMBER 5

And I prayed unto the LORD my God, and made my confession, and said, O Lord, the great and dreadful God, keeping the covenant and mercy to them that love him, and to them that keep his commandments.

Daniel 9:4

After prompting and preparation, here we see the preface to Daniel's prayer. He prefaces his prayer by remembering Who he's talking to. The Bible says we're to enter into His gates with thanksgiving and into His courts with praise (Psalm 100:4), because as we reflect on the greatness of God, the problems that seemed so big to us shrink radically.

I encourage you to spend time prefacing your prayer by reflecting upon and remembering the greatness of God. After all, if He spans the universe in His hand, He can surely handle whatever challenges face you (Isaiah 48:13).

NOVEMBER 6

And now, O Lord our God, that hast brought thy people forth out of the land of Egypt with a mighty hand, and hast gotten thee renown, as at this day; we have sinned, we have done wickedly.

Daniel 9:15

"We've sinned," Daniel says. And yet Daniel is one of the few men in all of the Old Testament of whom no sin is recorded. That doesn't mean he didn't sin, but that he lived an incredibly impeccable life. Here, however, he identifies himself with the people around him.

Wouldn't it be radical if we did that - if we really saw ourselves as one Body? When you drop a hammer on your toe, the rest of the body doesn't say, "What a jerk you are, toe." No, the rest of the body immediately begins to aid the toe. The whole body gathers around the hurting member. But what do we in the Body of Christ do? When someone drops the proverbial hammer, we find fault. That ought not to be.

If I'm finding fault with people, there's a problem with me. Daniel, a truly righteous man, said, "We have sinned, Father," and in so doing, models linkage and covering.

NOVEMBER 7

O my God, incline thine ear, and hear; open thine eyes, and behold our desolations, and the city which is called by thy name: for we do not present our supplications before thee for our righteousnesses, but for thy great mercies.

Daniel 9:18

What does Daniel request? Mercy. The purpose of prayer is not primarily to move the hand of God but rather to hold the hand of God. People say that prayer changes things. The reality, however, is that prayer changes *us*. Here, Daniel is coming to a place where he's saying, "I want to be in harmony with You, Father. I read in Jeremiah that our time here is almost over. I'm confessing our sins, Lord. I realize the jam we're in is because we're rebellious. So remember us, Lord." He's not commanding or ordering God to do something. He's simply placing himself in harmony with the will of the Father. And that is what true prayer really is.

Don't think you have to give God a reason to bless you. Approach Him solely on the basis of His mercy. Otherwise, Satan will quench the spirit of prayer in you by saying you have no right to pray.

NOVEMBER 8

And whiles I was speaking, and praying, and confessing my sin and the sin of my people Israel, and presenting my supplication before the LORD my God for the holy mountain of my God; yea, whiles I was speaking in prayer, even the man Gabriel, whom I had seen in the vision at the beginning, being caused to fly swiftly, touched me about the time of the evening oblation. And he informed me, and talked with me, and said, O Daniel, I am now come forth to give thee skill and understanding.

Daniel 9:20-22

As we take our final look at Daniel's petition, we see perspective from prayer. Daniel was praying concerning the seventy year captivity. But God sent Gabriel with a message that dealt with something much vaster - the entire history of the Jewish people prophetically.

This frequently happens in prayer. We come, concerned about a particular matter, but as we spend time in prayer, God shows us other things and ministers to us so deeply and intimately that we leave with an entirely different perspective. That's why prayer is so important. Daniel went his way blown away by what he learned in the place of prayer.

Daniel's entire prayer takes less than three minutes to read. Granted, Daniel was fasting. It's a given that he was intense with sackcloth and ashes. But I would encourage you to not think that, in order to receive revelation from the Lord and be impacted by Him, you need to pray for three hours.

The problem is, Satan comes to us and says, "All you have is five minutes? You really think God is going to meet you in five minutes?" So we commit to pray for an hour. But the hour never comes, or the alarm doesn't go off, or we drift off. Therefore, I encourage you to commit to praying even five minutes. Set your face. Bow your knee. Approach God on the basis of His mercy - and watch how you will leave that place a changed individual.

NOVEMBER 9

And he said unto me, O Daniel, a man greatly beloved, understand the words that I speak unto thee, and stand upright: for unto thee am I now sent. And when he had spoken this word unto me, I stood trembling. Then said he unto me, Fear not, Daniel: for from the first day that thou didst set thine heart to understand, and to chasten thyself before thy God, thy words were heard, and I am come for thy words.

Daniel 10:11-12

"The first day you prayed, your words were heard," the angel told Daniel. Yet, according to Daniel 10:2, for twenty-one days, there was no answer.

God can answer prayer directly and immediately. Or He can deny the prayer in His sovereignty, knowing what we ask for will be detrimental. Or He can delay the answer. Why does the Lord delay answers to prayer? Oftentimes, the Lord just wants us to spend time with Him and He knows that if we come cruising into His presence and get what we want immediately, we'll grab the goods and run away quickly. Therefore, oftentimes, I believe the Father says, "It's nice to see you again. Slow down. Don't rush off."

Sometimes, answers to prayer are delayed because God wants us to think through what it is we really want from Him. I remember when my kids were little, every Christmas they gave me wish lists consisting of everything they saw on TV, heard about from other kids, and saw in toy catalogues. How did I know what they really wanted? As Christmas got closer, the lists became condensed as they were able to determine the things they really wanted to see under the tree. I believe the same is true with prayer. We come with a torrent of thoughts, ideas, and requests, but sometimes the Lord delays the answer as if to say, "What do you *really* want?" It's not that He doesn't know. It's that He wants us to discover that which is truly on our own hearts.

Answers to prayer can be delayed because the Lord wants us to spend time with Him, because He wants us to recognize what it is we truly seek - or because of demonic spiritual forces. Such was the case with Daniel . . .

NOVEMBER 10

But the prince of the kingdom of Persia withstood me one and twenty days: but, lo, Michael, one of the chief princes, came to help me; and I remained there with the kings of Persia.

Daniel 10:13

In Ephesians 6, we read that we wrestle not against flesh and blood but against principalities and powers and spiritual wickedness in high places. There are angels, yes. But there are also demons. And they are very real. They're apparently highly organized into principalities, powers, rulers, and spiritual wickedness in high places. The Bible seems to teach that countries have specific demons that oversee or undermine them. Here, the angel says to Daniel, "The day you prayed, I was sent, but I was intercepted by the prince of Persia and for twenty-one days I wrestled with him." That is, the demon who oversees Persia, or present-day Iran, intercepted him and kept him from coming until Michael, the archangel of God, came to reinforce this angel and free him from the grasp of the prince of Persia.

Thus, the answer to prayer was hung up in a Heavenly conflict. What would have happened had Daniel quit praying after eighteen days? I believe the answer would never have come. He had to pray through. There are demons at work, gang. We are not wrestling against people, against flesh and blood. It's not your boss's personality, your husband's insensitivity, or your wife's inadequacies that are irritating you. Rather, there are demons in place that are causing all kinds of irritations, improper evaluations, and very real frustrations. If you're wrestling against people, you're fighting the wrong battle. It's the demons you need to war against, not flesh and blood.

James tells us that we have not because we ask not (4:2). In the original text, it's clear that Jesus taught us to keep asking, keep seeking, keep knocking (Matthew 7:7). Part of the reason we're taught to keep praying is because there is a war going on that, although we don't see it with our eyes, we feel its effects. If we give up in prayer, much of the blessing and release that would have come our way won't make it. Daniel discovered this.

NOVEMBER 11

Then there came again and touched me one like the appearance of a man, and he strengthened me, and said, O man greatly beloved, fear not: peace be unto thee, be strong, yea, be strong. And when he had spoken unto me, I was strengthened, and said, Let my lord speak; for thou hast strengthened me.

Daniel 10:18-19

His strength sapped, an angel comes and tells Daniel to be strong, to not be afraid, that he is greatly loved.

"No wonder an angel came to Daniel," you might say. "He was a great man, loved by God. But me? I'm weak. I struggle. The Lord would never speak to me or be able to use me." But check this out: the same angel ministering to Daniel, a messenger angel known as Gabriel, later came to Mary and said, "Hail, thou that art highly favored," or literally, greatly loved. Then he shared with her how she was chosen among all women to bring forth the Christ child (Luke 1). *Charitoo*, the Greek word translated "highly favored," appears only one other place in the New Testament . . .

To the praise of the glory of his grace, wherein he hath made us accepted in the beloved.

Ephesians 1:6

The same word spoken to Daniel and to Mary is spoken concerning you. This means you're loved every bit as much as Daniel. You're favored every bit as much as Mary. Because you are in Christ, He'll come to you and use you as surely as He did them.

NOVEMBER 12

And I heard, but I understood not: then said I, O my lord, what shall be the end of these things? And he said, Go thy way, Daniel: for the words are closed up and sealed till the time of the end. Many shall be purified, and made white, and tried; but the wicked shall do wickedly: and none of the wicked shall understand; but the wise shall understand.

Daniel 12:8-10

"Daniel, go your way. Seal up this prophecy. The wicked will keep on behaving wickedly. The righteous will behave rightly. And the wise will understand at the right time. But Daniel, shut the book. It's not for your day," the angel said.

Compare this with what John was told concerning the revelation he received . . .

And he saith unto me, Seal not the sayings of the prophecy of this book: for the time is at hand. He that is unjust, let him be unjust still:

and he which is filthy, let him be filthy still: and he that is righteous, let him be righteous still: and he that is holy, let him be holy still.

Revelation 22:10-11

Daniel was told to seal the book while John was told not to seal the book. Why? We live in a day when Daniel is no longer an impossible book to understand because so much of it has already come to pass. Therefore, the Book of Revelation is opened to us because the Book of Daniel provides the key.

So too, in your own Bible reading, there might be many things you read that you don't understand. The dietary regulations of Deuteronomy, for example, might be a mystery to you. So you wonder why you should even read about them. But there will come a time in your own pilgrimage, in your own walk when those things will begin to make sense. You'll read in the New Testament about the kinds of things we should be taking in and thinking on, staying away from certain activities and meditating on others - and you'll begin to make connections between them and the regulations in Deuteronomy. If you're not reading the Bible consistently, you'll never make those connections. But if you're reading consistently - even if you don't understand what you're reading today - there will come a time a year or two or five down the road, when it all makes sense. Even though it might be sealed up today, even though you might not understand it now, there will come a time when you hear the words, "Seal not up the book. The time is at hand. I'm going to show you how this applies to your life."

Keep reading - even though you're not fully understanding. The Holy Spirit will honor you for having that information and He'll begin to make application.

NOVEMBER 13

Then said God, Call his name Lo-ammi: for ye are not my people, and I will not be your God.

Hosea 1:9

Lo-ammi means "not mine." Even as Lo-ammi was not Hosea's, so too, the Lord says to Israel, "If you will not let Me be your God, you will not be My people." Be it a nation or an individual, the Lord doesn't force His love on anyone. He offers Himself to be Lord, Father, God, Redeemer, Savior - but He will not force Himself upon anyone.

"Behold I stand at the door and knock," Jesus said. "If any man hear my voice and open the door, I will come in and sup with him and he with Me" (see Revelation 3:20). Jesus knocks persistently, but gentlemanly. If anyone chooses to open the door, He will come in and be their Lord and live in their heart - but He won't kick in the door.

I'm always amazed by how polite the Lord is. He constantly gives every one of us the choice to give Him entry into our lives or into any part of our lives. But the choice is always ours.

NOVEMBER 14

Therefore behold, I will hedge up thy way with thorns, and make a wall, that she shall not find her paths.

Hosea 2:6

In Job 3, we see this same hedge of protection when God declared that He would plant a hedge around Job so that the enemy would not be able to harm him more than what the Lord allowed.

There is a hedge around every believer that protects us from the attacks and attempts of the enemy to destroy us. If Satan could, he would strike every one of us with disease or death. He would show no mercy whatsoever. But the Lord has a hedge around us and only what God allows for His purposes in strengthening our faith or developing our ministry can touch us. That is why the Bible tells us to give thanks in everything (1 Thessalonians 5:18). Nothing can come into our lives except that which the Lord allows.

NOVEMBER 15

I will go and return to my place, till they acknowledge their offence, and seek my face: in their affliction they will seek me early.

Hosea 5:15

It was in the house that the prodigal son left his father. It was in the pigpen that He decided to return (Luke 15). So too, it was prosperity that caused God's people to forget Him (Hosea 4:7) - and it was affliction that brought them back.

Our Father, being infinitely more loving than we could ever be as earthly parents, desires to bless us beyond all we can ask or even think. Yet, when the blessings He gives turn our hearts from Him, He reluctantly withdraws His hand of blessing in order that we will once again seek Him. The question then becomes not "Why is God so hard?" but "Why are we so dumb?"

NOVEMBER 16

Come and let us return unto the LORD: for he hath torn, and he will heal us; he hath smitten, and he will bind us up.

Hosea 6:1

Speaking through Hosea, the Lord shows He is truly *Jehovah-ropheka*, or the God Who heals (Exodus 15:26). The Lord wants to heal these people, but before there can be healing, there must be tearing. Before there can be binding, there must be cutting. Even as cancer must be dealt with severely, the Lord says, "Allow Me to have My way. Allow Me to do what needs to be done even if it's painful - for that is the only way you will be healed."

Maybe you have felt some of that pain as the Lord cut certain things from your life, allowing the Sword of the Spirit, the Word of God - to operate on specific areas. It's a painful process, but healing is sure to follow. That's always the way of the Lord.

NOVEMBER 17

Therefore have I hewed them by the prophets; I have slain them by the words of my mouth: and thy judgments are as the light that goeth forth. For I desired mercy, and not sacrifice; and the knowledge of God more than burnt offerings. But they like men have transgressed the covenant: there have they dealt treacherously against me.

Hosea 6:5-7

"It wasn't your sacrifices and burnt offerings I was after," the Lord says. "I wanted you to be a people who show mercy toward each other and have a passion for Me."

The word "knowledge" speaks not of knowing about the Lord but of knowing Him intimately. Even as these people were serving Baal, they were still going to the Temple of God religiously. They were there for worship every Sunday morning and Bible study every Wednesday night. They were serving on committees and singing in the choir - but their hearts were far from God. Over and over in the prophecy of Hosea, we hear the heartbeat of God, saying, "I want your love."

NOVEMBER 18

Strangers have devoured his strength, and he knoweth it not: yea, gray hairs are here and there upon him, yet he knoweth not.

Hosea 7:9

Israel wasn't even aware that her vitality and vibrancy were gone. In Judges 16, we see the same thing happen in the life of Samson. One of the saddest verses in the Bible is where we read that he stood up and "wist not that the Spirit of the Lord was departed from him" (see Judges 16:20). His hair was cut and now he was powerless - but he didn't even know it until it was too late.

This is what's tricky about losing our spiritual vitality. We don't even know it until the enemy is there. We realize only too late that our strength is gone. To the people of Israel, Hosea says, "Yes, you're celebrating your liberality right now and enjoying your material prosperity. But you don't realize the enemy is at the gates. You're going to stand up like Samson, thinking you'll be able to take them on, but you're going down. A stranger will devour you." Indeed, just as the Philistines devoured Samson, so the Assyrians would devour Israel.

If we ignore our walk with the Lord - our devotional life, times of prayer, times of fellowship - there will be an enemy from hell on the way. When he comes, we can't stand up to him if we have no backlog, no history, no consistency in our walk with the Lord. And we'll go down as a result.

The disciples found this to be true. When Jesus was on Mount Hermon, the disciples below were trying to cast out a demon from a boy. But they were powerless to do so. When Jesus came down, He cast out the demon - and the disciples asked, "Why couldn't we do that?"

"This kind does not come out except by prayer and fasting," Jesus answered (see Matthew 17:21).

The question obviously is, "How could the disciples have known this would happen?"

And that's the point Jesus is making. We should be living a life of prayer and fasting because we don't know when we're going to be face to face with the enemy. We need to have a history, a backlog, a discipline of fasting and prayer so that when the enemy does come, when the opportunity does arise, we'll have the power to deal with the challenge.

Israel mistakenly thought that, because she was prospering, she would be invincible. Little did she know that in a matter of years Assyria would destroy her. Don't be like Israel. Don't find yourself sidelined by the enemy because you didn't take seriously the message of Hosea. Don't think that you don't need to pray or seek the Lord with intensity but that you'll just cruise into church occasionally. If you do, like Israel, you'll be half-baked. Like Samson, you'll be powerless.

NOVEMBER 19

When Israel was a child, then I loved him, and called my son out of Egypt.

Hosea 11:1

As we see in Matthew 2:15, this verse prophetically refers to Jesus Christ. When the wise men came to worship the Babe of Bethlehem, Herod told them to tell him where Jesus was so he could worship Him too. But the wise men were warned in a dream not to return to Herod because Herod was not out to worship Jesus but to destroy this rival to his throne. So the wise men went home a different way. When Herod discovered this, he was so incensed that he ordered the death of every child two years old and younger. But, before the soldiers arrived on the scene, Joseph was warned to take Jesus into Egypt and remain there, fulfilling Hosea 11:1. *Israel* means "governed by God." Truly, Jesus was the One who was perfectly governed by God.

Why was this prophecy given?

I suggest it is because Egypt symbolizes the world. You see, Jesus, the Son of God, spent time in Egypt and was called out of Egypt. This reminds me that Jesus is a High Priest who is touched with the difficulties we go through because He was tempted in every point as we are, yet without sin (Hebrews 4:15).

Maybe you feel like you're in Egypt. Maybe you think your sin is incredibly tough, that no one could possibly understand it. But Jesus does. No matter what you're facing, no matter how brutal your sin might be, no matter how heavy your bondage might feel, Jesus has tasted it. Every single sin anyone has ever faced, Jesus Christ dealt with. Others might be horrified but Jesus understands. It was when we were in Egypt - before we had any under-standing of spiritual things - that God called us. It was while we were yet sinners that Christ died for us (Romans 5:8).

NOVEMBER 20

As they called them, so they went from them: they sacrificed unto Baalim, and burned incense to graven images. I taught Ephraim also to go, taking them by their arms; but they knew not that I healed them.

Hosea 11:2-3

"I called My people," the Lord declares. "I carried them in My arms. I taught them how to walk. But they didn't acknowledge Me. They served Baal instead."

If you asked God's people in Hosea's day if they loved God, they would say, "Absolutely! We celebrate all of the feasts and go to the Temple reli-giously." And if you asked them about the little idol on their mantels, they would probably say it was just something to inspire them. They were going through the motions of loving God, but their hearts were divided.

NOVEMBER 21

And my people are bent to backsliding from me: though they
called them to the most High, none at all would exalt him.
How shall I give thee up, Ephraim? How shall I deliver thee,
Israel? How shall I make thee as Admah? How shall I set thee
as Zeboim? Mine heart is turned within me, my repentings
are kindled together. I will not execute the fierceness of mine
anger, I will not return to destroy Ephraim: for I am God,
and not man; the Holy One in the midst of thee: and I will
not enter into the city.

Hosea 11:7-9

Admah and Zeboim were two cities destroyed when God judged Sodom
and Gomorrah. If I were God, I would say, "My people continually backslide from Me and rebel against Me. That does it. I'm through." But I'm a
man and not God. And, praise be to His name, He's God and not a man.
Therefore, He would not enter the city to destroy it. This, however, presents
a Divine dilemma - for if God is the Holy One, how could He love such
sinful people?

The story is told of a man in World War II gunned down by the Nazis
outside of Paris. Two of his friends picked up his body after the skirmish
was over and walked half a mile to a small church outside the village. They
knocked on the door and asked the priest if they could bury their friend.

"Was he Catholic?" the priest asked.

"No, he was a Methodist," they said.

"You can't bury him in our cemetery," the priest said. "But you can bury him
outside the fence."

So his two friends did just that.

A couple of weeks later, these same two friends, marching back through the
area wanted to pay their respects at the grave of their friend. They went to
the church and walked along the fence but couldn't find the grave. So they
knocked at the door of the church and said, "We're confused. We buried our
friend a couple of weeks ago, but we can't find his grave."

The priest answered, "That night, after you left, I couldn't sleep a wink. So the next day I got up and moved the fence. He's inside now."

That's what the Lord did for us. How could He be fair and equitable and yet loving and merciful? He moved the fence. How? Through the Cross of Calvary. We're inside because of the blood Jesus shed in our place.

NOVEMBER 22

Therefore they shall be as the morning cloud, and as the early dew that passeth away, as the chaff that is driven with a whirlwind out of the floor, and as the smoke out of the chimney. Yet I am the LORD thy God from the land of Egypt, and thou shalt know no god but me: for there is no saviour beside me. I did know thee in the wilderness, in the land of great drought. According to their pasture, so were they filled; they were filled, and their heart was exalted; therefore have they forgotten me.

Hosea 13:3-6

Here, the Lord says, "When you were in the wilderness you sought Me. I knew you in the hard times. But when your pastures were green, when times were good, you forgot Me."

The pitfall of prosperity must be understood. Yes, the Lord wants to bless you. There's no question about it. He will withhold no good thing from those who love Him (Psalm 84:11). The problem is, when He blesses us, if we're not very careful, we'll be enamored with His blessings rather than with Him.

NOVEMBER 23

Who is wise, and he shall understand these things? Prudent, and he shall know them? For the ways of the LORD are right, and the just shall walk in them: but the transgressors shall fall therein.

Hosea 14:9

The transgressors will stumble indefinitely, but those who are wise will hear.

C. H. Spurgeon visited one of his parishioners and saw a weather vane on the man's barn inscribed with the words "God is love."

"Are you trying to say that God's love changes?"

"Oh, no," the farmer said. "I'm saying that no matter which way the wind is blowing, God is still love."

That is the message of Hosea. God's people would break His heart. And yet, just as Hosea was not to give up on his rebellious wife Gomer, God would not give up on His people. His love remained consistent toward them - just as it does for you.

Hear the heart of your Father. Come back to Him. Let Him love you.

NOVEMBER 24

And I will restore to you the years that the locust hath eaten, the cankerworm, and the caterpillar, and the palmerworm, my great army which I sent among you.

Joel 2:25

The Book of Joel sums up a year in the life of a nation. The people of Israel had been plagued by a swarm of locusts that had devoured the land. The crops were destroyed to the point that even the bark of the trees was stripped. There was nothing left. All of the energy and effort of the previous year had been eaten up in a matter of weeks. So too, maybe as you look back at the past year of your own life, you feel like locusts have descended upon it. Maybe you put a lot of energy into a relationship only to have nothing to show for it now. Maybe you gave a lot of yourself to your job but were passed by for a promotion. Maybe the creeping, gnawing, crawling, stripping locusts have left virtually nothing behind of that which you so lovingly planted, to which you so energetically gave yourself.

But, as He said to His people in Joel's day, God says to you this day, "I will restore the years the locust has eaten. I'll not only give you a fresh start, but will restore to you the years that were lost, the energy that was wasted."

When my daughter, Mary Elizabeth, was about two years old, I remember telling her a bedtime story about a big, red bear who came in the house and said, "Mary, grab my neck. We're going for a walk." So in the story, little Mary grabbed the bear's neck and they went for a walk through Jacksonville and all the various stores and shops. At the end of Jacksonville, they went into the Jacksonville Trader. Inside the store, the bear saw a big box and in the box was a beautiful baby doll. The bear grabbed the box, had the people wrap it, and gave it to Mary.

At that point, Mary jumped up excitedly and said, "Where is it, Daddy? Where is it?"

"Where's what?" I asked.

"The dolly!" Mary said, as she looked under the chair, under the bed, and in her closet. You see, Mary was so into the story that she believed what I was saying had actually happened.

The next day I bought the doll.

"If you, being evil, know how to give good gifts to your children, how much more will the Heavenly Father give good gifts to His?" Jesus asked (see Luke 11:13).

If you're saying, "Wow! Beautiful! Thank You, Lord!" as you read promises like this one in Joel, you can be sure He's going to be so delighted by your faith that blessing you will be His joy (Matthew 8:10).

NOVEMBER 25

For lo, he that formeth the mountains, and createth the wind, and declareth unto man what is his thought, that maketh the morning darkness, and treadeth upon the high places of the earth, the LORD, The God of hosts, is his name.

Amos 4:13

God declares His thought to man. How does one declare a thought? The only way is by a word. How did God declare His thought, how did He reveal His heart? In the beginning was the Word and the Word was with God and the Word was God (John 1:1). He did it in the Person of Jesus Christ. That's why Jesus had to come - not only to die for our sin, but also because everyone had their own idea of what God was like. So God revealed His thought by becoming the Word incarnate.

How do I know what God is like? By studying the life of Jesus Christ, by listening to His words, by seeing what He did in situations. Without Jesus, we could only argue and hypothesize about the character of God. But because Jesus came, we can know what God is like.

"Show us the Father," Philip said.

"Oh, Philip," Jesus answered. "Have I been with you so long? Don't you know that he that hath seen Me hath seen the Father. I and the Father are one" (see John 14:8-9).

How do we know the thought, the heart, the mind, and the intent of God? Through Jesus Christ. He is God's final Word.

NOVEMBER 26

They that swear by the sin of Samaria, and say, Thy god, O Dan, liveth; and, The manner of Beer-sheba liveth; even they shall fall, and never rise up again.

Amos 8:14

The reason for the famine of hearing the Word was that God's people worshipped idols from the north in Dan to Beer-sheba in the south. Consequently, because they filled themselves with idol worship, they could no longer hear the Word of the Lord.

You may wonder why you're not hearing the words of the Lord, why the Bible is so dry, why there is a famine in your land. As seen here, a very possible reason is that you are worshipping an idol of compromising literature, of questionable entertainment, of overworking to make more money. In Mark 4, Jesus said the Word of God is like seed thrown into the soil of men's hearts. But the cares of this world, the deceitfulness of riches, and the lust for material things can choke its growth.

When you experience a famine in hearing the Word of the Lord, it's His loving signal that something is amiss. When Scripture is no longer vibrant or important, when the impressions are no longer real or understandable, when spiritual truths are meaningless to you, the Lord in His love says, "That's the first sign I'm giving you that something is wrong in your life. The path you're on will eventually destroy you."

If this is where you're at, seek the Lord. Let Him point out to you the sin of Samaria, the gold calf of Dan before it destroys you. If you turn from it, your appetite for the Word will return. The seed of the Word will flourish once more, bringing forth much fruit.

NOVEMBER 27

The pride of thine heart hath deceived thee, thou that dwellest in the clefts of the rock, whose habitation is high; that saith in his heart, Who shall bring me down to the ground? Though thou exalt thyself as the eagle, and though thou set thy nest among the stars, thence will I bring thee down, saith the LORD.

Obadiah 3-4

The Edomites lived in an area southeast of Israel, an area in present-day Jordan - a rocky, rugged area. They became a powerful, prolific people and developed three cities: Bozrah, Teman - which was known as a center of knowledge and wisdom in the ancient world - and their capital city of Petra. Petra was thought to be the safest place in the world; it was hidden in a volcano's crater and had only one way in, that being a narrow mountain pass, which was only twelve-feet wide in many places. Historians tell us it would take only twenty men to defend the city of one million because the Edomites would stand on the cliffs surrounding the city, that ranged in height from two hundred to one thousand feet, and pelt any intruders with boulders.

As a result, the Edomites were extremely proud and arrogant. So the Lord sent His humble servant, Obadiah, to address them.

Just like the Edomites, we will go down if there is pride in our hearts because we will become independent from God and insensitive to others.

What's the solution? Confession of sin. I find that daily, constantly, and specifically confessing my sin to God keeps me in a place of constant humility. "Lord, I wasn't listening to that person. I overreacted to that situation. I ignored that need." You will not walk around with a puffed up head or puffed out chest if you are constantly confessing your sin. That's why God desires it.

> Confess your faults one to another, and pray one for another, that ye may be healed.
>
> James 5:16 (a)

We are to humble ourselves in the sight of God, but we are also to confess our faults to one another. There is nothing more humbling than confessing our faults to a close brother or sister. Everyone has problems, struggles, and difficulties. We're all in this together.

NOVEMBER 28

But Jonah rose up to flee unto Tarshish from the presence of the LORD . . .

Jonah 1:3 (a)

Jonah fled from the presence of the Lord out of fear. However, it was not the cruelty of the Ninevites Jonah feared, but the mercy of God toward them. You see, Jonah knew that if the Ninevites turned to God, He would forgive them, and the last thing Jonah wanted was to see the Ninevites blessed. He wanted to see them blasted.

Jonah put patriotism above evangelism. But before we are too quick to judge, we must search our own hearts. What if the Lord said to you, "I have a mission for you: Go to the most anti-American country and give your life to them in My name"? If you're like Jonah - or me - you would have a very hard time with that request. But our Father says, "I love this world - including all of those who shout, 'Death to the Great White Satan America.' You may not understand them, but I do."

We have to be careful of a "Moral Majority mentality" that says, "America is always right and everyone else needs to see things our way." We're part of something bigger than the USA, gang. We're part of the Kingdom of God; and our King is merciful, compassionate, slow to anger, and desirous that all be saved (2 Peter 3:9).

NOVEMBER 29

But the LORD sent out a great wind into the sea, and there was a mighty tempest in the sea, so that the ship was like to be broken.

Jonah 1:4

God sent a storm.

> For he commandeth, and raiseth the stormy wind, which lifteth up the waves thereof. They mount up to the heaven, they go down again to the depths: their soul is melted because of trouble. They reel to and fro, and stagger like a drunken man, and are at their wits end. Then they cry unto the LORD in their trouble, and he bringeth them out of their distresses.
>
> Psalm 107:25-28

Sometimes God sends storms of severity in order to bring His children into port safely. Such was Jonah's case. This storm was not God's punishment of Jonah, but showed His patience *with* Jonah. You see, had Jonah listened, through the howling wind of the storm, he could have heard God's voice saying, "I'm not going to let you go, Jonah. I love you too much. So blow, wind, blow."

Not every storm, however, is the result of rebellion. Jesus sent His disciples into storms on more than one occasion, not because they were sinning, but because they had need of strengthening - not to destroy them, but to develop them (Matthew 14:24; Luke 8:23).

Some of the most beautiful trees I've ever seen are the cypress trees of the Monterey Peninsula. The longer the wind blows these trees, the more shapely and beautiful they become. The stronger the wind blows, the deeper their roots go. Thus, the cypress become incredibly sturdy and very lovely because of the constant wind upon them.

The same is true of us. God's stormy winds upon our lives are meant not to destroy us, but to develop us. If you are in the midst of a storm even now, take hope, dear saint. God is either using it to bring you back to His safe port or He's using it to make your life into a beautiful trophy of His grace.

NOVEMBER 30

Then Jonah prayed unto the LORD his God out of the fish's belly.

Jonah 2:1

Jonah didn't pray the minute he was swallowed. Three days and three nights passed before he prayed. Why do you suppose he waited so long? I suggest it was for the same reason we do.

When we're in a place where we know we have rebelled against the will of the Lord and we're in a tight spot because of it, we think, "No doubt I have blown it so badly and grieved God so deeply that He won't listen to anything I say. Therefore, why pray? If I were God, I wouldn't listen to me, either."

We have the mistaken idea that God hears the prayers of "good people" but turns a deaf ear to those who are in a place of rebelliousness or weakness.

So often I mistakenly think my relationship with God is based upon the subtle supposition that if I'm really "good" - if I'm reading my Bible, going to church, and praying a lot - God will hear my prayers. But if I'm not, then He's not interested. But that's just not true - for, as Jonah is about to experience, God is gracious and merciful, kind and compassionate, ready to forgive and eager to respond to His children no matter where they're at or why they're there.

DECEMBER 1

And the LORD spake unto the fish, and it vomited out Jonah upon the dry land.

Jonah 2:10

The whale suddenly felt the "urge to regurge," and Jonah was deposited on the beach. So too, if you feel that nothing is working out with your job, your relationships, or your family; if you feel that your life is going nowhere, that nothing is making sense, take heart - for even when we think nothing is working out, God has promised that it's all working out (Romans 8:28). You see, while Jonah felt forsaken and forgotten, blinded and in the dark - for three days and three nights when he thought his life was going nowhere - the whale was moving.

Where was it going? It was swimming from somewhere out in the middle of the Mediterranean off the coast of Spain back to the place where God had wanted Jonah all along. Jonah didn't have a clue that anything was happening until suddenly he was on the beach at Assyria.

The same is true for you. If you call out to the Lord and say, "Lord, I need You," you'll find that eventually you'll be right where you were supposed to be - that, through the days and nights when you thought nothing was happening, unbeknownst to you, the whale was moving.

DECEMBER 2

And the word of the LORD came unto Jonah the second time . . .

Jonah 3:1 (a)

Our God is the God of the second chance.

I remember reading that General Motors Corporation only gave one chance. That is, according to the article, candidates for executive positions were taken out to lunch where their every move was scrutinized - down to the seasoning of their soup. If they salted their soup before tasting it, they supposedly demonstrated the behavior of one who makes decisions before having the facts. One false move like that, and they'd be out!

I'm thankful God isn't like that because we would all be dust, curtains, toast, finished. We wouldn't have a chance! And, lest you think Jonah was an exceptional case, please note that giving people a second chance is God's usual mode of operation . . .

Abraham denied that Sarah was his wife and watched her carried off to kings' harems - not once, but on two separate occasions (Genesis 12:15; 20:2). Moses murdered a man and tried to cover his sin by burying the body in the desert sand (Exodus 2:12). David committed adultery and subsequently murdered Uriah (2 Samuel 11:4, 15). Peter denied Jesus by the enemy's fire (Matthew 26:74). John Mark left Paul and Barnabas stranded when he ran home to Jerusalem (Acts 13:13). Yet in each of these cases, God used these men *after* their mistakes.

Why? Because giving people a second chance is God's delight. God loves to use the foolish things of the world to confound the wise and the weak things to confound the strong (1 Corinthians 1:27).

God loves to use people like you and me - with flaws, failures, and short-comings. And here, He's about to use Jonah who, only three days earlier, had been sailing in the opposite direction from where he should have been going.

But maybe you read this account and say, "That's nice that God gave Jonah a second chance. But what if Jonah would have blown it a third time or an eighth time? I understand that the Lord gives second chances, but what about a tenth chance or a hundredth chance? What would have happened if, after being deposited on the beach, Jonah went to the nearest port and bought another ticket to sail as far away from Nineveh as he could get?

I think the Lord would have had another whale for him, another situation all set up to bring him back again - a third, a fourth, a thirtieth, a fortieth, a three hundredth, a four hundredth time. God's mercy is inexhaustible. He just keeps working with us and remaking us. He doesn't give up on us. He just doesn't.

DECEMBER 3

*And he shall judge among many people, and rebuke strong
nations afar off; and they shall beat their swords into
plowshares, and their spears into pruninghooks: nation
shall not lift up a sword against nation, neither shall they
learn war any more.*

Micah 4:3

This verse is inscribed on the United Nations building in New York City.
The problem is, they left out the first part of the verse - which is the key to
the entire verse. No matter how organized she becomes, no matter how po-
litically involved she is, even the Church will not be able to usher in peace
on this earth. Oh, there will be peace internally, as the Holy Spirit floods
peoples' hearts individually, but there won't be peace nationally until the
Prince of Peace comes back.

The only way a person can have peace internally is to allow Jesus Christ,
the Prince of Peace, into his life personally. And the only way the world can
experience peace globally is for Jesus to come back and reign in Jerusalem
- as seen in this prophecy.

DECEMBER 4

*He hath shewed thee, O man, what is good; and what doth
the LORD require of thee, but to do justly, and to love mercy,
and to walk humbly with thy God?*

Micah 6:8

To do justly simply means to do what's right. Do justly, but love mercy. In
other words, "You do what's right, but when it comes to others, look for
every opportunity to show mercy." We are not by nature merciful. Our tendency is to want to get back at people who hurt us. To walk humbly means
to walk in dependency upon God.

Jesus reduces Micah's three commandments to two: love God with all your heart and soul and mind and strength, and love your neighbor as yourself (Matthew 22:37-40).

Precious people, it all gets down to a single syllable: Love. Paul said, "If I have the tongues of men and angels but have not love, it's nothing. If I give my body to be burned because I'm so radical in service but I don't have love, it's to no avail. If I have enough faith to do miracles but have not love, it doesn't amount to a hill of beans. It all gets down to love" (see 1 Corinthians 13).

"Uh-oh," you say. "If it all gets down to love, I'm in trouble."

That's what Peter thought . . .

"Do you love Me, Peter?" Jesus asked.

"What can I say, Lord? I denied You. I disobeyed You. How can I say I love You?" Peter answered.

A second time Jesus said, "Peter, do you love Me?"

And a second time, Peter answered, "Lord, You know I like You."

The third time Jesus asked the question, He framed it a little differently, saying, "Peter, do you even like Me?"

"Yes, Lord, You know I like You," Peter answered.

"I'll accept that," Jesus said. "Feed My sheep" (see John 21:15-17).

God so loved us that He gave His only Son to die for our sins - including the sin of not loving Him.

DECEMBER 5

Who is a God like unto thee, that pardoneth iniquity, and passeth by the transgression of the remnant of his heritage? He retaineth not his anger for ever, because he delighteth in mercy.

Micah 7:18

The reason God pardons sin as horrendous as Israel's and as hideous as mine is single: He delights in mercy. The justice of God took the wrath I deserved and poured it on Christ Jesus, His Son, who was slain for my sin. When Jesus cried from the Cross, "My God, My God, why hast Thou forsaken Me?" He was feeling the anger God should have hurled on me. Thus, God can say, "I delight in mercy" - not, "I have to develop it, discipline Myself to feel it, or determine to show it. No, I *delight* in mercy because the price of your sin was fully paid on the Cross by My Son."

After praying so intensely that it caused His blood vessels to burst, Jesus saw a company of men coming toward Him. Suddenly, from out of the company, one stepped forward and kissed Him on the cheek. Knowing exactly what Judas was doing (John 6:70), Jesus nonetheless said to him, "Friend, wherefore art thou come?" - even then giving Judas an opportunity to respond to His unfathomable love (Matthew 26:50).

Jesus called Judas "friend." Amazing.

Jesus calls me "friend" (John 15:15). Incredible.

Who is our God?

Micah was right. There is none like Him.

December 6

God is jealous, and the LORD revengeth; the LORD revengeth, and is furious; the LORD will take vengeance on his adversaries, and he reserveth wrath for his enemies.

Nahum 1:2

God is love. But His love is not a sloppy sentimentality. His love is righteous and true. Thus, His very jealousy is part of His love, for He would not be loving if He were not jealous.

"I'm confused," you say. "I thought jealousy was a sign of carnality, a sin of the flesh." Jealousy is a sin as it relates to you and me (Proverbs 6:34), but not as it relates to God.

You see, when I get jealous it is because I am worried someone is going to take something or someone from me. Not so with God. God the Father, God the Son, and God the Holy Spirit are completely content in and of themselves. God isn't saying, "If I lose Jon, My whole world will collapse and I'll be miserable." No, God is all-sufficient. He has need of nothing. This means His love for me is not based upon my satisfying Him or my fulfilling a void in His life. Therefore, because He needs nothing, God's jealousy is vastly different than man's.

God is jealous not because He's worried about His loss, but because He's concerned about our hurt. Think of it this way: If we were at the zoo and a cobra slithered out of its cage and was face to face with my kids, I'd be very jealous for them. It's not that I would worry that the cobra would steal them away from me or that they'd like the snake better than me. No, I would simply be concerned that the cobra would hurt them.

That's the kind of jealousy God has. "Kids," He says, "I'm not concerned that you'll hurt Me but that you'll be hurt in leaving Me. The cobra is sure to strike, so I will deal with those things that will hurt or harm you. I will take vengeance on My enemies in order to protect My children."

DECEMBER 7

The LORD is good . . .

Nahum 1:7 (a)

After Nahum declares God's power, a reminder is given: The Lord is good. I like that! When you're talking about the awesomeness of His judgment, always keep in mind that the Lord is *good*. The first verse I taught each of my kids was Psalm 73:1 - Truly God is good. Why did I choose that particular verse? Not only because it's simple to learn but because it's foundational to their understanding of who God is.

The goodness of God is the first truth Satan attacks. "Has God said you're not to eat of that fruit?" he asked Eve. "He knows in the day you eat it, you'll have new revelation." In other words, "God is holding back something good from you, Eve" (see Genesis 3:1-5).

And that's what Satan still does today. He slithers up beside you and hisses in your ear, "Isn't that a little narrow and restrictive? Isn't there a more exciting way to live? Is God *truly* good?"

"I know mentally that God is good, but emotionally sometimes I doubt His goodness," said the psalmist. "But then I go into the sanctuary. And when I'm in God's presence with God's people, I'm reminded of His goodness all over again" (Psalm 73). Haven't you found the same thing to be true? You come to the place where God's people are studying and worshipping - and suddenly you see it again: God is good!

DECEMBER 8

. . . and he knoweth them that trust in him.

Nahum 1:7 (c)

God not only knows those who trust in Him, but He thinks about them. How often? As many times as there are grains of sand on the shores of the sea . . .

> O LORD, thou hast searched me, and known me . . . How precious also are thy thoughts unto me, O God: How great is the sum of them! If I should count them, they are more in number than the sand . . .
>
> Psalm 139:1, 17-18 (a)

God says, "When I'm on the seashores of Waikiki, Bora Bora, or Tahiti, I'm thinking about you more often than the number of grains of sand beneath My feet."

Those who study such things tell us there are 10^{25} grains of sand on the seashore worldwide. They also tell us there are 10^{25} stars in the heavens. I find this more than coincidental, for God promised Abraham that his seed would be as the sand on the seashore and as the stars in the heavens (Genesis 22:17).

So next time you're at the beach, remember that there's a star for every grain of sand. And for every star, there's a thought about you in the heart and mind of your Father. In other words, you're always on His mind and in His heart.

DECEMBER 9

Behold ye among the heathen, and regard, and wonder marvellously: for I will work a work in your days, which ye will not believe, though it be told you.

Habakkuk 1:5

I'm convinced God doesn't tell us what He's doing because He knows that if He told us what would be happening in our lives five years from now, we wouldn't believe it - or we would argue about it. In Isaiah 55:8-9, the Lord declares that His ways are not our ways, that His thoughts are higher than ours. This means God does not have an obligation to give us an explanation about our expectation. His promise is simply relaxation.

"Be anxious for nothing," Paul would write, "but in everything with prayer and supplication let your requests be made known to God. And the peace of God which passes understanding shall keep your hearts and minds in Christ Jesus" (see Philippians 4:6-7).

In other words, God says, "When you're anxious or uptight, I promise you not a peace that comes from your understanding but a peace that passes your understanding. I'm going to bypass your puny brain, so to speak, and infuse you with a deep peace in your heart."

DECEMBER 10

I will stand upon my watch, and set me upon the tower, and
will watch to see what he will say unto me, and what I shall
answer when I am reproved.

Habakkuk 2:1

"I need an answer," said Habakkuk, "so I'm going to go up into my tower and seek My Father."

Please note three key components of this verse. The first is determinati. When he needed an answer, Habakkuk said, "I will stand upon my watch." He didn't say, "Maybe I should spend some time with the Lord next week - or whenever it's convenient or if I can break away from work or if I can find some time." No, he said, "I need an answer and I'm determined to get one. I *will* seek the Lord."

The Lord promises that we shall find Him when we search for Him with all our heart (Jeremiah 29:13). But so often we lack determination. Oh, there's an acknowledgement in our minds that we should seek the Lord. There's an intention that we probably will seek the Lord sometime. But we don't get answers to the questions with which we wrestle because we lack this key component of determination.

Second, notice Habakkuk's isolation. He got away from his telephone, radio, and TV and went up into a tower. He got away from all the distractions that would otherwise bombard him. I believe we don't hear the voice of God because there are so many other voices constantly ringing in our ears. If you really want to hear from the Lord, there is no alternative to a quiet time, a quiet place, and a quiet heart.

Finally, notice Habakkuk's expectation. He said, "I will see what the Lord will say to me," not "what He *might* say to me," not "what I *hope* He will say to me," not "what I *wish* he would say to me," but "what He *will* say to me."

Hebrews 11:6 declares that without faith, it is impossible to please God, for he that comes to God must believe that He is and that He is a rewarder of them that diligently seek Him. There are many ways to please God, but none apart from faith. If you don't believe God is going to speak to you and deal with you, you're not going to hear anything from Him.

How do you know if God will speak to you or not? Here is a very simple test: when you seek the Lord, do you have a journal with you, a pencil and paper before you? You see, if I don't really expect God to speak, I'll just kind of show up, casually slumped in my chair, saying, "Wonder if there's anything in the Word for me today . . . Probably not . . ."

We adopt a laid-back mentality in seeking God and then wonder why we never hear from Him. But those who expect to hear from God have pencil and paper in hand. They are on the edge of their chair or on their knees in a posture of expectancy rather than in a spirit of complacency and lethargy.

Habakkuk said, "I am going to seek God. I will get away and I will hear what He has to say to me." That's the kind of faith that honors God. That's the kind of faith that clears the wax of the world out of the ears of the inner man.

DECEMBER 11

. . . but the just shall live by his faith.

Habakkuk 2:4 (b)

This verse is a key component of New Testament understanding. The just shall live by faith - not puffed up with pride concerning their abilities or spirituality, but solely by faith. For Habakkuk, this was not the theological base of salvation that we understand from Paul when he quotes this verse in Romans and in Galatians, and from the writer to the Hebrews who quotes it in chapter 10. Rather, the context here for Habakkuk deals directly with his own situation specifically. That is, God is saying, "Habakkuk, the Babylonian is proud and puffed up. But the just shall live by faith. You, Habakkuk, are going to live by faith."

This is the hinge upon which this entire book swings. God is not saying, "You should live by faith," or "I want you to live by faith," but "you *will* live by faith." He's saying, "You won't always have answers to your questions, Habakkuk. You won't always have solutions to your problems. You are going to live not by intellect, sight, feelings, or touch. You're going to live by faith. That means, you won't always know what I'm doing, how I'm working, where I'm going, or why I'm doing what I'm doing. You will live by faith - like it or not!"

"That sounds cruel," you say.

Not at all.

God says to us throughout Scripture that our physical senses - our eyesight, touch, and hearing - will be irrelevant in the ages to come. Faith is the currency of eternity and He wants us to be rich people. Therefore, He desires us to hear Him with the ears of faith, see Him with the eyes of faith, and touch Him with the hands of faith. He says to us, "I'm not going to appear before you like you want Me to because that won't do you any good in the ages to come. I want you to be a people who are spiritually developed and the only way I can do that is to force you to walk by faith."

God is weaning us, gang. Just as a mother lovingly weans her baby, our Father desires to wean us from the sights and sounds and feelings upon which we are so dependent in order that we might grow strong in faith. And since faith is the substance of things hoped for, the evidence of things not seen (Hebrews 11:1), it's an entirely different dimension than anything we've known.

God says to Habakkuk, "I realize you're wrestling, but the just shall live by faith. I'm going to help you, Habakkuk, develop spiritually because it will come in handy in the next billion years to come. Let the Babylonians be puffed up with their military plans, their strategy, their economy, their ability - but the just shall live by faith, simply trusting Me."

DECEMBER 12

Although the fig tree shall not blossom, neither shall fruit be in the vines; the labour of the olive shall fail, and the fields shall yield no meat; the flock shall be cut off from the fold, and there shall be no herd in the stalls: yet I will rejoice in the LORD, I will joy in the God of my salvation.

Habakkuk 3:17-18

The Hebrew word translated "rejoice" literally means "to jump up and down." The Hebrew word translated "joy" literally means "to spin around." These words, spoken by a trembling Habakkuk on the eve of the destruction of his country, constitute one of the boldest declarations of faith to be found in all of Scripture.

"Lord, You are my hope. I have seen You. I will rejoice in You. I will joy in *You*," Habakkuk declares.

"*In* everything give thanks," Paul told the Thessalonians (1 Thessalonians 5:18, italics added) - not *for* everything. I can give thanks in everything because I know that God can redeem the situation and can work out the problem. Although I may not be able to rejoice in the problem, I can always rejoice in the Lord.

DECEMBER 13

The LORD God is my strength, and he will make my feet like hinds' feet, and he will make me to walk upon mine high places.

Habakkuk 3:19 (a)

Contrast, if you will, two prophets who struggled with God's will: Jonah and Habakkuk . . .

Jonah ran *from* God when he heard what God would do.

Habakkuk ran *to* God, wondering what God would do.

Jonah saw the salvation of God *to* the Gentiles.

Habakkuk saw the sovereignty of God *through* the Gentiles.

Jonah's story ends in *foolishness* as he worries about a gourd.

Habakkuk's story ends in *faith* as he trusts in God.

The difference between Habakkuk and Jonah - between you and the person who's despairing - is simply this: Jonah had to learn in the fish. Habakkuk learned in the high tower. You and I have a choice. God is going to teach us because the just *shall* live by faith. Where do you want to live? Where do you want to learn your lessons about faith?

I have a choice. I can either seek the Lord with determination and expectation in the tower, or I can get tossed around in the storm in the belly of the great whale and wonder, "Why is my life always going through storms? Why is there always seaweed around my head? Why do I always feel cramped? Why am I always in the dark?"

The reason people are always in the storm is because they're never in the high tower. The message here is simple: Habakkuk's problems were greater than Jonah's, his message much more difficult, but he ends in victory because he learned the secret of seeking God.

The Lord wants us to seek His face, to hear His voice, to see His vision that no matter what is happening around us, we might be oases of tranquility and peace that passes understanding. No matter how bad the news might be, He wants us to rejoice in Him. *He* is our strength and our joy.

Have you discovered that when you seek the Lord about a problem, by the time you're finished talking it over with Him, as you worshipped Him and spent time with Him, you forgot what you came for in the first place? His fellowship is so rich. No matter what happens, He is our joy. In seeking Him, we find what we longed for all along.

DECEMBER 14

And it shall come to pass at that time, that I will search Jerusalem with candles, and punish the men that are settled on their lees: that say in their heart, The LORD will not do good, neither will he do evil.

Zephaniah 1:12

"Settled in their lees" refers to the process of wine-making used in Zephaniah's day whereby a winemaker would allow wine to settle for a period of time before pouring it into another vessel, leaving the dregs behind. If the winemaker poured the wine from vessel to vessel too soon, the "lees," or dregs, would still be afloat in the wine. But if he waited too long, the wine would take on the taste of the dregs. Thus, it was a very exacting process that was repeated up to seven times until the wine was crystal clear.

With this in mind, hear the Lord saying, "I will punish the men that are settled on their lees," for not only were the people of Zephaniah's day too material, too sinful, and too vocational, they were too comfortable. Sitting still in their barrels, unruffled and untouched, they had taken on a bad flavor and were beginning to stink.

Saint, that's why God suddenly pours you as well. Your life is going along just fine - until your boss says, "You're out of here," or your girlfriend says, "Pack sand."

"How can this be?" you ask. "I thought God loved me?" He does. In fact, He loves you so much that He won't allow you to get too comfortable or too settled because He knows if you do, your life will become clouded with lees and you will lose the clarity you once had. So things get shaken up as He pours you from one vessel to another. And you are left saying, "What's going on? I better seek the Lord." And you wait upon Him with renewed intensity.

DECEMBER 15

The just LORD is in the midst thereof; he will not do iniquity: every morning doth he bring his judgment to light, he faileth not . . .

Zephaniah 3:5 (a)

Even though people are foolish and fickle, even though they neither call upon nor trust in Him, the Lord is still in the midst of them. He is faithful even when His people are faithless (2 Timothy 2:13). Don't you love God for that? Even when we are squirming and floundering, flopping and flailing, God is faithful, morning by morning - making His ways known to us, blessing and convicting us, nudging and correcting us. God is faithful, no matter what!

DECEMBER 16

In that day it shall be said to Jerusalem, Fear thou not: and to Zion, Let not thine hands be slack. The LORD thy God in the midst of thee is mighty; he will save, he will rejoice over thee with joy . . .

Zephaniah 3:16-17 (a)

How I love this verse! Here, we see the Redeemer of Israel in her midst - and He is rejoicing. We have a tendency to think God is worried about us. We picture Him with furrowed brow and frowning face. We envision Him watching, wondering, and wringing His hands, reacting to our every mistake. We hear Him saying, "Is Jon going to make it? I'm not sure, but I'm ready to belt him if he gets out of line." Yet nothing could be further from the truth! The Lord in our midst is rejoicing, singing, and resting because He sees us in our glorified state. That is, He already sees the finished product.

Suppose I put some ants in one end of a shoebox, some peanut butter at the other end, and a few barriers and blockades in the middle. If I sat for a while and watched the ants, I would see them begin their journey, scratch their heads, and wonder if they would ever make it. I would see them struggle and crawl, fight and fall as they questioned all the while if anything was worth such effort. Before long, however, even though many ants would still be struggling and striving in their journey, I would see huge smiles break out on the faces of the first ones to reach the peanut butter and I would know they would all get there eventually.

So too, God sees us marching through time. We wonder if we will make it, convinced that our neighbor probably won't. We snap at each other; we get uptight and worried - but all the while God is rejoicing because He sees the peanut butter. Our vision is obstructed and shortsighted indeed for we can only see our way to the next obstacle. Not so with God. He sees all of time and eternity at once. Yes, He sees our failing; surely He sees our faltering; but He also sees our finishing. He sees us already in glory with Him. That is why He can rejoice over us with great joy.

DECEMBER 17

Thus speaketh the LORD of hosts, saying, This people say, The time is not come, the time that the LORD's house should be built.

Haggai 1:2

Notice that the people weren't saying the Lord's house shouldn't be built. They were simply saying that, due to the enemies on the outside and the contention within, this wasn't the time to do it. "We'll get to it later," they said. "We'll do it sometime - maybe even soon. But not right now."

The same thing can still happen. One of the favorite attacks of the enemy is to whisper in our ears, "Next month, next year - after you buy your house, develop your career, have your family - then you can really engage yourself in doing what the Lord has called you to do." But, gang, it's never the wrong time to do the right thing.

By the age of thirty-three, Alexander the Great had conquered the world. Later, he was asked by the historians who traveled with him to tell them the secret of accomplishing so much by such a young age. He is said to have responded that the secret lay in three words: Do it now.

What has God called you to do? What has He placed on your heart to accomplish in serving Him? What has He gifted you to do for His glory? Procrastination is what the enemy will use to hinder you from doing it. He won't say it's not worth it. He'll just tell you to do it later.

Maybe it's been fifteen years since you started doing what the Lord called you to do but you have since neglected it. Do it now. Be obedient to what He's told you to do. If He's called you to pray, pray. If He's called you to study the Word with intensity, get back to studying. If He's called you to witness, witness. If He's called you to be a singer, write songs and sing. If He's called you to be hospitable, open your house regularly. If He's called you to the mission field, go. Don't say the time is not now. Neglecting to do what He's called you to do will lead to great emptiness in your life.

DECEMBER 18

And he shewed me Joshua the high priest standing before the angel of the LORD, and Satan standing at his right hand to resist him. And the LORD said unto Satan, The LORD rebuke thee, O Satan; even the LORD that hath chosen Jerusalem rebuke thee: is not this a brand pluckt out of the fire?

Zechariah 3:1-2

Here, we see Joshua standing before Jesus with Satan ready to resist, or accuse, him. According to Revelation 12:10, one of Satan's main occupations is accusing believers. In fact, the word *devil* actually means "slanderer."

When Satan talks to you about God, he lies. He tries to get you to think that God is some kind of cosmic killjoy who wants you to be miserable. He whispers in your ear that God is mad at you, disappointed in you, through with you. But when he talks to God about you, he speaks truth. "Look at Jon Courson," he says. "He's supposed to be Your child. But did You hear what he said? Do You know what he thought? Did You see what he did?"

As Jesus answers the accuser, He doesn't liken Joshua to a mighty redwood or a majestic oak. No, He says, "See this little twig? I plucked him out of the fire - just like I chose insignificant Jerusalem to be My capital city."

Our security and significance don't lie in who we are, gang, but in Whose we are. Ephesians 1:4 declares that before the foundation of the world, God elected us and adopted us into His family. Before we did anything or were anything, God ordained that we would be part of His Kingdom. Therefore, we don't have to convince ourselves or others that we're something we're not.

DECEMBER 19

Now Joshua was clothed with filthy garments, and stood before the angel.

Zechariah 3:3

The people didn't think Joshua's garments were filthy. On the contrary, they thought his robes were beautiful, ornate, significant. But in the presence of the Lord, even his priestly robes became as filthy rags. Why? Isaiah gives us the answer . . .

> But we are all as an unclean thing, and all our righteousnesses are as filthy rags; and we all do fade as a leaf; and our iniquities, like the wind, have taken us away.

Isaiah 64:6

All of our efforts at religiosity or generosity might make us seem like good people. But in the presence of the Lord - as our motives are suddenly exposed - all of our righteousness takes on the appearance of filthy rags.

The picture painted here is very important because Jesus, a Greater-than-Joshua, would come on the scene and tell the people that unless their righteousness exceeded that of the Pharisees, they couldn't enter the Kingdom (Matthew 5:20). "Be ye therefore perfect," He said, "even as your Father in Heaven is perfect" (Matthew 5:48). In other words, if you're going to try and make it into Heaven on your own religious merit, good luck. You've got to be perfect. But once you see you are a sinner, clothed in filthiness, the door is opened for you to see your need for a Savior, a Redeemer. That's what salvation is all about - knowing we can't make it on our own. The entire purpose of the Sermon on the Mount was to drive us to Jesus not as a wise teacher or an astute philosopher but as our Redeemer, our Savior, our only hope.

DECEMBER 20

And he answered and spake unto those that stood before him, saying, Take away the filthy garments from him. And unto him he said, Behold, I have caused thine iniquity to pass from thee, and I will clothe thee with change of raiment. And I said, Let them set a fair mitre upon his head. So they set a fair mitre upon his head, and clothed him with garments. And the angel of the LORD stood by.

Zechariah 3:4-5

Notice that the Lord didn't tell Joshua to go to his room and clean up. That's what we think the Lord says to us. When we hear the accusation of the slanderer, we think we have to somehow cleanse ourselves before we can ever pray, worship, or serve. Not so. As Joshua just stood passively, realizing his robes of religiosity were filthy, he heard the Lord say, "I will clothe him with robes that are righteous."

I will greatly rejoice in the LORD, my soul shall be joyful in my God; for he hath clothed me with the garments of salvation, he hath covered me with the robe of righteousness, as a bridegroom decketh himself with ornaments, and as a bride adorneth herself with her jewels.

Isaiah 61:10

Salvation is not a matter of trying to clean up my act or ironing out my problems and wrinkles. It's a matter of realizing I'm a sinner and letting Jesus robe me with the garments of *His* righteousness.

Therefore if any man be in Christ, he is a new creature: old things are past away; behold, all things are become new . . . For he hath made him to be sin for us, who knew no sin; that we might be made the righteousness of God in him.

2 Corinthians 5:17, 21

This is essential to understand. You are the righteousness of God not because of what you do or don't do but because of where you are. When you opened your heart to Jesus, He came in to you. But, more importantly, you were placed in Him. You are in Christ. Therefore, when the Father looks at us, He doesn't see us in our sin. He sees us in His Son.

> My little children, these things write I unto you, that ye sin not. And if any man sin, we have an advocate with the Father, Jesus Christ the righteous: and he is the propitiation for our sins: and not for ours only, but also for the sins of the whole world.
>
> 1 John 2:1-2

In the Heavenly scene, Satan is the prosecuting attorney, calling judgment upon me, pointing out the faults within me before God, the Judge of all men. But when my name comes up, I have a defense lawyer, Jesus Christ, Who steps up and says, "Father, I died for Jon and My blood has covered his sin. He is in Me."

Hearing this, the Father says, "Case dismissed for complete lack of evidence."

And I am free.

DECEMBER 21

And the angel of the LORD protested unto Joshua, saying, Thus saith the LORD of hosts; If thou wilt walk in my ways, and if thou wilt keep my charge, then thou shalt also judge my house, and shalt also keep my courts, and I will give thee places to walk among these that stand by.

Zechariah 3:6-7

"Don't be condemned about the Temple lying in ruins for the past fifteen years," the Lord says to Joshua. "Don't let that slow you down, but keep going and you'll be used in even greater ways - among Heavenly beings in the ages to come."

This life is simply preparatory for eternity, gang. If you walk with the Lord now, He will greet you in Heaven with the words, "Well done, good and faithful servant . . . enter into the joy of the Lord" (see Matthew 25:23) and you will rule and reign significantly with Him. If, on the other hand, you just cruise through life, living for your own self, your own pursuits, your own pleasures; when you get to Heaven, although you'll be happy, your capacity to enjoy Heaven will be greatly diminished.

Your usefulness and capacity to enjoy the ages to come are being determined right now. That's why Paul said, "When I became a man, I put away childish things" (1 Corinthians 13:11) and why he pressed on "toward the mark for the prize of the high calling of God in Christ Jesus" (Philippians 3:14). When Paul had a vision of Heaven (2 Corinthians 12:2-4), his life was suddenly changed. He knew that only one thing mattered: obeying the leading and command of the Lord. What we do for ourselves will all burn. But what we'll never once regret is what we did for the Kingdom.

DECEMBER 22

The hands of Zerubbabel have laid the foundation of this house; his hands shall also finish it; and thou shalt know that the LORD of hosts hath sent me unto you.

Zechariah 4:9

Through Zechariah, the Lord said to Zerubbabel, "I know what you're thinking. Sixteen years have passed and the project you began is now stalled. But I have good news for you. I am going to complete that which I began. And your hands will be the hands I use to do it. Therefore, be patient. Don't despise the day of small things. Just be faithful. How will all of this come about? Not by your might or by your resolve. The stalled project will be completed by My Spirit. Just as the oil from the olive trees passes through the lamps apart from human effort, so too, I will work apart from anything man does."

I know there is a time in virtually all of our lives when the Lord lays something on our hearts. A promise is given. A dream is placed on our minds. A vision is set before our eyes. It might be a business or a marriage, a family or a ministry. We begin. We lay the foundation - but then the difficulties come. As the months and years pass, we say, "It's not going to happen." And our hearts sink.

But, just as He said to Zerubbabel, the Lord would say to us, "I am going to allow the hands that laid the foundation to finish the work. You are going to bring the capstone - the finishing piece - with shouts of grace at the end. It's all by My grace. So don't despise the days of small things, of small beginnings. And don't give up."

DECEMBER 23

Then answered I, and said unto him, What are these two olive trees upon the right side of the candlestick and upon the left side thereof? And I answered again, and said unto him, What be these two olive branches which through the two golden pipes empty the golden oil out of themselves? And he answered me and said, Knowest thou not what these be? And I said, No, my lord. Then said he, These are the two anointed ones, that stand by the Lord of the whole earth.

Zechariah 4:11-14

As Zechariah ponders the vision, he is told that the branches by which the oil of the Spirit flows are the two anointed ones. Historically, this speaks of Joshua and Zerubbabel. Prophetically, Revelation 11 refers to this verse in relation to the two witnesses who will be raised up in the tribulation. But most importantly, symbolically, the two olives trees speak of the anointed Ones - Jesus Christ and the Holy Spirit. "I am the vine," Jesus declares. "Ye are the branches" (John 15:5). We're to be the branches through which the oil of the Spirit flows into the reservoir so that the light, the Church, might burn brightly. Therefore, if we want to be filled with the Spirit, we must position ourselves as did Joshua and Zerubbabel - in the place of service. You will find that the Church burns brighter, that the Kingdom is expanded, and that your own life takes on significance when you do this.

When you realize it is only by the power of the Spirit that anything will happen, you'll quit trying to muscle your way through your ministry. Instead, you'll get on your knees before the Lord and say, "It's only by the work of Your Spirit, Lord, that anything will take place in my life." And it is then that the mountain will be removed; the lamp will burn; the Temple will be completed - and the Lord will be glorified.

DECEMBER 24

Thus saith the LORD of hosts; Let your hands be strong, ye that hear in these days these words by the mouth of the prophets, which were in the day that the foundation of the house of the LORD of hosts was laid, that the temple might be built.

Zechariah 8:9

To these people who had grown weary of building the Temple, Zechariah comes on the scene with the word of the Lord, saying, "What you're doing has huge significance. All of history is flowing down the channel of prophecy and the Temple you're hesitating to build will be the very place from which the Lord will rule. A Branch will come. The Kingdom shall be established. Old people will walk in dignity. Kids will play in safety. Every person will experience prosperity. Therefore, what you're doing will impact all of eternity."

So too, if you're at a point where you're wondering why you should keep teaching Sunday school or carving out time for family devotions, why you should labor in this ministry or that calling, I believe the Lord would say to you that what you're doing is of great significance to Him. It might seem small to you, but don't despise the day of small things because it's a foundation for what He will do - culminating in the coming of Christ, in the establishing of His Kingdom. We have a huge destiny, gang. Let us press on, robed in His righteousness, empowered by His Spirit, seeing the big picture of where it's all going.

DECEMBER 25

Ask ye of the LORD rain in the time of the latter rain; so the LORD shall make bright clouds, and give them showers of rain, to every one grass in the field.

Zechariah 10:1

In Israel, there were historically two rainy seasons. The first was from October through December and was called the former rain. The latter rains fell in April and May. These rainy seasons caused Israel to be a land of lush vegetation. After the Jews were dispersed by the Romans in AD 70, the Turks gained control of the region and began to tax the people there according to the number of trees on their property. It didn't take people long to figure out that it was in their best interests to chop their trees down. As a result, the ecology changed. The soil eroded. There was no more evaporation. The latter rains stopped altogether and the former rains were so drastically diminished that the land became arid and dry. That is why, when they became a nation again, the first project of the Israeli government was re-forestation. They still plant millions of trees every year. The ecology is beginning to change and the latter rains have returned.

Spiritually, the latter rain speaks of the outpouring of the Spirit that will take place in the last days (Joel 2:23-28). We are living in a time when the Holy Spirit is being poured out afresh. Yet, although we can observe this and study it, we will not experience it unless we ask the Lord to send the latter rain upon us personally.

I think of Noah. Talk about rain! For forty days and forty nights rain fell upon him. Wondering if the storm had abated, he let out a dove. Throughout Scripture, the dove is a picture of the Holy Spirit. When the dove found no place to land, it returned to Noah and in Genesis 8:9, we read that he pulled the dove in unto him. Noah didn't sit in the ark with folded hands saying, "Dove, if you want to land on me, I'm open." That's the way some people approach the Holy Spirit. And then they wonder why the Holy Spirit never empowers or uses them. Noah reached out and grabbed the dove and brought it to himself. We must do the same. How? Simply by asking.

If ye then, being evil, know how to give good gifts unto your children: how much more shall your heavenly Father give the Holy Spirit to them that ask him?

Luke 11:13

When the Holy Spirit was poured out on the disciples in the Upper Room, they had been praying and waiting for ten days (Acts 2). We no longer have to wait for the Holy Spirit. He's already been given. But we must wait on the Holy Spirit. That is, we must say, "Lord, is there something in my life preventing You from pouring out Your Spirit upon me?" If you want a fresh anointing, a greater empowering for service, talk to the Lord about it; all you have to do is ask, and He'll take it from there (Matthew 5:6).

DECEMBER 26

And he shall pass through the sea with affliction, and shall smite the waves in the sea, and all the deeps of the river shall dry up: and the pride of Assyria shall be brought down, and the sceptre of Egypt shall depart away. And I will strengthen them in the LORD; and they shall walk up and down in his name, saith the LORD.

Zechariah 10:11-12

The Jews would indeed "pass through the sea with affliction." When they saw the clouds of the holocaust forming, many Jews got into boats and headed to Palestine. But when the British mandated that no more Jews would be allowed entrance, one of the great tragedies of history occurred when their boats were turned back.

The seasoned saint, Zechariah, standing in the place of seeing prophecy passing before him is once again calling the people of God to see the big picture. And he calls us to do the same. We're headed for Heaven, gang. Never grow weary of reading the prophets. They call us to remember where we're headed. We want something practical. We want to read about how to have a better marriage, how to raise better kids, how to find a better job. But the prophets speak of the mystical rather than the practical because you'll be a better husband if you remember you're headed for Heaven, a better mom if you remember you'll live eternally. John tells us it was because Jesus knew from whence He came and where He was going that He was able to wash the feet of those who were too busy jockeying for position to serve one another (John 13:3). That is why our Father sent prophet after prophet to talk about the mystery of eternity, to remind us to set our hearts on things above (Colossians 3:2).

DECEMBER 27

And the LORD said unto me, Cast it unto the potter: a goodly price that I was prised at of them. And I took the thirty pieces of silver, and cast them to the potter in the house of the LORD.

Zechariah 11:13

In the small town of Carioth, a boy grew up. Educated and refined, in his twenties he began following an itinerant Rabbi named Jesus of Nazareth. Chosen by the Master to be one of His twelve disciples, he was the only one from the southern part of the nation. People from the north were thought to be uncouth, unteachable, unyielding. Eleven of the men Jesus chose were from Galilee in the north. Judas of Carioth was not one of them. No doubt he spoke with the accent of an intellectual sophisticate. Maybe that is why he was appointed treasurer of the group. No doubt it would seem that at the beginning of Jesus ministry, Judas would be His right-hand man.

But we know, of course, that Judas was, in fact, His betrayer. Why did Judas betray Jesus? Perhaps it was because he was disillusioned with Jesus. Maybe he thought that when Jesus was made King, he would have the prestigious post of secretary of the treasury. But when Jesus began to say that His Kingdom was not of this world, when He purposely went to small towns that had no political importance, Judas' heart must have sunk.

The same thing can happen to us. When Jesus doesn't work the way we think He should, we can become disillusioned and vulnerable to a degree of betrayal as well. When Jesus sat at the Last Supper and told His disciples that one of them would betray Him, they didn't say, "It's Judas." He wasn't even suspected. Instead, they looked to themselves and said, "Is it I?" I must ask this question as well. "Am I using You to do my own thing, Lord? Search my heart."

After realizing he had betrayed innocent blood, Judas brought the thirty pieces of silver to the chief priests and elders. When they refused to take it, he cast the money down on the floor of the Temple. In Matthew 27:10, we read that a potter's field was purchased with this money - exactly as Zechariah prophesied. Thus, a prophecy given 520 years earlier was fulfilled to the letter.

Culturally, being paid the price of an injured slave was insulting to Zechariah. Prophetically, however, it was exacting. But personally, it is incredibly comforting. You see, the potter's field was the field outside the house of the potter wherein broken or flawed pottery and clay were thrown. The potter's field was the least valuable piece of property in the area because, filled with pottery accumulated over centuries, the soil was useless. In Jeremiah 18, God likens Himself to a Master Potter and us to lumps of clay He shapes into vessels for His use. If, however, we refuse to respond to the shaping He desires to do in our lives, as worthless pieces of pottery, we find ourselves in the potter's field.

Yet what did Jesus do? The money that was used to betray Him was then specifically used to buy the most worthless piece of property, the place filled with cracked pots and marred vessels. That's what Jesus always does. His blood purchased people like you and me - people with nicks and chips, flaws and failures - and then He reshapes, remolds, and renews us. If I were Jesus, I would have bought beachfront property. He, however, bought me.

If you feel broken, remember Zechariah's prophecy - and never forget Jesus' unspeakable love.

DECEMBER 28

The burden of the word of the LORD to Israel by Malachi.

Malachi 1:1

We don't know very much about Malachi personally. But we do know his name means "Messenger" and, in a sense, that is all we need to know, for it's not the messenger but the message that matters. It's the message that makes the difference.

If you heard a knock on your door and opened it to find a FedEx driver standing there with an envelope in his hand addressed to you, you wouldn't ask him about his ancestors, his favorite foods, or his political leanings. Your interests would lie with the message he carried for you. The enemy, however, comes to each of us and whispers, "Who do you think you are, witnessing? Who do you think you are to be teaching or serving?" The enemy's tactic is to condemn us constantly in an effort to neutralize us (Revelation 12:10). But we must realize that it's the message with which we've been entrusted that matters. Therefore, be faithful in what the Lord has given you to do. Pass on what He's entrusted to you. Don't get sucked into the lie that, because you're not spiritual enough, you can't do or say anything on behalf of the Lord.

DECEMBER 29

And your eyes shall see, and ye shall say, The LORD will be magnified from the border of Israel.

Malachi 1:5

"When did You love us?" the people had accusingly asked the Lord in verse 2. Here, He says, "Look over the border of Israel and see that while you are blessed, the land of Edom is impoverished."

When depression knocks, instead of answering the door, I believe we simply need to stand on our tiptoes and look around at our world, our neighbors, our colleagues, and our own society to see that people are impoverished and hurting, depressed and enslaved by their own carnal desires. We have been blessed, gang. Yes, we have struggles and trials, but we are a people of destiny. God has a purpose and a plan for us. He has forgiven us. He has liberated us. He's blessed us. Therefore, don't hang your head and say, "When has God loved me?" Instead, stand on your tiptoes. As you contrast your situation with that of those around you, you'll say, "Lord, thank You that I'm part of Your family."

DECEMBER 30

Even from the days of your fathers ye are gone away from mine ordinances, and have not kept them. Return unto me, and I will return unto you, saith the LORD of hosts. But ye said, Wherein shall we return?

Malachi 3:7

How would the people return? In this case, it would be through giving. Why? Giving is not God's way of raising money. It's His way of raising kids. You see, because we're sinners, each of us has the tendency to be selfish, small, greedy, and materialistic. But God is a giver (John 3:16) and He wants His children to be like Him.

In the Bible, there are over four hundred fifty verses on faith and over five hundred fifty verses on prayer. But there are over twenty-one hundred verses on giving. One of every ten verses in the New Testament deals with giving, money, or possessions. Of the thirty-eight parables Jesus taught, sixteen deal directly with giving, money, or possessions. Why is the Lord so emphatic about this? Because Jesus said that wherever a man's treasure is, there will his heart be also (Luke 12:34). He wants us to give to Him - not because He needs our money but because He wants our hearts.

DECEMBER 31

Behold, I will send you Elijah the prophet before the coming of the great and dreadful day of the LORD: and he shall turn the heart of the fathers to the children, and the heart of the children to their fathers, lest I come and smite the earth with a curse.

Malachi 4:5-6

The scribes understood that this verse spoke of the coming of Messiah. Therefore, Jesus' disciples asked Him why the scribes said that before Messiah came, Elijah would come.

"Elijah is coming and has already come," Jesus answered (see Matthew 17:10-12).

John the Baptist came in the same spirit, with the same power and the same kind of ministry as Elijah. But he wasn't literally Elijah. When will Elijah come? Revelation 11 tells us two witnesses will come on the scene in the tribulation period who will have the power to stop the rain, to cause plagues to fall on those who come against them, and to call down fire upon any who attack them. One will be Elijah - the man who prayed both drought and fire down from Heaven (1 Kings 17; 2 Kings 1). Most likely, Moses will be the other - no stranger himself to plagues (Exodus 7-11).

Elijah will come with a ministry of getting things right, of setting things straight lest the Lord comes with a curse. That's the way the Old Testament ends. How does the New Testament end? "The grace of our Lord Jesus Christ be with you all." The Old Testament ends with a curse. The New Testament ends with grace.

The Old Testament ends with a curse because, in essence, it's the Law of God being given to proud and pompous mankind who think they're pretty good. But the Law, God's standard of righteousness and holiness, actually strikes and curses us when we realize we can't keep it. So it is the Old Testament Law that sets the stage for the New Covenant - when He Who knew no sin would be made sin for us that we might be made the righteousness of God in Him (2 Corinthians 5:21).